# REFERENCE

**Introducing Management**

# Introducing Management
## A Development Guide

## Kate Williams

## Third edition

ELSEVIER

AMSTERDAM • BOSTON • HEIDELBERG • LONDON • NEW YORK • OXFORD
PARIS • SAN DIEGO • SAN FRANCISCO • SINGAPORE • SYDNEY • TOKYO
Butterworth-Heinemann is an imprint of Elsevier

Butterworth-Heinemann is an imprint of Elsevier
The Boulevard, Langford Lane, Kidlington, Oxford, OX5 1GB
30 Corporate Drive, Suite 400, Burlington, MA 01803, USA

First edition 1999
Second edition 2004
Third edition 2006
Reprinted 2007, 2009

Notice
No responsibility is assumed by the publisher for any injury and/or damage to persons
or property as a matter of products liability, negligence or otherwise, or from any use
or operation of any methods, products, instructions or ideas contained in the material
herein. Because of rapid advances in the medical sciences, in particular, independent
verification of diagnoses and drug dosages should be made

**British Library Cataloguing in Publication Data**
A catalogue record for this book is available from the British Library

**Library of Congress Cataloging-in-Publication Data**
A catalog record for this book is available from the Library of Congress

ISBN: 978-0-7506-6880-4

For information on all Butterworth-Heinemann publications
visit our website at books.elsevier.com

Printed and bound in *Great Britain*

09  10  11  12   12  11  10 9 8 7 6 5 4 3

Working together to grow
libraries in developing countries

www.elsevier.com | www.bookaid.org | www.sabre.org

ELSEVIER     BOOK AID
             International     Sabre Foundation

# Contents

# Preface

Organizations need a skilled, flexible and responsive workforce in order to survive and thrive in today's competitive markets. Effective and efficient management is key to an organization's success and its ability to meet changing business demands.

The role of a manager is both challenging and complex and the aim of this book is to assist new and existing managers to make sense of their role through a greater understanding of management. This book provides an introduction to the theories and concepts of management and explores the primary responsibilities of a manager.

This third edition has been fully revised and contains updated and new material in line with the latest edition of the Occupational Standards for management and leadership. This book is an essential resource when studying for a recognized management qualification through, for example, the ILM, Chartered Management Institute or an S/NVQ. You will find this book beneficial to your learning and development as it is closely linked to the knowledge requirements for first-line manager qualifications.

Management is essentially a practical skill and, as with the first two editions, this book reflects this. You will find case studies and practical examples representing different industry sectors that enable you to apply the concepts and principles to your own work situation.

We hope you find this book helpful in assisting you to make sense of the complexities within your role. Use it as a measure of your own performance as you continually explore new and improved ways of working.

Finally, I would like to thank my husband for his advice, encouragement and patience through the revisions of this edition.

*Kate Williams*

# Learning structure

**Introducing Management: a development guide** has an easy-to-follow learning structure to guide readers through their introduction to the management role.

The book is divided into five sections, as follows:

**Section 1: Managing in Context** starts with a brief explanation of the work managers can expect to do and the results for which they are responsible. It describes the way in which changes in the wider world affect organizations and how they may impact on the job of a manager. It explains the varying structures of organizations and the influence of culture on decision-making and methods of working. As the title suggests, the purpose of this section is to set the manager's job into the context of the whole organization and beyond. For many managers it is easy to get caught up in the day-to-day, hour-by-hour activities and over-look what the organization expects them to achieve in the longer term and the influence of external factors. Section 1 is intended to put that right and encourages the reader to consider the bigger picture.

**Section 2: Providing Direction** begins by examining the skills needed to develop as a professional manager, covering developing self-awareness, the importance of reflection, valuing equality and diversity, and tips for achieving work/life balance. Effective communication is critical to an organization's success, so the principles of effective communication are explored together with different situations at work when a high level of communication skill is required. A manager needs to demonstrate clear direction and effective leadership. The section explores a range of ideas about leadership, how the people issues of management fit within the context of the job of management and some techniques for effective delegation. Motivation is defined, and some theories of motivation are introduced as well as examining problems that may be encountered in trying to motivate staff. The final chapter looks at the importance of developing productive working relationships.

**Section 3: People and Performance** – teams deliver results, and Section 3 starts by looking at the manager's role in building a successful team. It examines ways to improve individual performance and how to manage under-performance through the disciplinary process. The impact of change on organizations is discussed as well as ideas for successfully involving people in the change process. A range of problem-solving and decision-making techniques are offered, including the important aspect of generating and evaluating alternatives. The final chapter of the section provides an overview of the steps to be taken in recruiting new staff to the team.

**Section 4: Effective Resource Management** offers advice on effective ways of managing and controlling resources, including information and time. The transformation of inputs into outputs is explored as well as the concept of 'adding value'. It shows how accurate, timely and relevant information is an essential basis for quality decision-making and the financial implications of the process of making strategic as well as operational decisions. It looks at budgets and the controls and decisions that have to be made to effectively manage them.

**Section 5: Focusing on Results** – managers achieve results through people and other resources. This section looks at the results managers should achieve, how they can make the best use of people and what they need to do to ensure that work achieves the desired objectives. It stresses the importance of identifying customers, both internal and external, and satisfying their needs and expectations. Taking a fresh look at the workplace by focusing on ways of improving design and layout is explored within the context of the manager's responsibilities in maintaining a healthy and safe environment. The final chapter examines the important role the manager has in continuous improvement.

**Introducing Management** includes the following features to assist your learning:

---

### Chapter Objectives

Bullet points at the beginning of each chapter serve as a guide to the content and the learning that will be covered.

---

### Insights

Short anecdotes about different situations a manager may find themselves in followed by questions to generate possible solutions.

---

### Case Studies

These are used to bring a real-life aspect to the information and, as with the Insights, are intended to contextualize the reading for the learner. They are also followed by questions which require more thinking and time.

---

### Review Your Learning

Each chapter ends with review questions. These reinforce and check the understanding from the chapter that has just been read.

---

### Theory to Practice

These activities relate the knowledge gained back to the workplace for the reader. This helps to contextualize the learning and encourages the reader to reflect and improve on their own management style and skills.

**LEARNING STRUCTURE**

**Resource Bank**

Located at the end of each section, these are intended as a bank of resources for the reader including reference sources, additional reading and website addresses.

# Section 1 Managing in Context

- *What is management?*
- *What do managers do?*
- *What resources do managers have?*
- *Where do resources come from?*
- *Who are our customers?*
- *What do they buy?*
- *How does culture affect an organization's performance?*
- *What is the significance of organizational culture to you as a manager?*
- *What affects an organization's success or failure?*

# 1 Achieving results

We begin this book by examining the role of the manager; this will help you to have a better understanding of management, what managers do and the impact effective management has on an organization. You may not necessarily have 'manager' in your job title. In fact many organizations avoid the term, particularly for jobs that have a management element at a junior level. For example, the Civil Service typically uses the titles 'Administrative Officer' and 'Executive Officer' for such positions. Many companies call their junior managers 'supervisors' or 'team leaders'. On the other hand, in some small firms, the Directors are also responsible for day-to-day management.

That's all very well but not particularly helpful without some understanding of what the management role involves. There are many differing views amongst writers on management, which help towards an overall understanding.

Many of the early writers on management have significantly influenced the way we view the management role. For example, in the first European book on management, Henri Fayol (1916) stated that management involved:

- Forecasting and planning
- Organization
- Command
- Control
- Co-ordination.

**MANAGING IN CONTEXT**

E. F. L. Brech (1953) described management as:

*A social process entailing responsibility for the effective and economical planning and regulation of the operations of an enterprise, in fulfillment of a given purpose or task.*

Koontz (1914), on the other hand, in his book *Towards a Unified Theory of Management*, argued that management was:

*... the art of getting things done through and with people in formally organized groups.*

More recent definitions include:

*Management is ... the organ of society specifically charged with making resources productive.*
Drucker (1954)

*Deciding what should be done and then getting other people to do it.*
Stewart (1999)

*Management is fundamental to the effective operation of work organizations.*
Mullins (2002)

As you can see, there is a common thread that links these views:

- Management involves making plans and decisions about the future needs of the business
- Management is about making cost-effective use of resources through efficient organization and control
- Management is about getting the best out of people to achieve objectives.

## Your role as a manager

It is the content of your job which makes you a manager not simply your job title. Regardless of the title, a genuine management job involves:

- Forecasting the future nature of the business and of your operation and the challenges (environmental factors) affecting it
- Planning the targets and objectives your operation will deliver either in the short term (day-to-day) or in the medium to long term, or both

- Ensuring you have the resources (people, equipment, budget, materials) to meet your objectives
- Making cost-effective use of those resources
- Giving clear and relevant instructions to your staff
- Gaining and maintaining staff commitment to the organization and to their work.

These activities reflect the content of a manager's job whatever the level. However, the balance of activities varies according to whether we are considering a junior, middle or senior manager. Research in America, by Rosemary Stewart, shows that junior managers are much more involved in short-term, relatively simple, day-to-day decisions. At higher levels, decisions take longer to make and put into practice.

Decisions at the lower levels are often more clear cut. They usually have to be done quickly and there is less uncertainty about the result than at higher levels. Downsizing and streamlining across a number of different industry sectors has led to a reduction in the number of management levels and has pushed decision-making responsibility and leadership roles further down the organization. Nevertheless it is still the case that:

- First-line managers are mainly responsible for day-to-day and hour-by-hour decisions
- Their decisions tend to be followed by immediate action which allows an early chance to see if they have worked
- First-line management decisions usually deal with fairly straightforward issues where the results and effects of the decision are obvious.

At the same time, not all decisions at a junior level are of this short-term, straightforward nature. Increasingly, managers at this level are being expected to make or suggest improvements to working practices, the use of resources and the quality of their output and to take responsibility for longer-term issues like staff recruitment and customer satisfaction.

However, not all the work a manager does is truly management work. Consider this situation:

**Insight**

Ranjit Khan is the manager of a small neighbourhood supermarket. Each morning he comes in early to open the shop and

serves at the checkout until his staff arrive. He then gives them their duties for the day. During the day, he meets sales representatives and places orders for next week. When the shop is busy, he refills the shelves. In quiet moments he prepares wage packets, checks stock levels and pays bills.

**Which of Ranjit's jobs are management jobs?**

The following are the management elements we see in Ranjit's job:

- *Using Resources*
  This involves opening the shop, checking stock levels and placing orders.

- *Working with People*
  This involves giving his staff their duties and presumably supervising them during the day.

- *Providing Direction*
  Ranjit's presence in the shop enables him to assess the extent to which it is providing customer satisfaction and to make improvements.

- *Managing Information*
  The jobs of preparing wage packets and paying bills are not management jobs. However, they may encourage him to seek more effective ways of managing the payroll or keeping accounts.

In a small operation like this it would be unrealistic to expect that the manager will manage all the time. Ranjit is not managing when he serves at the checkout or refills the shelves. But those activities do keep him close to customers and aware of the issues and problems facing his staff when they do the same jobs. This is one of the main considerations which have led to the delegation of decision-making – decisions should be taken by the people affected by them and who will understand the consequences.

For many junior managers the jobs they do are an uncomfortable mix of managerial and 'hands-on' work. It is important to be aware of the difference. Managerial work involves the activities of forecasting, planning, managing resources and managing people that have already been described. 'Hands-on' work involves the basic tasks that keep the operation running.

Check your understanding of this chapter by completing the
following:

1 Henri Fayol listed five elements of management. What words
did he use to describe the following activities?

(a) Look to the future and deciding what to do about it ..........

(b) Get together the necessary resources and procedures to
deliver objectives .....................

(c) Give instructions and granting authority .....................

(d) Check results and take corrective action .....................

(e) Keep everything and everybody working towards defined
goals .....................

2 List the four types of resources managers manage.

3 What is the main consideration when delegating decision-
making?

Apply this chapter to your own experience by answering the
following:

1 Identify the main activities you undertake at work. Decide
roughly what percentage of the working week you spend on
each. What percentage of the week do you spend on managerial
activity?

2 What do you know about the aims of your organization?

3 Which aspects of your role enable you to contribute to the
achievement of these aims?

4 How far can you influence the resources you manage?

5 What are your responsibilities to and for the people you manage?

**MANAGING IN CONTEXT**

# 2 Using resources

| Chapter Objectives | • *What resources do managers have?* |
| | • *Where do resources come from?* |

Increasingly in today's competitive markets there is a need for managers to **add value** through the work that they do. In fact this does not only apply to managers. The main idea is that the only way people can justify their employment is by producing something that is more valuable or desirable than the raw materials they started with. Here are some examples:

- An assembly line worker adds value by turning lengths of wood into table legs.
- An accounts clerk turns orders and delivery notes into invoices – which are of greater value to the organization because they ultimately result in income.
- A haulage driver adds value by moving goods from their starting point to where they are wanted.
- A good waiter adds value by providing a superior level of service whilst projecting a sparkling personality.

The manager's contribution to this process of adding value is to ensure that through the process of 'transformation' the final result is worth more than the combined cost of the raw materials and the resources used.

This process of transformation involves:

- Making sure the tools, machinery or equipment are in place to change them into something more valuable
- Getting hold of the necessary raw materials
- Managing the people involved
- Continually checking that the final result meets the expectation of customers and their willingness to pay.

**INTRODUCING MANAGEMENT**

You will find ideas and thoughts that illustrate the process of transformation and adding value throughout this book. For the moment though, let's concentrate on the resources on which managers depend, where they come from and how difficult they are to get hold of. This will then lead us into looking at how the organization and the environment have an effect in the final two chapters of this section.

In the previous chapter we saw that managers depend on the resources of:

- People
- Equipment
- Budget
- Materials.

These four are all **inputs**. They form the resources which are then transformed into the products and services needed by customers. Inputs or resources can be split into two categories:

## Consumable resources

As the name implies these are used up as the process of transformation takes place. Some examples of consumable resources are:

- Raw materials
- Energy in the form of heat and light
- Time
- Budget (which pays for energy and time).

## Renewable resources

These are resources necessary for the transformation process but which can be used repeatedly over time. Examples are:

- Equipment or machinery
- Staff experience and expertise
- Premises, space
- Furniture, computers, telephones.

Insight

Picture the staff canteen in a corporate headquarters office block. The canteen is subsidized and serves morning coffee, afternoon tea, snacks and lunches.

What inputs does the canteen need?

Which are consumable and which are renewable?

What differences would it make if the canteen were expected to make a profit?

One view could be as follows:

The canteen's *consumable resources* would consist of:

- Raw materials like instant coffee, teabags, water, milk, sugar, meat, vegetables, salad and so on
- Energy – gas or electricity to heat drinks and cook the food
- Pre-packed snacks like biscuits, cakes or sandwiches – assuming the canteen staff do not make sandwiches themselves
- The canteen staff's time
- Money – the budget to subsidize the canteen.

*Renewable resources* would be made up of:

- Teapots and coffee urns
- Cups, saucers, plates, cutlery – unless the canteen uses disposable versions which would be thrown away after use and therefore would be consumable resources
- Cookers
- Refrigerators and freezers
- Canteen furniture – tables and chairs
- Dishwashers
- The cooks' expertise in preparing and cooking food
- Serving staff's ability to, for example, operate the tills, serve the food and clear the tables.

If the canteen were not subsidized, two main differences would come into play. First the prices in the canteen would increase as the canteen would have to make a profit in order to fund itself. The office staff would therefore become customers who could choose to

10

use the canteen or go elsewhere. Which raises the second difference. We said just now that part of the manager's role in managing resources was to make sure that products or services satisfied customers. If the canteen received no subsidy it would be even more important that the quality and value offered by the canteen met customer expectations and compared successfully with competitors outside. We shall return to this theme both briefly in the next chapter and at greater length in Chapter 24.

# Obtaining resources

Managers often complain that they have insufficient resources to meet their particular needs of the business. Lack of necessary resources is an understandable source of frustration. However it is important for managers to recognize the wider context in which their operations take place.

The amounts an organization can afford to spend on resources are partly the result of past income and expenditure and partly the result of external constraints. In an ideal world senior managers would predict their likely resource needs in future years and set money aside to pay for them. However, such an ideal situation often does not apply.

| Example | A commercial business may not achieve the sales turnover and resulting profit it expected. In years of really poor sales performance it may even trade at a loss. As a result money that should have been set aside for future resources will either not be there or will be used to keep the business running. |
|---|---|

Government-funded bodies such as the health or defence services are generally not allowed to put money aside to spend in future years. Any surplus budget at the end of a financial year is lost. Consequently, the amount of money a Civil Service department has available to spend, for example, on new or extra resources depends on the generosity or otherwise of government at the time that year's budget is prepared. In other words, the obtaining of resources depends on the 'political' environment, i.e. the agendas and 'rules' within that company – a factor we shall return to in the final chapter of this section.

**MANAGING IN CONTEXT**

Publicly funded operations often find that the demand for their services is greater than they have forecast. There are several possible reasons for this. In the health service progress in diagnosis and treatment has meant that doctors can now treat diseases that were previously incurable. The treatment will be available but at a greater cost than that forecast because the treatment did not exist when the forecasts were made.

For road maintenance programmes, severe weather may demand greater road maintenance than anticipated. As their processes become more sophisticated employers may need greater numbers of staff with degrees. As a result society expects more people to attend university. Any of these causes of higher-than-forecast demand will mean that past money set aside for resources will be inadequate.

Consider this situation:

**Case Study**

> The Copy Shop is an independent business offering a printing and photocopying service in the small town of Swinford. It was set up five years ago with two leased photocopiers and a reconditioned printing press. Last year was a profitable one. So the owner set some of his profits aside to buy a new printing press because the current reconditioned machine needs expensive maintenance and is no longer able to produce the quality customers expect. Unfortunately a national chain has set up a printing and photocopying branch in the town. The Copy Shop has lost two major customers, turnover has dropped by 20% and it is currently trading at a loss.
>
> The owner calculates that he can afford to continue paying his staff for another four months without touching the reserves he has put aside for the new printing press.

**What choices are open to the owner?**

**What would you advise him to do?**

We might see these as the decisions between which the owner has to choose:

- Buy the new printing press, keep his staff and mount a marketing campaign to restore the lost business. A high-risk decision but commercial decisions are risky by definition!

- Forget the new press and use the money to pay his staff for longer than four months. But he may find it difficult to maintain and increase his business if the quality produced by the old press is not competitive.

- Find ways of reducing the cost of resources: for example, could the new press be leased rather than bought? This may be more expensive in the long term but cheaper in the short term. Will staff accept a drop in wages – or can they find better-paid jobs elsewhere? Can new materials such as paper and ink be bought more cheaply – or will the quality suffer?

- Cut back on the scale of his business. Ending the lease on one of his photocopiers, making staff redundant or even moving to smaller premises would all reduce overheads – although the photocopier lease almost certainly contains a penalty clause for early termination, staff will be entitled to redundancy payments and there will be costs involved in moving premises.

Faced with these alternatives, what advice would you give? There is no 'right' answer to this question. However, any action to reduce costs without attempting to rebuild the business is likely to lead to a further decline in the Copy Shop's turnover and profit. But at the same time the owner cannot afford to upgrade his resources, keep all his staff and pay the costs of an advertising campaign. The only approach to this crisis which is likely to have any chance of success will need to combine cost savings, the development of a more competitive service and major marketing activity.

# External factors

That last case study shows that historical success in building up reserves to increase or upgrade resources can often be hindered by external factors outside an organization's control. So far in this chapter we have mentioned the impact of:

- Customer choice
- Political decisions
- Technological improvements
- Competitor activity
- Social change
- The weather.

All of these affect an organization's operations by affecting the cost and availability of resources.

---

**Example**

A coffee manufacturer will find raw materials (coffee beans) scarce and expensive if bad weather leads to crop failure.

New improved operating methods may require staff with different expectations and qualifications. If the country's education and training system has not caught up with the changes, staff with relevant backgrounds will also be hard to find and costly.

Both of these problems (raw materials and staffing) will be aggravated if competitors are seeking the same resources.

Many governments have now limited or banned the exploitation of natural resources like hardwoods. Organizations with processes that depend on them need to find alternative sources or to redesign their processes.

---

## Resources and you

This chapter has presented a 'big-picture' view of resources, emphasizing an organization's need to be aware of external influences when planning resource needs or seeking to obtain them.

You may be wondering what these strategic considerations have to do with you. There are two answers to this question. The first is that managers do not work in isolation. To be effective, managers need to have an interest in, and understanding of, the wider world they are in, so that they can effectively plan resource needs. Such an understanding is essential if managers are to make sense of decisions taken elsewhere in the organization, and be able to explain them to their staff. As far as using resources is concerned, these decisions may involve:

- Changes to products or new materials
- Changes to processes
- Changes to budgets
- Why necessary resources can or cannot be made available.

These references to change lead on to our second answer. Management is an ever-changing, dynamic process. Much of a manager's work should involve looking for, making or recommending improvements. In order for improvements to be relevant and desirable, they need to take account of the organization's past performance, future plans and the environment in which it operates.

**Review your learning**

Check your understanding of this chapter by completing the following:

1 Managers are responsible for a_ _ _ _ _ v_ _ _ _ through the work that they do.

2 Resources are also known as i_ _ _ _ _ .

3 What are the two categories of resources?

4 List four external factors that might affect resource availability.

5 Give two reasons why managers need to understand the context in which their organizations operate.

**Theory to practice**

Apply this chapter to your own experience by answering the following:

1 What resources do you manage?

2 What changes are you responsible for?

3 How does your organization fund extra or upgraded resources?

4 What improvements would you like to see to the resources you manage?

5 How practical are those improvements in view of the context in which your organization operates?

6 What are the foreseeable changes for your organization which may affect availability of resources?

# 3 Customer focus

| Chapter Objectives | • *Who are our customers?* |
| --- | --- |
| | • *What do they buy?* |

Many managers have little or no contact with their organization's external customers. In fact, for many organizations, like government departments and hospitals, the idea that the people they serve are customers at all is a comparatively recent one.

However, in the past few years, management thinking and management literature have placed considerable emphasis on the need for 'customer orientation', i.e. basing the majority of actions and decisions on the needs and wants of the customer. Here are some statements which make the point:

*There have always been strategic advantages in staying close to customers. Good customer relationships reverberate not only in current sales but also in future effectiveness and growth. Satisfied customers are the single best source of new business. Timely knowledge of changing customer requirements makes it possible to guide production more efficiently, reducing waste, inventory costs and returns.*
Kanter (1989)

*We believe in making a difference … We deliver a quality service by empowering our employees and we facilitate and monitor customer feedback to continually improve the customer's experience through innovation.*
(Virgin.com website)

*To say that 'the customer is king' is an understatement of many of our successful companies. For them good customer relations and a deep knowledge of the market in which they operate are essential, routine and unquestioned parts of their day-to-day method of doing business.*
Goldsmith and Clutterbuck (1985)

There are two themes that are important to this emphasis on customers. The first is the theme of change. As Kanter stresses, all organizations now operate in environments where change is massively unpredictable and taking place at a bewildering speed. Secondly, in order to keep their operations relevant, organizations must check constantly on their customers' expectations and requirements because customer satisfaction should be their primary goal.

The second theme is that of total quality management or continuous quality improvement. The TQM philosophy is also based on the principle that customer satisfaction is the main objective of any organization. But it goes further; total quality management starts from the position that everybody in an organization is somebody else's internal customer. A closer look at some of these internal customer–supplier relationships reveals some important issues.

*Most internal service problems are a result of 'silo' mentality where people and departments work in isolation, consider only their own priorities and think others are sitting around twiddling their thumbs with nothing to do ...*
Donna Earl (2005)

The TQM theme is related to the theme of change because it is founded on the idea that internal relationships make up a supply chain which ultimately leads to the external customer. If that supply chain is working properly to identify customer needs at each stage, the whole organization will be able to adapt to the changing needs of external customers. We shall return to the topics of customer satisfaction and the internal supply chain in Section 5.

Therefore, an organization is full of customers. Your colleagues are your customers and you are their customer. They can fulfil your needs and requirements by carrying out their role efficiently and vice versa. For example:

**Insight**

Katie works in the internal communications department in the Head Office of a large retail company. Her job involves editing and collating all the information from the relevant departments in order for it to be clear, understandable information that can be sent out to all departments. In this scenario, the members of staff working in the other departments are Katie's customers. She serves their needs and requirements in order for them to carry out their jobs efficiently. However,

Katie is also a customer. She is a customer of the IT department. They need to keep her PC and printer in good working order so that she can input all the data to enable her to extract the information to disseminate to the departments. The IT department needs to ensure that they serve Katie's needs and requirements so that she is a satisfied customer.

Because they all work for the same company everyone here is an internal customer.

### Who are your 'internal' customers?

On the other hand, we are all the 'external' customers of, for example, supermarkets. If a supermarket is continually out of stock with empty shelves then it does not serve our needs or requirements satisfactorily. We will cease to visit it. It won't get any customers and eventually will make so little money that it will be forced to close.

Just as Katie relied on the IT department to keep her computer functioning in order for her to distribute information, the supermarket relies on us in order to make enough money to sustain itself. For the moment we shall explore the needs of external customers and how these are affected by their environment.

## Customers and quality

The TQM literature takes as its starting point that customers buy quality.

It is important to understand what quality means in this context. It does not mean the same as 'high quality', 'top quality' or even 'good quality'. Instead TQM emphasizes that quality should be 'satisfactory' – in other words, it should meet the needs of customers. Quotations from two of the early total quality gurus clarify this point.

Juran defined quality as 'fitness for purpose or use'. Crosby used the phrase 'conformance to specification'.

From the customer's viewpoint, therefore, quality describes the extent to which a product or service *meets their needs* or *satisfies their expectations*.

> Two friends have gone shopping to buy cutlery – sets of table knives, forks and spoons. The first wants them for a holiday caravan the family has just bought, which they plan to use for their annual holidays and occasional weekends. The second wants them to give to a nephew as a wedding present.

**Based on this limited information what do you think would constitute 'quality' in each case?**

Without being able to ask the customers, we have to make some assumptions. It seems reasonable to assume that cutlery for the holiday caravan should ideally be robust and relatively inexpensive, without needing to look particularly special. The cutlery for the wedding present on the other hand will need to be impressive, a well-known brand, possibly silver plate and with the weight and design to give a positive message about the good wishes and generosity of the givers.

# External influences

Of course making assumptions like these are subjective and unreliable. That is why in Section 5 we shall go into greater detail about the need to carry out proper and frequent research into customer requirements. But it is also essential to recognize that customer needs are in part a reflection of the external factors affecting customers. Here are some examples:

**Example**

- More rigorous drink–driving laws in the UK have increased pub sales of soft drinks.

- Greater public awareness of environmental issues has led to an increase in supermarket sales of recyclable products and organically farmed foods.

- Tourism revenue in the UK during 2005/06 is predicted to rise from an increase in visitors from China following China's decision to allow 'ordinary' citizens visas to travel.

**MANAGING IN CONTEXT**

In each of these cases something in the wider world has changed. Customers, manufacturers and suppliers will have had little or no influence on that change. However the change has either increased or reduced the amount of a product or service that customers were willing to buy. In other words, external factors brought about a change in customer expectations or requirements.

In a similar way, external factors can influence what customers see as 'satisfactory quality'. For many employees a company car delivers satisfaction in a number of ways:

- As a means of transport for getting from A to B
- As a source of comfort on journeys
- As a status symbol.

Any car will meet the first requirement. The second is to.do with a range of considerations like seat design, whether the car has air conditioning, the smoothness of the ride. The third requirement has historically been met by a combination of size and brand.

Today the requirements of a company car remain the same in terms of comfort and status but a change in external considerations has added an extra requirement and brought different expectations. Company cars are often seen as:

- 'Gas guzzlers'
- Wasteful of national resources
- Environmentally damaging.

Big company cars are consequently seen as reflecting badly on the environmental sensitivity of both their drivers and the employing organizations.

**What response to this change would you expect from customers and car manufacturers?**

The typical customer response was to move to smaller cars which offered the same standard of comfort they had been used to in their previously preferred larger cars. However, manufacturers like Jaguar and BMW did not make smaller cars. As a result their sales declined. In response, they broke with tradition by developing their own compact models – the X type in the case of Jaguar and the 1 series in the case of BMW. Once again a change in the external environment forced suppliers to change their product range in order to remain responsive to customer requirements. Alternatively and more charitably you would argue that prestige car manufacturers had predicted and planned for changes in customer requirement but slightly mis-timed their response.

Comparable changes in the external environment have resulted in other changes in customer definitions of 'satisfactory quality'.

| Example | • Internet shopping has led to fast and easy access to a wide range of products and services. |
|---|---|
|  | • Competition from Japanese car manufacturers led customers to expect higher basic specification levels of equipment from European made cars. |
|  | • Privatized public transport has led to higher customer expectations of service, convenience and price. |

## Your contribution to customer satisfaction

As was mentioned at the start of this chapter, many managers have little or no contact with external customers. And if your organization has not moved along the total quality route you may have no formal way of identifying the requirements and expectations of your external customers. Nevertheless, this does not remove your need to be aware of what your organization's customers expect from your products or services.

So, **what can you do?** There are three steps you can take:

In **Step 1**, you need to recognize that all organizations have customers:

- Patients are the customers of hospitals and GP surgeries.
- Taxpayers are customers of the Inland Revenue.
- Road users are the customers of local council road maintenance departments.
- Churchgoers are the customers of their local vicars.

You will notice we have deliberately chosen examples from non-profit making sectors in order to emphasize the fact that *all* organizations have an obligation to identify and satisfy their customers' expectations and requirements.

At **Step 2,** you make yourself aware of what those customer expectations and requirements are. Building on our earlier examples:

- Patients expect prompt and courteous attention, successful and relatively painless treatment.
- Taxpayers expect accurate advice delivered in a supportive and understanding way.
- Road users expect safe, smooth roads maintained with the minimum of inconvenience.
- Churchgoers expect stimulating sermons, lively hymns and comfortable pews.

**Who are your organization's customers?**

**What do they expect?**

**How do you and your team contribute to meeting their expectations?**

**Step 3** is to find out the external factors which are likely to influence those customers' expectations and requirements. Of course, that is not always easy. All well-run organizations monitor their own and their customers' external environment in order to identify:

- What the future demand for their products and services will be.
- How easily they will be able to acquire the resources to meet that demand.
- How much they will have to pay for those resources.
- The satisfaction their customers expect from their products or services.
- What competition they will face.
- Any external factors which will influence their customers' expectations.
- How those expectations will change as a result.

They do all this as part of the strategic planning process in order to forecast the nature and volume of future demand. Not all organizations make this information available to their staff. Consequently, in order to carry out the third and final step you will need to do one or more of the following:

- Use your employer's published report and accounts to find out its view of the opportunities and threats facing it.

- Pay attention to internal publications like a staff newsletter to gain the same insight.

- Find out if your organization runs a marketing customer awareness or TQM course at your level. If so arrange to attend it!

- Gain access through your organization's policy development strategic planning or marketing team to future environmental and customer demand forecast.

- Find out who your organization views as its customers. Then read the business sections in the newspaper or the internet regularly to see what informed outsiders believe is likely to affect them and what external factors may have an impact. For example, interest rates on consumer spending.

You may be wondering why you should put yourself to the trouble and inconvenience of going through this discovery process. It would indeed be foolish to pretend that the three steps we have described are simple or require no effort. The opposite is clearly the case. So, **what's the point?** There are three answers to this. The first is painfully practical. The second and third are more philosophical and go to the heart of the nature of management.

Our first answer goes back to the principles of total quality management. Any operation in any organization should contribute ultimately to customer satisfaction. And as we pointed out in Chapter 2, managers are responsible for ensuring that the operations they manage add value to the supply chain, which results in customer satisfaction. This 'added value' concept implies that operations that do not add value are both unnecessary and redundant. Even in an organization that has not made its operations subject to outside competition, it will not be long before an operation that does not add value is removed from the supply chain. It costs money but contributes nothing.

Our second answer confirms a point made in previous chapters. For managers to be able to forecast and plan, they must understand the external environment in which their organization operates. Only then will they be able to make effective decisions about the future direction of their own operations.

Finally, success and progression in management involve the ability to take an increasingly wider view of the external environment.

<table>
<tr><td>

**Review your learning**

</td><td>

Check your understanding of this chapter by completing the following:

1 How would an organization benefit from investing in monitoring customer expectations?

2 Everybody has two types of customers – what are they?

3 How does Juran define quality?

4 List five factors that make up the external environment.

</td></tr>
<tr><td>

**Theory to practice**

</td><td>

Apply this chapter to your own experience by answering the following:

1 How does your operation contribute to increasing customer satisfaction?

2 How much do you know about your organization's external customers?

3 How could you find out more?

4 What external factors affect demand for your organization's products or services?

5 Is that demand likely to increase, decrease or remain the same? Why?

6 How will this impact on your part of the organization?

</td></tr>
</table>

# 4 Understanding the culture

| Chapter Objectives | • *How does culture affect an organization's performance?* |
|---|---|
| | • *What is the significance of organizational culture to you as a manager?* |

In an environment of rapid change such as we described in the previous chapter, organizational success depends on the ability to respond quickly and appropriately to changes in resource availability, demand levels and customer requirements.

We also suggested earlier that the best decisions are most likely to be made by those people who are close to the situation, affected by the decision and who understand the implications. It is for this reason that organizations are increasingly delegating decision-making responsibility and accountability to lower levels of management and to non-managerial staff.

However, regardless of how desirable it may be, it is not possible simply to stick-on speed of decision-making and delegation like a first-aid dressing to improve effectiveness because the culture of the organization may prevent this from happening.

Working in an organization, whether private or public sector, at any level, means being part of the organization's culture. As a manager it is important for you to understand your organization not only in terms of its functions and procedures but also what its values and beliefs are, and how they underpin the organization.

## What is organizational culture?

The following quotes provide a good starting point in helping us to understand what is meant by 'organizational culture':

*The glue that holds the actors together, it provides people with a continuing sense of reality. It gives meaning to what they do.*
Hunt (1995)

*A pattern of beliefs and behaviours, assumptions and routines ...*
*which are distributed across the organization, usually in an uneven*
*pattern.*
Galunic and Weeks (2001)

So culture is all about 'the way we do things around here'. This is
the result of an organization's

- History
- Size
- Ownership
- Purpose or function.

### History

It is obvious that all organizations were established at particular
moments in history. Each moment had its own prevailing philosophies or management. For example, an organization set up a hundred years ago may have a tradition of making decisions centrally at
a high level in the expectation that they will then be obeyed without
question.

### Size

Small organizations present different management challenges from
large ones. A small organization will typically have a 'hands-on' style
of management simply because it is neither big enough to afford, nor
operationally requires, several tiers of management. Large organizations on the other hand, particularly those operating from several
sites like retail chains, are likely to have sets of formal rules and procedures to ensure consistency of decision-making.

### Ownership

Differences in ownership have several implications. Publicly owned
and funded organizations (government departments, schools, hospitals) usually place great emphasis on ensuring that taxpayers'
money is not wasted. As a result, decisions are carefully monitored
and controlled to check that they give good value for money. On the
other hand, businesses owned by their senior managers have much
greater freedom to make entrepreneurial decisions.

### Purpose

Some organizations exist to provide largely routine and repetitive products or services. Think, for example, of simple manufacturing processes, or rubbish collection, or the processing of invoices. Any of these activities offers limited scope for creativity. On the other hand, picture an advertising agency, or a training department, or an architect's practice. All these functions depend for their success on creative and innovative thinking. In these cases it is essential for 'the way we do things around here' to allow freedom to experiment with the potential risk of expensive failure.

# Handy's four cultures

Many writers have attempted to define organizational culture and this chapter now introduces you to just one of them – Charles Handy.

Handy, an eminent management thinker, described four main organizational cultures. He stresses that no one culture is preferable to the others. Instead, he points out that each brings its own advantages and disadvantages. The secret is to make sure that the culture of an organization is a suitable match for its size, stage of development and the external environment in which it operates.

### Power culture

Handy likened this type of culture to that of a spider's web.

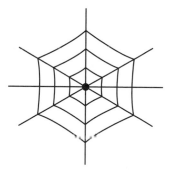

*Figure 4.1*

This culture depends on a strong leader and so the spider at the centre of the web is a single senior manager or a very small group of them. As with a real spider, the managers at the centre will be sensitive to everything that happens in the organization. Faced with a problem or an opportunity, they will make quick decisions based on their own intuition or experience. They will be quick to reward or punish, often arbitrarily. A power culture has few or no rules and procedures. What happens happens because the manager says so.

Examples of a power culture can often be found in small entrepreneurial businesses or family-owned companies. Those employed in such organizations need to be able to 'buy in' to the culture and be able to anticipate what is expected of them and perform accordingly.

A power culture is responsive and opportunistic. Little or no power or authority is delegated. It can only work in a small, centralized organization because decision-making relies on managers 'walking the job' to keep up to date with everything that goes on. It also depends for its success on having a strong, capable leader at its centre. Examples of individuals who could be said to have established power culture within their organizations are Bill Gates, Chairman and Chief Software Architect of Microsoft, and Richard Branson, founder of Virgin Records and Virgin Atlantic Airways.

### Role culture

The role culture is the opposite of the power culture. In this type of culture roles are given precedence over individuals and logic, reason and procedures govern people's behaviour. Examples of this type of culture are commonly seen in large organizations such as banks, and public sector environments such as the Civil Service.

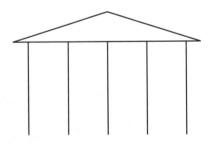

*Figure 4.2*

Handy illustrated this type of culture as a Greek temple; with each of the pillars of the temple representing a different function, e.g. production, sales, administration, personnel. Work in a role culture is controlled by formal rules and procedures, typically with large procedure manuals that specify exactly what actions to take in every imaginable situation. Each function operates independently, with co-ordination being carried out by senior managers at the top of the structure – represented by the temple roof. A role culture is good at achieving consistent decisions based on its comprehensive set of rules and can offer significant job security. However, staff are rarely treated as individuals but rather as payroll numbers expected to carry out specific tasks according to procedure. As you can imagine it is difficult for role cultures to respond quickly to change. Procedures are tightly defined, therefore nothing can change until new procedures have been worked out and written.

### Task culture

A task culture is most frequently found in organizations that place a premium on innovation and creative thinking and are often found in creative businesses such as advertising and marketing companies. They are often the culture underpinning project teams where the development of innovative or revolutionary approaches is a primary requirement. Consequently, task cultures work well in an environment of rapid change because their principal strength lies in finding different ways of doing things.

Handy illustrated this type of culture by way of a net.

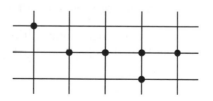

*Figure 4.3*

The net, with people where the cords cross, suggests that in a task culture people depend on each other. It is also flat, indicating that hierarchy or status are not issues. Instead, people respect each other for their knowledge and expertise – their ability to come up with the right ideas to get things done.

Task cultures are not all good news though. Because they are non-hierarchical and respect expertise rather than status, they are notoriously difficult to control. They are also expensive. Creative solutions may work – or they may not. Task cultures come up with more than their fair share of costly failures. That, after all, is the price of a culture founded on experimentation.

**Person culture**

In this culture it is the individual rather than the organization that matters. This is the least common of the four cultures. Handy's symbol for this culture is a cluster – a series of unrelated blobs representing the people in the organization. This type of culture is found in small groups of specialized professionals, for example, doctors, lawyers, architects, who come together to form a business.

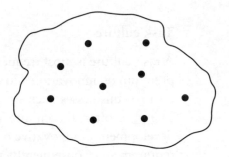

*Figure 4.4*

Person cultures are hardly organizations at all. No one is in charge, decisions can only be taken with the full agreement of all the members and there is no control: everyone can do their own thing without reference to others.

None of these four cultures is ideal. As circumstances change each will seek to adapt by borrowing approaches from others. For example:

- As a power culture grows in size, it may well introduce formal performance monitoring procedures from the role culture.
- Faced with rapid change, a role culture may introduce change groups or project teams from the task culture.
- When money is tight, a task culture may introduce financial controls from the role culture.
- Faced with a crisis decision, a person culture may introduce a dynamic leader from the power culture.

Consequently, the majority of organizations present uneasy cultural blends. A dominant culture may have bits of other cultures tacked on. Or different departments of the same organization may exhibit different cultures, for example the finance section of an organization may operate within a role culture where staff work within clearly defined parameters. The marketing department within the same organization may well operate a task culture with an emphasis on teamwork, innovation and informality. As a result, when the departments meet they negotiate from totally different sets of values and expectations.

# The significance of organizational culture to you as a manager

As a manager you need to understand how the culture works within your own organization in order for you to achieve what you are required to do. As has been shown, it is not just about understanding your organization in terms of its functions and procedures but also about understanding how the values and beliefs impact on and underpin the organization.

For example, if you are a manager in an advertising agency you may be fairly relaxed about working procedures within your team as long as they achieve results. On the other hand, if you are a manager within a bank you will need to ensure that your team adheres to the laid-down procedures in achieving objectives.

In recruiting new members to the team awareness of the culture will help you to select appropriate people who will 'fit' within the culture.

One of the tasks for you as a manager is to assess whether the culture of your operation fits:

- The needs and future direction of your organization
- The capability of your team
- The extent to which the controls to which they are subject allow for mistakes, experimentation and waste
- Your ability to make decisions and give direction
- The changes taking place in the environment in which the organization operates.

We shall explore later in the book how your leadership and management styles can impact on, and influence, the culture within your own organization.

**MANAGING IN CONTEXT**

31

# Changing organizational culture

As many managers and organizations have found, changing the culture is not an easy process! We have seen many examples of organizations reluctant to change 'the way they do things'; Marks & Spencer is one example within the retail sector that has had to significantly, albeit reluctantly, change operating practices in order to retain market share. So organizations need to adapt their cultures over time, but culture is derived from history and tradition among other things. As a result, it is deeply rooted within an organization and therefore difficult, time-consuming and often costly to change.

Consider the following situation:

**Insight**

> Alpha Industrials is a manufacturer of electrical components. Owned for several years by a multinational company and now on the edge of financial collapse, the business has been sold to its managers. Previously, instructions were issued by the multinational company owner, and Alpha Industrials obeyed. In order for the business to survive the new owners want to involve their staff in proposing and implementing some radical changes to operating methods.

**What culture changes will this involve?**

**How difficult will they be to introduce?**

Applying Handy's identified cultures to this situation produces these ideas:

In recent years, Alpha Industrials has probably been either a power or a role culture. Its multinational owner may have issued instructions and expected obedience. Or it will have been a role culture with operating methods contained in a procedures manual. In either culture, staff will have been expected to do as they were told.

Under its new management Alpha Industrials wants to introduce a task culture with an emphasis on managing change, innovation and problem-solving. In the past, suggesting a different approach may well have been frowned upon; now it is going to be welcomed. Cultural changes like this do not happen overnight. Staff will need to be encouraged, rewarded and probably trained to view their jobs differently. Alternatively the new owners could decide for themselves the new operating methods they wanted and give the orders (a power culture but with a new centre of power) or else issue a new set of procedures (a role culture). Of course, both these alternatives raise a range of issues. Neither involves staff in the decision-making process. Both assume that the new owners know exactly what operational changes need to be made. It may be that following the buy-out staff have been looking forward to involvement in making improvements. Either alternative will disappoint them if this is the case.

Successful cultural change is likely to require:

- Time to implement
- A visible change in management attitude
- Explanation and training for staff
- Willingness to accept confusion and misunderstanding
- Some expensive mistakes.

Handy's four cultures provide us with a useful starting point in understanding the complexities of organizational culture. They are descriptive, and he does not suggest that one is better than another and therefore should be adopted. In practice, no organization falls neatly into one of these cultures. Instead, the model offers a way of looking at organizational culture.

**Review your learning**

Check your understanding of this chapter by completing the following:

1 Organizational culture means; 'The way we d_ t_ _ _ _ _ _ a _ _ _ _ _ h_ _ _.'

2 List the four factors which determine an organization's culture.

3 Handy described four types of culture; briefly describe each type.

**Theory to practice**

Apply this chapter to your own experience by answering the following:

1 Which aspects of Handy's classification of culture fit with your organization?

2 Obtain a copy of your company's mission statement. What does the statement tell you about its purpose and core values?

3 How does the culture of your organization impact on the day-to-day operation?

# 5 Understanding the environment

| Chapter Objectives | • *What affects an organization's success or failure?* |
|---|---|

Organizations do not exist in a vacuum. They are subject to a wide range of external factors and influences which will have an effect, either positive or negative on:

- The cost and availability of resources, including raw materials, equipment, staff, property and money
- The demand for the organization's products or services
- Its turnover and profitability
- How cheaply and efficiently it can run its business.

These factors and influences are commonly called the 'PESTLE' factors:

Political
Economic
Social
Technological
Legal
Environmental

It would of course be a mistake to assume that each of these categories is watertight and has no influence on others. For example:

- Political decisions can have an impact on economic conditions.
- Changes in technology can affect the physical environment.
- Legal judgments can change people's working conditions as part of the social environment.

Nevertheless, for the remainder of this chapter we shall attempt to keep the six categories separate, simply pointing out where one is heavily influenced by others.

# Political factors

Directly or indirectly, political decisions can influence the economy, society, the law and the physical environment. In fact, there can even be a political impact on technological development when governments decide to put public money into specific research and development initiatives.

Political decisions may make specific markets more or less attractive. For example, French and German governments' actions in banning the import of British beef during the 2001 outbreak of foot-and-mouth disease resulted in the closure of many farms and the subsequent loss of farming and related sector jobs within the UK.

In the Budget the Chancellor may introduce or remove opportunities for organizations to make tax savings. Recent budget proposals in the UK have focused on giving incentives for businesses to invest, and lowering the levels of corporation tax.

Governments may offer financial incentives to encourage firms into areas of high unemployment (a good example of a political decision with social consequences). Such incentives may take the form of reduced local taxes, the offer of property at artificially low rents or even a subsidy to cut the cost of wages. Other political initiatives with social consequences include:

- Government sponsored training schemes
- Jobseeker's allowances
- Publicly funded careers guidance
- Equal opportunities legislation.

If central banks keep interest rates high, borrowing becomes more expensive both for consumers (buying things like cars and houses) and for businesses planning to invest.

Governments can take alternative views on the benefit of offering public support to businesses.

- Some seek to encourage competition
- Redistribute wealth

35

- Encourage enterprise
- Lower taxation.

The implications of a government's philosophies upon business could include:

- Higher or lower investment in technology and new products
- More or less emphasis on efficiency
- More or less encouragement to enter foreign markets
- Less or more state intervention in the decisions made by organizations.

All of these considerations affect an organization's long-term strategy and its day-to-day operations. As a country approaches the time of election, any uncertainty about the philosophy of the next government will cause a marked slowdown in economic activity. This is because individuals will delay purchase decisions, businesses put investment on hold and public services draw up alternative plans for the use of resources.

# Economic factors

The state of the economy depends in part on political factors. It is affected by political decisions such as:

### The level of individual taxation

Income tax in the UK has been reducing for the past two decades. In order to maintain government income, successive administrations have increasingly taxed expenditure through VAT and excise duties on commodities such as alcohol and petrol. This has had a major effect on businesses in the beverages and transport markets.

### The level and nature of corporation tax

Increasingly, UK governments have tried to give firms incentives to invest in technology and research and development. This has been done through the granting of tax relief on profits reinvested in the firm. Such tax relief has made it more attractive to retain and reinvest profit, therefore paying less out to shareholders.

### The government's attitude to unemployment

High unemployment nationally leads to reduced consumer demand. However, in recent years writers on politics, economics and management have argued that governments have far less impact on a nation's economy than they would like to think. There is significant logic in this argument. Governments have little or no influence over:

- The economies of other countries
- Levels of demand from other countries
- The level of competition from businesses at home or abroad
- Social change and consequent shifts in demand. For example, divorce rates, numbers of children in families, where people choose to live, the age of the population
- The overall rate of technological development
- Customer preferences
- Customer confidence and willingness to spend money.

As a result, although we realize that political decisions have some impact on the economic environment, we can see that it is reasonable to treat economic factors as independent and worthy of separate consideration.

# Social factors

Society is made up of people – individuals, families, communities. Sociology is the study of people – which means that it includes a very wide variety of topics. The following is a representative list of the social factors that influence an organization's customer base, nature and level of demand, staff availability and expectations.

### Age of the population

Throughout Europe populations are getting older. In the UK the proportion of the population aged 65 and over continues to increase, whilst the proportion of the population below the age of 16 is less now than 30 years ago. This in turn leads to significant implications for both businesses and society as a whole. Predictably, the nature of the products and services people want and need is influenced by age. For example, a younger population has a greater need for maternity services while an older population has more need for hip replacements and elderly care. With an ageing population employers who traditionally recruited school-leavers now have to be prepared to take on older staff.

### Education and training

The standard of education which people receive influences their lifestyle and their leisure activities. Higher standards of education tend to increase demand for specialist books and the arts like theatre, ballet and opera. Currently in the UK schools and universities are placing greater emphasis on giving students the skills necessary for work. The quality and quantity of training available have increased, partly in recognition of the need to compete in the international marketplace. At both local and national levels standards of education and training influence the nature of demand and the availability of qualified and competent staff.

### Family composition

Twenty years ago a typical UK family was made up of husband, wife and 2.4 children. That stereotype no longer applies. This has resulted from a range of social changes, including:

- An increase in divorce
- Decline in marriage, as couples choose to live together in preference to marriage
- Increase in the numbers of gay and lesbian couples
- More people living alone
- Working women delaying the start of a family
- Single parent families.

The organizational impact of these changes has included an increased need for more flexible and part-time working and workplace crèches, a further need for smaller housing units, increased demand for labour-saving devices like microwave ovens and dishwashers and for convenience foods.

### Wealth and status categories

Traditionally we have separated society into simple categories, like working class, middle class, upper class. Today, social researchers use more sophisticated methods of analysis and separation. Nevertheless old-style and new-style social categories both recognize that people's lifestyle, purchasing power and the nature of the things they buy are dependent on their wealth and status. Over time the size and importance of different social categories change. A hundred years ago it was the nobility who had most money and, as a result, products and services were largely designed, produced and priced to appeal to them. A combination of the expense of maintaining their family homes, extravagant living, death duties and the growth of the middle classes has turned the nobility into a minor and specialist market.

## Insight

Alan Thornton has decided to use his experience of computer manufacture to start a business making electronic components. He has found a possible factory site on a small industrial estate in the North East. What questions should he ask about political, economic and social factors before finalizing his plans for the business and its location?

**It would be sensible for Alan to find out:**

- Whether there are any financial incentives from local or national government available for his chosen location.

- Whether the components he plans to make are the subject of severe competition, either from the UK or abroad.

- Whether the markets he intends to service are experiencing fast, slow or negative growth.

- Whether there are enough people available in the local job market to satisfy his recruitment needs.

- Whether they have the right training and experience.

- How easily and cheaply he will be able to buy the raw materials he needs.

- Whether most of his sales will be to national or overseas customers.

- If selling to overseas customers, the export regulations he will be required to obey and the cost and inconvenience of doing so.

# Technological factors

Developments in technology significantly affect:

- Production and distribution methods
- Customer demand and expectation
- Product desirability and price
- Administrative efficiency.

| Example | **Production methods** |
| --- | --- |

**Production methods**

The introduction of computer control into manufacturing and stock management has reduced the need for people to do repetitive, semi skilled production line jobs; improved production control and output quality; given scope to change production specifications more easily and quickly; improved the accuracy of stock control thereby reducing stockholding.

**Distribution technology**

This has mainly affected information transfer and mechanical handling. Orders are now often placed and processed using electronic data links. Most warehouses of any size are now operated from a central control point, using computer systems and electronic switching to move products around.

**Customer demand and expectations**

These change as new technology becomes available. Customer expectation is for immediate availability of goods and services. Shopping on the Internet has significantly increased choice and access to a wide range of goods and services and also had an impact on, for example, sales of compact discs (CDs) as customers can download and copy music from the Internet.

All of the above are examples of product desirability rising and falling as competition changes in response to technological development. As technology becomes more sophisticated and widespread, so it becomes easier and cheaper to produce highly specified products. The majority of mobile phones now offer a broad range of functions, including digital camera and video player – they are no longer simply a mobile method of communication.

Conversely, new technology may lead to simpler products which respond to the buying public's environmental awareness (a theme we shall return to a little later) and making new types of product available to developing countries. Examples of this are wind-up radios and torches which are powered by a simple mechanical action and have no need of batteries or mains electricity.

# Legal factors

In Europe, the United States and, increasingly, the Far East there is a large body of legislation which governs the decisions managers are allowed to take concerning their organizations. It is vital as a manager to be aware of the range of legislation that impacts on the day-to-day operation of the business.

### Company law

Company law lays down rules which specify how different types of organizations – charities, partnerships, private companies, sole traders, public limited companies – must behave. It affects such things as the preparation and publication of accounts, the issue of shares, liability in case of bankruptcy and the actions needed in order to set up an organization legally.

### Contract and trading law

This aspect of law is likely to have a greater impact on you either as a manager, a customer or both.

Contracts are an important part of business life. They establish agreements between the organization and its employees, its suppliers, customers and other businesses. UK contract law is based on two assumptions: that everyone is free to choose which contract they enter into and the terms on which they do so. Fundamental to this philosophy is the idea that if two parties cannot agree an acceptable contract, they are free to take their business elsewhere. It is this idea which has led to competition law in the UK and anti-trust law in the United States, both of which are designed to ensure that no single business controls so much of a market that customers cannot go to another supplier. Contract law also sets out to ensure that if one of the parties to a contract is in a weak bargaining position (for example a single member of staff negotiating with a big employer), their rights are strengthened.

A legal contract must have six ingredients. It must involve:

- Agreement (one party makes an offer; the other accepts it)
- Consideration (each side must promise to give or do something to the other's benefit)
- Intention (the parties must intend their agreement to have legal consequences)
- Form (some contracts must be in writing)
- Genuineness of consent (no one can be forced into a contract)
- Capacity (the parties must be legally capable of entering into a contract) – for example, many contracts with young people under 18, those with recognized mental health problems, or those under the influence of alcohol, cannot be legally enforced.

Some examples of the day-to-day implications of contract law are as follows:

| **Example** | <ul><li>Businesses intending to expand their operations may find themselves prevented from doing so by competition law.</li><li>A bankrupt organization may not be entitled to continue trading.</li><li>Employees cannot be forced into accepting changes to their contracts of employment.</li></ul> |
| --- | --- |

Trading law relates primarily to the supply and sale of goods and services. Legally goods and services must be:

- of satisfactory quality (in other words they must do what might reasonably be expected of them)
- fit for the purpose (that is, they must meet the customer's needs if the customer has specified these needs and relied on the supplier to provide something suitable)
- in accordance with their description (a 'leather suitcase' must not be made mainly of plastic)
- consistent with a sample (for example, if you inspect a display table in a furniture store and the store then orders one for you from the manufacturer, the table you get must be of the same specification as the one you inspected).

These legal requirements are of particular relevance to marketing and advertising (description); sales (fitness for purpose); but also to manufacturing and production (merchantable quality) and to quality assurance (samples and specification).

### Employment law

It is this category of legislation which is likely to have the greatest and most frequent impact on you as a manager. In Europe and the United States the following are all against the law:

- Discrimination on the basis of sex, race, religion, disability
- Sexual harassment
- Providing unsafe working conditions
- Unfair dismissal.

Other requirements, which apply in some countries but not others, apply to: written contracts of employment; rights to paid holidays and sick leave; union recognition; redundancy procedures; age discrimination; minimum wages.

This diverse range of employment law requirements have implications for one-off events like the recruitment of a new member of staff; for regular events like appraisal and the provision of training; and for the day-to-day management of staff. Consequently, as a manager you need to ensure you know the law that applies to your particular situation and take early advice from human resources or personnel colleagues in cases of doubt or difficulty.

# Environmental factors

This heading refers to society's concern for the physical environment. As we mentioned earlier, some governments have passed laws to, for example, reduce exhaust emissions from cars and lorries; protect natural resources like slow-growing hardwoods, limestone and peat; prevent the destruction of areas of national beauty by limiting the building of roads, houses and factories.

Public concern for the environment has resulted in demands for recyclable packaging; ozone-friendly cleaning products; improved public transport; reduced use of chemicals in food production; a more cautious approach towards developing genetically modified food.

Manufacturing responses have included the development of electric cars; emphasis on the use of renewable raw materials; more efficient use of energy; improved methods of waste disposal.

You may not be involved in the design and development of products or services. You will certainly not be involved in deciding the location of new premises for your organization. However, since continuous improvement is a central part of a manager's job, you may well be able to introduce or influence:

- More energy efficient production methods
- Reductions in waste
- Reduced use of consumable items (even basic things like paper, cleaning materials, telephone usage)
- Simpler, less wasteful administrative procedures.

## Review your learning

Check your understanding of this chapter by completing the following:

1 List six categories of external factor that affect an organization's performance.

2 List four aspects of the economy over which government has little or no influence.

3 Which are the four developments in technology which can affect organizations?

## Theory to practice

Apply this chapter to your own experience by answering the following:

1 How have your organization's products or services changed in recent years? What influence have external factors had on those changes?

2 Is your organization finding it harder or easier to recruit staff? Which external factor has brought about that change?

3 What impact have technological developments had on your organization?

4 How confident are you in your knowledge of employment law? How could you find out more?

5 What could you do to improve energy efficiency in your operation?

6 How could you reduce waste in your operation?

# Resource bank

## References

Brech, E. F. L. (1953) *Principles and Practice of Management*, Longman
Crosby, P. (1979) *Quality is Free*, McGraw-Hill
Drucker, P. F. (1954) *The Practice of Management*, Butterworth-Heinemann
Fayol, H. (1916) *General & Industrial Management*, Pitman
Galunic, C. and Weeks, J. (2001) 'A Cultural Evolution in Business Thinking: Mastering People Management', *Financial Times* (London), 29 October, pp. 2–3
Goldsmith, W. and Clutterbuck, D. (1985) *The Winning Streak*, Penguin
Handy, C. (1985) *Understanding Organizations*, Penguin
Hunt, J. (1995) *Managing People at Work*, McGraw-Hill
Kanter, R. M. (1989) *When Giants Learn to Dance*, Simon & Schuster
Koontz, H. (1914) *Towards a Unified Theory of Management*, McGraw-Hill
Mullins, L. (2002) *Management and Organization Behaviour*, FT Prentice-Hall
Stewart, R. (1999) *The Reality of Management*, Butterworth-Heinemann

## Website addresses

**www.bh.com**
Business and management publisher providing a range of textbooks and flexible learning resources on related subjects

**www.businesslink.gov.uk**
Provides impartial advice for small businesses

**www.DonnaEarlTraining.com**
US training consultant

**www.FT.com**
*The Financial Times* – provides UK and international news and reports

**www.juran.com**
Official website of the Juran Institute

**www.virgin.com**
The Virgin Airline website

# Section 2 Providing Direction

- *How can I develop as a professional manager?*
- *In what ways can I improve my communication skills?*
- *How can I communicate more effectively at work?*
- *What is the difference between a manager and a leader?*
- *How do I get the best out of my staff?*
- *What is motivation?*
- *Why is motivation so important?*
- *What motivates people?*
- *How do I manage conflict?*

# 6 Developing professionally

| **Chapter Objectives** | • *How can I develop as a professional manager?* |
|---|---|

*Personal and professional development is a journey, not a destination!*

The overall focus of this book, as shown in Section 1, is about the role of the manager from, for example, making the best use of resources, motivating the team, managing projects to focusing on customers. However, the starting point of that role is developing self-awareness of your own strengths and challenges as an individual and as a manager. For example, how do you reflect on your experience, how do you cope with stress and how do you achieve a balance in your work and life?

This chapter examines the skills you need to manage yourself, developing as a professional benefiting not only yourself, but also your team.

## Developing self-awareness

How can you manage, motivate and inspire others if you are not aware of your own values and behaviours?

Organizations are generally placing greater value on the sensing/emotional side of management and a body of literature has emerged focusing on recognizing and developing our emotional intelligence in order to manage more effectively.

*self-awareness is the vital foundation skill for three emotional competencies ...*
Goleman (1999)

**PROVIDING DIRECTION**

Goleman identified these as:

- *Emotional awareness* – being able to recognize how our emotions actually impact on our performance and understanding how our values affect decision-making.

- *Accurate self-assessment* – being able to have a sense of our own strengths and limitations, having a vision of how we need and can improve and having the ability to learn from experience.

- *Self-confidence* – the strength that comes from knowing our own capabilities, values and what we want and need to achieve.

So knowing your own strengths and limitations as well as those of your team members enables you to undertake and allocate tasks, effectively delegate and make the best use of your own strengths and those of your team. Recognizing your limitations and those of your team enables you to identify areas for development and use learning opportunities appropriately.

Goleman suggests that self-confidence is '*a strong sense of one's self-worth and capabilities*'.

We can all think of occasions when we have had that strong *sense* and have been able to tackle day-to-day issues and problems decisively, but there are also other occasions when lack of confidence as a manager results in us doubting our own abilities and the decisions that we make. There is a balance to be found between that lack of self-confidence and being overly confident, which can portray arrogance.

Leech (2004) suggests there are keys to building and maintaining a level of self-confidence:

- *Recognize that no one is confident all the time, even though they may appear to be.*

- *Avoid comparing yourself to other people. They have their strengths, you have yours.*

- *Acknowledge your own strengths, skills and abilities – use them and build on them.*

- *Always remember that if you look and sound confident, that's how people will perceive you.*

# Managing your own training and development

Identifying training and developing needs for your team applies equally to what you should expect for yourself. For example:

Do you know the objectives and standards expected of you? More specifically, do you know what is set out in your job description? If you do not have one or it is not clear, have you asked your manager?

Do you know how well you are performing against those standards? Do you regularly seek feedback from your:

- Manager?
- Colleagues?
- Your team, who will be in the best position to tell you how effective you are as a manager?
- Have you identified your own training needs?

You can do this, first of all, by comparing your performance with expected standards. Secondly, by looking ahead to see how your job will change and identifying any new knowledge and skill requirements arising from the changes.

Have you decided what your career aspirations are? Where do you want to be in, say, two years and five years? What development will you need to get there?

Are you making the best use of your organization's performance review process? Do you prepare effectively for your review? Can you give relevant answers to your manager's questions about your training and development needs?

How much thought do you give to how these can be met in practical terms? What knowledge and skills do you need? What additional experience? Would further qualifications help you achieve your career objectives?

# Reflecting on experience

One of the most important aspects of being a professional is that you are able to continually update your knowledge and skills to meet the changing demands of the environment in which you work. A crucial way of doing this is through the ability to learn

51

from experience – this enables you to grow from 'apprentice' to professional manager.

By reflecting on your experience as a manager you will be constantly reviewing your own level of competence, your knowledge and skills and how effectively you manage the differing problems you encounter on a day-to-day basis.

A cautionary note – experience does not necessarily result in learning. You can probably think of people you have worked with who have many years' experience but who appear not to have learned anything in that time!

**So why is reflection important?**

First, reflection is a key component in the learning process. By reflecting on issues at work for example, you can build up your own ideas which can then be put to the test in new situations.

Secondly, by reflecting and considering other people's ideas and theories many of which are outlined in this book, you can then put these ideas into action.

Thirdly, reflecting on your job as a manager enables you to question the way you do things and whether the way you are doing it is, for example, the most cost-effective way.

You will find the Theory to Practice activity at the end of each chapter a practical way of reflecting on and improving your own management style and skills.

# Valuing equality and diversity

Diversity at work is about recognizing and valuing that people are different and adapting work practices accordingly; it is not just about race or gender.

As a manager you should reflect, through the way you conduct yourself and how you manage your team, the principles of:

- Dignity at work
- Equal opportunities
- Equal treatment
- Inclusion

- Managing flexibility
- Respect for the individual
- Valuing diversity.

*Managers need to work to ensure diversity drives inclusiveness and co-operation, and is about more than just box ticking and employment quotas, instead diversity focuses on changing working cultures and embracing difference.*
CIPD

So how can you incorporate these values into your day-to-day work and into the management of your team?

Managing diversity is not a 'one-off', it is a process of improvement that encompasses aspects such as behaviour in the workplace, communication and training.

As a manager you should ensure that you:

- Set standards of behaviour that are based on respect and dignity, focusing on fairness and inclusion
- Look for ways of addressing the diverse needs of your team and those of your customers, both internal and external
- Develop open communication channels using team meetings, for example, to ensure your team are kept up to date with diversity policies and practices
- Encourage your team to embrace the concepts and practice of diversity through handling different views, perceptions and ideas in a positive way.

*Clients are increasingly looking for innovative and creative services and products. Diverse teams are more likely to come up with creative ideas and solutions as there will be more debate within them.*
PricewaterhouseCooper (Incomes Data Services 2004)

- Keep up to date with changes in the law and participate in your organization's monitoring and evaluation processes.

Importantly, you need to be prepared to challenge your own views, beliefs and attitudes. Be honest, check your own assumptions and identify where you need to change.

*Being able to value diversity means being able to widen your view of what is normal to include the rich diversity of human life.*
Leech (2005)

# Managing stress

Stress is something we all experience in varying degrees in both our working and daily lives. But we tend to be bombarded with conflicting messages about stress:

*Stress is good for you, it keeps you on your toes, it's challenging.*

On the other hand we are told:

*Stress is bad for you, it can lead to burn out and serious illness.*

This would suggest that stress is either wholly good or bad, which is not the case. We need a certain amount of pressure to motivate us but it is widely accepted that the problems arise when these pressures develop into stress. So an understanding of stress, how we react to it and how we can manage it in others is an important aspect of developing ourselves.

First, we need to define stress:

*the adverse reaction people have to excessive pressure or other types of demand placed on them.*
HSE

Pressure is part of everyday work: pressure to meet a deadline, pressure to achieve a target, pressure to exceed customer expectations. But when does this pressure become stress which results in us unable to perform our jobs properly?

In 2004/5 12.8 million working days were lost to stress, depression and anxiety in the UK, according to the HSE (Health and Safety Executive). So how does pressure lead to stress? How can we identify the stressors?

**Case Study**

> Mary has just returned to work in the small local branch of the bank she used to work in following a career break of five years whilst she had two children. Her role is customer services team leader, which is a new role for Mary as previously she worked in the mortgage section of the branch. She was the most hard-working and popular member of the mortgage team.

Her eldest child has just started school and is having problems settling and the youngest is looked after by a childminder.

Mary has been back at work about a month and feels she is struggling with her new role. The staff at the bank have all changed since she was last there, her team don't work well together, the branch manager is relatively new and Mary is finding that she is constantly interrupted in her work and feels that she has been given very demanding targets to achieve.

Mary feels under pressure both at work and at home.

**What are the pressures Mary is under and what can she do about them?**

Initially Mary may respond well to the pressures at work and feel stretched and challenged by her new role. She will want to achieve the targets and succeed as she had done in her previous role. However, if she is not able to resolve some of the issues and the pressure continues then she may become anxious, indecisive with negative feelings of incompetence – leading to stress.

Mary needs to recognize the pressures she is under and look at ways of managing this. It will probably involve talking to her manager, gaining support and cooperation from the team and looking at different ways of managing her workload.

At home Mary may well be struggling with balancing her role as parent and employee. She needs to perhaps seek additional help from family members.

It is important that we recognize the impact different levels of pressure have on our performance. Conversely, too little or too much pressure can impact on our performance leading to stress. as shown in Figure 6.1.

The HSE has developed a set of Management Standards for Work-related Stress which cover six key areas of work design which, if not properly managed, are associated with poor health and well-being, lower productivity and increased sickness absence.

The six key areas are:

- *Demands* – This covers issues such as workload, work patterns and the work environment. For example, the standard is that *'employees indicate that they are able to cope with the*

| LOW PRESSURE | OPTIMUM | HIGH PRESSURE |
|---|---|---|
| Under stimulation | Effective performance | Over-stimulation |
| Tiredness | Energized | 'Burn-out' |
| Boredom | Creative | Tension |
| Dissatisfaction | Flexible | Poor decision-making |
| Stagnation | Satisfaction | Exhaustion |
| | Receptive to change | Illness |
| STRESS | | STRESS |

PERFORMANCE

PRESSURE

*Figure 6.1*

*demands of their jobs'*. To achieve this one of the HSE recommendations is that *'people's skills and abilities are matched to the job demands'*.

- *Control* – This relates to how much say a person has in the way they do their work.

- *Support* – This includes the encouragement, sponsorship and resources provided by the organization, line management and colleagues.

- *Relationships* – This standard includes promoting positive working to avoid conflict and dealing with unacceptable behaviour.

- *Role* – This is about whether people understand their role within the organization and whether the organization ensures that an individual does not have conflicting roles.

- *Change* – This is how the organization manages and communicates change, large or small.

All of these aspects are part of the principles of good management and you will find the tools and techniques for achieving these as you study this book.

## Achieving a work/life balance

Figures from the HSE show that:

*Workers in the UK work the longest hours in Europe.*

*DTI research has highlighted the link between long hours and stress.*

*One in six workers in the UK work more than 60 hours per week.*

### Why has this situation arisen?

The world of work and work patterns are changing. Increasingly businesses are operating long hours and outside of the traditional 9 to 5 pattern. Banks and supermarkets for example, are now having to offer a 24 hour service to satisfy customer expectation and needs. Increasingly people are finding they are having to juggle their responsibilities at home and work.

This can result in:

- Feelings of guilt in relation to child care
- Taking work home, extending the working day even more
- Limited social life because of working long hours
- Frustration from trying to have a perfect home life and be the perfect manager and succeeding at neither.

Fortunately both organizations and central government are taking steps to help both employers and employees achieve a balance.

There are clearly a number of benefits to a business in introducing policies that underpin work/life balance issues. These include:

- Higher productivity and competitiveness
- Increased flexibility and customer service
- Increased morale and motivation amongst the workforce
- Reduction in absenteeism
- Meeting legal requirements.

Many organizations have developed supportive, flexible working environments, embracing family-friendly practices, flexi-time, and a mix of part- and full-time opportunities.

Evidence suggests that flexible working can benefit all concerned. A survey undertaken in 2001 found that 70% of those who work flexible hours scored higher than their full-time colleagues on resilience, leadership and commitment – and also produced more work.

### The legal implications

From April 2003 the law requiring employers to incorporate work/life balance provision was significantly extended to cover aspects of employment such as:

- Annual leave
- Working time

- Parental leave
- Time off for dependent care
- Maternity leave
- Paternity leave
- Adoption leave
- Right to request flexible working
- Part-time work.

So how can you find the right balance? You can begin by answering the following questions:

- What are your life goals over the next five years?
- What are your work goals?
- Which are the areas of your life that you want to give more or less attention?
- How do you distribute your time between the various aspects of your life?

Once you start to achieve a balance then you will be able to promote this with your team, encouraging flexibility, engaging and empowering them.

*A balanced life is one where we spread our energy and effort – emotional, intellectual, imaginative, spiritual and physical – between the key areas of importance. The neglect of one or more areas, or anchor points, may threaten the viability of the whole.*
Halpin (2005)

**Review your learning**

Check your understanding of this chapter by completing the following:

1 Which are the three emotional competencies of self-awareness that Goleman identified?

2 What is the HSE definition of stress?

3 List the six key work design areas identified in the HSE Management Standards for Work-related Stress?

4 Give three business benefits of introducing work/life balance policies.

**Theory to practice**

Apply this chapter to your own experience by answering the following:

1  How do you identify your own strengths and limitations?

2  Develop an action plan, with time-scales, for addressing your limitations.

3  How do you embrace the concept of valuing diversity in your day-to-day activities at work?

4  How can you encourage more flexible working in your team whilst still achieving organizational objectives?

PROVIDING DIRECTION

# 7  Principles of effective communication

<table>
<tr><td>Chapter<br>Objectives</td><td>● In what ways can I improve my communication skills?</td></tr>
</table>

Effective communication is central to an organization's success. An essential skill of an effective manager is the ability to communicate well with your team, your customers and suppliers and at all levels within the organization.

Communication is part of our everyday working lives; it tends to be something that we take for granted, often with little thought given to the processes involved. Consequently we frequently find examples of bad communication and it is one of the major aspects that many organizations fail to get right.

*Among managers, communications competence strongly distinguishes star performers from average or poor ones; the lack of this ability ... can torpedo morale.*
Goleman (1999)

So, as a manager not only do you need to be an effective communicator but you also need to understand the process as well.

In this chapter we look at the key aspects of communication and identify ways in which you can improve this vital skill.

The purpose of communication is not simply to transmit information, it is to achieve a result. The desired result may take any one of a number of forms, for example:

- An instruction to one of your team is intended to bring about action – they carry out the instruction.
- Congratulating your team on a job well done is intended to motivate them to continue working well.

- Pointing out unacceptable behaviour, perhaps as part of a disciplinary process, is intended to stop that behaviour in future.

- Management control information is intended to facilitate decisions about corrective action.

- An announcement to patients in a hospital waiting room that the clinic is running 30 minutes late is intended to forewarn them and prevent complaints.

Of course transmitting information may not have the desired effect. We can begin to understand why not and what to do about it by looking at a communication model.

# A communication model

The process of communication involves a sender and a receiver:

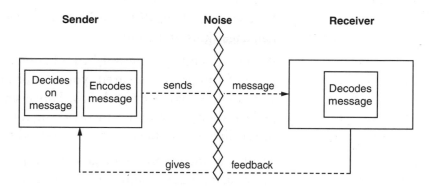

*Figure 7.1*

- The 'sender' is the person transmitting the information.
- The 'receiver' is the person for whom it is intended.
- The 'message' is the information itself.
- 'Encoding' is the process of translating the information in the sender's head into the message.
- 'Decoding' is the process by which the receiver interprets the message.
- 'Noise' is anything which gets in the way of the message being received and properly understood.
- 'Feedback' is confirmation that the receiver has understood the message.

The model itself is simple. However, each of the elements in it is rather more complex. Because effective communication is not a straightforward mechanical process, the most helpful way of exploring the complexities is to examine what can go wrong at each stage.

### Deciding on the message

If you are not clear in your own mind what you want to communicate, you stand little chance of getting your receiver to understand it. In that situation we often fall into the trap of either leaving out important information or giving the receiver so much information that the overall message becomes confusing or incomprehensible.

### Encoding the message

Receivers will have different levels of knowledge and experience, language skills and confidence.

If you are sending a message to a maintenance engineer to get a piece of equipment repaired, you do not need to explain how it works – the engineer will know. However, if you want an inexperienced operator to use the machine for the first time, it would be sensible to provide a basic understanding of the machine.

The basic rule about language is to keep it as simple as you can, avoiding ambiguous and emotive statements.

Direct messages will suit confident receivers. Those with less confidence may need a gentler and more reassuring tone.

You may come across the ABC of communication, indicating that a message should be:

- Accurate
- Brief
- Clear.

Of course, all messages should be accurate – but difficult messages may need some careful phrasing. How brief you can be will depend on how much your receiver needs to know, and what constitutes clarity will depend on things like knowledge, experience, education and language ability.

### Sending the message

We can transmit information by various media including:

- Sign language
- Pictures
- Braille
- Body language
- Telephone
- Facsimile
- Email
- Video conferencing
- The Internet
- Computer networking.

At this stage there are two important factors to consider. The first is the need to select the most suitable communication medium. Suitability will depend on:

- The purpose you want to achieve
- Whether you need immediate feedback
- The length and complexity of the message
- The urgency of transmitting the information
- The urgency of achieving your purpose
- Who your intended receivers are
- Where your receivers are located
- How close your working relationships are with your receivers.

The second factor to remember is to keep your message consistent. For example:

- With face-to-face communication your words must be consistent with your body language.
- With sales literature, a message designed to impress must be presented impressively.
- An urgent message must be transmitted in a way that conveys urgency.

### Noise

Messages can be distorted in many ways. For example:

- Physical distortions, like conveying a verbal message in a noisy location
- Using jargon that is not understood
- Transmitting a message to a receiver who is angry
- Transmitting a difficult message to someone who rejects it entirely or receives it selectively.

### Decoding the message

So far, we have concentrated on the responsibilities of the sender to get the message right and clear, and send it in a suitable and consistent way. But there is a burden of responsibility on the receiver, too. Decoding the message involves:

- Working out what the sender intended
- Highlighting any uncertainty or confusion
- Seeking clarification.

### Cultural differences

Increasingly managers are working in a global marketplace, and you may well have customers, suppliers and colleagues working in different countries. You may communicate in the same language but the cultural differences need to be understood to ensure that there are no communication pitfalls.

Being aware of cultural differences – for example, British and Americans require more personal space than other cultures, pointing with a finger is considered rude in China, an embrace is an acceptable greeting in some European countries – will enable you to communicate effectively and avoid cultural misunderstandings. The HSBC Bank has run a series of adverts that powerfully demonstrate the importance of cultural awareness.

### Feedback

All messages result in feedback, some aspects of which are more useful and valuable than others.

**Formal feedback** is a deliberate response to the message. It may be 'I understand and will do it now', or 'I do not know how to do that. Will you explain?' **Informal feedback** involves the interpretation of unintended signals from the receiver. For example, if you ask a team member 'Are you happy about doing that?' and your receiver says 'Yes' but with gritted teeth and clenched fists, the feedback is that your message has been badly received and the task may not be done, or be done badly.

As the descriptions suggest, **immediate feedback** may take the form of a response straight away in the case of telephone or face-to-face communication, or by return in the case of written communication. **Delayed feedback** may contradict a formal response, initially made after a week or two. The response may not be what was desired. If you send a message requesting action and still nothing happens even after a long period, the informal delayed feedback is 'No, I will not', 'I cannot be bothered', 'I am too busy'.

The most useful feedback is formal and immediate. It allows you to take corrective action which may take the form of further clarification or persuasion.

Delayed feedback is difficult to deal with. Your response to silence will depend on how well you know the receiver and your working relationship. You may respond by:

- Chasing for a reply
- Stressing the urgency of your message
- Going to someone else
- Changing the message.

# Informing, persuading and influencing

It is the human aspects of communication which make it succeed – or fail. Technically, there are some fairly simple guidelines to follow in encoding and sending a message.

Consider who is receiving your message:

- Their knowledge and experience
- Their level of confidence
- Their willingness to cooperate – or not
- Your relationship with them.

65

**Informing** people is not an end in itself. You inform to achieve a result. To achieve that result you need to understand the people involved. Nowhere is that more important than when your purpose is to change people's attitudes, opinions or actions, or to encourage them to do something which they had not thought of doing; in other words, when your purpose is to persuade or influence.

Managers are in the business of selling – not products or services in most cases, but ideas. You are selling an idea when you:

- Make a recommendation to your manager
- Suggest improvements to your team
- Make a case for additional resources
- Apply for a promotion.

If you want people to accept – or buy – an idea, they will only do so if they can see how they will benefit from it. Benefits result from satisfying people's needs.

We will examine the sorts of needs or expectations people have from work when we look at motivation in a later chapter. As far as **persuading and influencing** are concerned, the most relevant approach to motivation is that of Abraham Maslow, who said that people needed: *the basic requirements for life (food, shelter), security, acceptance and belonging, respect and recognition, and the opportunity for personal growth.* So, when you set out to sell your ideas, whether to your team, colleagues or your manager, you should be sure you know the answers to these questions:

- What is of greatest importance to those people? What is their greatest need?
- How could my idea, suggestion or request help them to satisfy that need?
- How can my message make the link between their need and my idea?

Insight

A rumour about large-scale redundancies has been circulating the organization which has worried your team. They are technical specialists and are concerned that finding alternative work may be difficult and time-consuming. You want them to work unpaid overtime.

**What do you see as your team's priority needs at the moment?**

**How might you persuade them to accept unpaid overtime working?**

Your team is likely to be most preoccupied with their basic needs (continuing to feed themselves and their families) and with the security of their jobs. If you can present unpaid overtime as a way of making their jobs more secure and maintaining their ability to buy their basic needs, you will go a long way in gaining their acceptance.

# Essentials of face-to-face communication

As a manager you will spend a considerable part of your working day communicating with people on a face-to-face basis. This will involve your team, colleagues, other managers, customers and suppliers. In all of these circumstances you need to be able to communicate effectively. So often in the workplace a simple message can be misunderstood with disastrous consequences. Communication is a two-way process and you need to ensure that you both deliver your message accurately and effectively, and that you listen actively.

### Listening skills

*'We have two ears and one mouth as a sign that we should listen twice as much as we talk.'*

That may be an exaggeration, but there is still a lot of truth in it! Communication is about achieving results and feedback is an important part of communication. Consequently, you should be ready to listen to:

- Suggestions from members of your team
- Objections to your own suggestions.

Effective listening demands some self-discipline. It depends on:

- A willingness to stop talking
- Showing interest in the other person by facial expression and body language
- Asking questions to encourage and clarify

- Patience, particularly in face of hesitant or inarticulate speakers
- Avoidance of prejudice; your least capable staff member may still have points worth listening to.

*Listening skills – asking astute questions, being open minded and understanding, not interrupting, seeking suggestions – account for about a third of people's evaluation of whether someone they work with is an effective communicator.*
Goleman (1999)

Questions to encourage and clarify are a topic in themselves, as shown in the following Case Study.

**Case Study**

> Team leader Judy has suggested to team member Naseem that he tackle a task differently. Naseem objects.
>
> Judy could respond in different ways, with:
>
> (a) So you're rejecting my idea, are you?
>
> (b) Why don't you think it will work?
>
> (c) How else could we speed up the job?

**Which of these responses would you recommend?**

The first response is not encouraging. It is aggressive and likely to lead to a yes or no answer.

The second may lead to further discussion of possible improvements but as it stands it sounds defensive and challenging.

The third response is the most likely to lead to a more productive exchange of ideas, because it is neutral and actively seeking suggestions.

**Interpreting non-verbal communication**

Research undertaken by Michael Argyle indicated that the way we transmit messages to other people can be broken down as demonstrated in Figure 7.2. Which means that, if we concentrate only on words and their meaning, we can potentially miss two-thirds of the messages others are sending us.

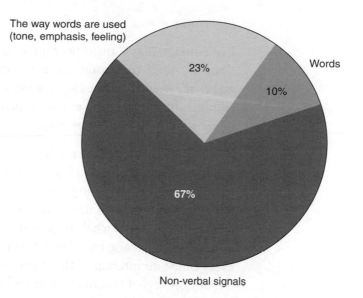

The way words are used
(tone, emphasis, feeling)

23%

Words

10%

67%

Non-verbal signals

*Figure 7.2*

Non-verbal communication includes use of space and touch, postures and gestures, facial expressions and eye contact.

## Space and touch

Personal space and touch are influenced by cultural rules. As a manager you need to be aware of what is acceptable behaviour but as a rule try not to invade the personal space of others, it can be very intimidating.

## Posture and gestures

These include the way we sit, stand and move. Standing with arms folded may indicate anger or defensiveness but be wary of misinterpreting gestures, it could simply mean that the individual is cold! A shrug of the shoulders may indicate ignorance or lack of interest. Looking at the ground may indicate shyness, discomfort or lack of interest.

## Facial expressions

These can indicate an individual's feelings. Smiles offer encouragement. Frowns may indicate disagreement or careful attention. Interestingly, the words spoken may be giving a very different message than that conveyed by facial expressions.

*Eye contact*

Eye contact plays an important part in non-verbal communication. We tend to search for eye contact when we are listening rather than when we speak. Again, eye contact can be subject to cultural differences, for example people from some cultures will lower their gaze to convey respect.

It is important for you to realize that individual non-verbal signals can be interpreted in a variety of ways. Moreover, it is possible to pay attention to body language and miss the point of what is actually being said. So as a manager you need to understand the significance of the non-verbal aspects of communication. You need an awareness that your own body language will be sending messages every time you interact with others, and also a greater understanding of non-verbal communication will help improve your interpersonal relationships within the organization.

# Essentials of written communication

Most of us avoid written communication as much as we can. There are some good reasons for this:

- Talking to people is quicker
- It requires less effort
- We get immediate feedback about people's reactions and attitudes
- It allows us to adapt our message according to the feedback we receive
- We are not always confident about our ability to get grammar, spelling and layout right.

Nevertheless there are also situations where written communication is at least preferable, if not essential:

- If you want to send the same message to a large number of people
- If, for legal reasons or to protect yourself, you need a record of your message
- If your message is too long or complicated to send over the telephone or face-to-face. If it is difficult for you to make direct contact with your intended receiver

- If you want your receiver to be able to refer several times to your message, without relying on memory.

In any of these situations your communication will be much more effective if you put it in writing.

### Effective written communication

Any message should be clear, concise, complete, correct and courteous. But these are especially important in the case of written communication, particularly as messages in writing are permanent and therefore will remain, either to your credit or to haunt you! Here is what the '5Cs' mean for a written message:

*Clear*

Keep your language simple and suited to your audience. Avoid pompous, complicated language, just because you are writing. Use abbreviations only if appropriate.

*Concise*

Decide what your reader needs to know and limit your message to that. Keep sentences short. But remember that difficult or unpopular messages may need more justification.

*Complete*

Unnecessary information is a source of confusion and a waste of time. But without all the necessary information, a written message cannot achieve its purpose. So make sure you include all the facts, evidence and conclusions your reader needs. If this message is one of a series or part of an ongoing correspondence, remember to put it into context.

*Correct*

Make sure your facts are accurate, your conclusions and recommendations justified. Check your grammar and spelling; if appropriate ask a colleague to read your draft. If your organization has a standard format for letters, memos and reports make sure you adhere to these.

*Courteous*

This is not just a matter of good manners. People react badly to rudeness which annoys them. Being courteous contributes to overall harmonious working relationships.

**What to put in writing**

You may need or choose to put information on to paper for the following reasons:

*To meet organizational requirements*

In most organizations there is a formal requirement to put into writing some or all of the following:

- The minutes of meetings
- Regular reports of achievement against objectives
- The outcomes of performance reviews
- Personnel attendance records
- Purchase orders
- Goods received.

In addition, certain written information is required by law and will therefore appear as a requirement somewhere in your organization's procedure manual. Examples are:

- Employment contracts
- Supplier contracts
- VAT returns
- Tax returns
- Accident records
- Details of disciplinary action.

Finally, organizations that have adopted formal quality assurance systems, either their own or the relevant version of ISO 9000, will require procedures to be documented and records to be filed and accessible so that an audit trail can be carried out.

*As a personal record*

You may attend a meeting with colleagues, your team or your manager. You will hold face-to-face and telephone conversations. During them, you may give an undertaking to do something or be told something of interest. It is more reliable and easier in the long run to jot down the details on paper rather than trusting to memory.

### To confirm agreement

We often discuss possibilities and reach tentative agreement with people face-to-face or over the telephone. This may concern something simple, like a hotel booking or a proposed visit. Or it may be more complex, like asking a colleague to give a presentation on a particular topic to your team. You could of course simply hope that the other party has taken their own personal records and will take the action agreed. It would be safer though to confirm details of the agreement in writing.

### To promote discussion

We have already mentioned that written communication is better for long, complex messages and can be circulated more cost-effectively to several people. But it also brings the drawback of delay. All of these factors combine to make written communication, in the form of discussion papers or recommendations for change, the best way of encouraging people to think carefully about alternative solutions to difficult problems or major long-term issues.

### To keep people up-to-date

We have stressed the importance of communicating only what people need to know or the information necessary to achieve your purpose. But that often goes beyond communicating just the 'bare bones' of a situation.

**Case Study**

Louise has been authorized by her manager to take on two temporary staff because her permanent staff have fallen behind with invoice preparation. Her temporary staff are inexperienced but Louise decides she can cope with this by carefully monitoring their work. But she becomes unwell and is off work for a week.

A little later, the complaints start to arrive in the Customer Relations team. Some customers have been invoiced for goods not received, some discounts have been wrongly calculated.

Her manager is called in to a meeting with senior management to discuss the situation. He is asked 'why has this happened?' but cannot answer the question.

### What should Louise have done differently?

In an ideal world, Louise would have found experienced staff. Less ideally, she would have asked a member of her team to supervise the temporary staff while she was off sick. Neither of these may have been possible. But even in the worst situation she should have made sure that her manager knew what was happening by communicating with him both verbally and in writing in view of the seriousness of the implications. Managers do not welcome surprises, particularly unpleasant ones!

The same principle applies to colleagues and team members. It is not suggested that you should pass on irrelevant information 'just in case it comes in useful'. Remember though that knowledge is power! If you have information which is likely to have implications for other people, remember to pass it on to give them greater control over their own futures and decisions.

### Writing memos

You should think of a memo as an internal letter to someone else in your organization. The person you are writing to is therefore likely to have a reasonable understanding of the workings of your organization, so, of the 5Cs of communication the most important for a memo are that it should be:

*Clear*

So that the receiver understands what it is about; the key information you want to communicate; the response (action or decision) you are looking for. In the case of a memo, jargon is acceptable, provided you are confident that the reader is familiar with it.

*Complete*

Containing all the necessary, but no more than the necessary, information. Most organizations have a standard format for memos, which will help to prompt you.

*Concise*

Some organizations demand that memos should be no longer than a single side. Your reader should know the background, so this will help. In any case, long and wordy memos tend to be ignored. Complicated messages may be better as a report.

Standard memo formats usually require:

- Who it is to and from
- A reference or subject heading
- The date.

In addition, memos normally only deal with a single subject and, as with any written message, should use simple language. Short paragraphs are also better and can be broken up with subheadings or numbered points if these make the memo easier to follow.

### Writing emails

We discuss in Chapter 20 how the developments in information and communication technology have increased the speed and ease of communication both internally and externally. Electronic mail (email) has increased our ability to communicate to a wider audience. However, the use of email has created a number of problems for many organizations.

*Today's employees receive a daily average of 64 emails, only half of which are necessary. All in all 36 billion emails are sent world-wide each day.*
Oldfield (2005)

So what has gone wrong? Why has this important form of communication almost spiralled out of control?

A study by Rand Corporation in the United States highlighted a significant attribute of email that distinguishes it from other forms of communication – its ability to evoke emotion in the recipient! Other studies have found that 50% of emails can be misinterpreted. A common complaint in many organizations is that employees feel overwhelmed by the sheer volume of emails they are receiving.

One problem is that people do not apply the 5Cs of communication when writing their message. Remembering to be clear, concise, complete, correct and courteous applies just as much to emails as it does to other forms of written communication.

It is important to think before you write; thinking about the message you are trying to convey and the recipients will help you to send a message that is both clear and useful. Lengthy messages are often inappropriate, so using the attachment facility will assist in transmitting files or reports, for example. Email is not necessarily confidential, this will very much depend on the policy and practices within your own organization but you should always consider whether email is the most appropriate medium when handling sensitive and confidential information.

As a manager you need to be aware of your own and your team's use and abuse of email, through monitoring and developing communication protocols if necessary.

**Writing letters**

Letters may be to suppliers, customers, job applicants, official bodies (government departments or trade associations) or other organizations. Most organizations also write letters to staff members on personal or confidential matters.

Writing letters may be a regular part of your job, or a rare event. In the first case, you will find it helpful to compare your standard approach with what follows. In the latter case, you may want to convert our suggestions into a checklist for future reference.

An effective letter depends on knowing the answers to three questions:

*Who am I writing to?*

If you know their name, use it. Write to 'Dear Mr Allen', rather than 'Dear Sir'. It is perfectly acceptable to write 'Dear Phil' if you know the person well and use their first name in conversation. The more personal you can make the letter, the better it will read.

Considering the person will also help you to use a suitable style and vocabulary. The general rule is to avoid jargon. But if the person is a long-standing contact, jargon is an acceptable way of shortening your message, provided your reader will understand it.

*Why am I writing?*

Is it to inform, persuade or influence? Remember the issues of needs and benefits we described previously.

Is this letter a response to someone else's, or the start of a correspondence intended to achieve your own purpose? If the former, include a reference to the earlier letter. If the latter, think about the content necessary to achieve your purpose.

Regardless of the situation, make some careful decisions about the information your reader will need and make sure you have all of it.

*How should the message be presented?*

When you have the necessary information, arrange it in a logical order. The first paragraph should explain the purpose, background or context. The middle paragraphs should contain the relevant facts, justifications or arguments, again arranged logically. The final paragraph should set out the desired action or response.

As with memos, ensure your letter conforms to your organization's standard layout (position of receiver's name and address; date and reference; spacing and margins; headings, subheadings and paragraph numbers; and so on).

Finally, remember your purpose. If you are writing to persuade or influence, you may be able to include sales literature; put the letter into a folder with supporting documents; arrange special binding. If you are writing to inform (perhaps about delivery schedules or changes to procedures), you may need to include charts, instructions or other enclosures.

Armed with the answers to these questions, you can then draft your letter. Remember to:

- Include a reference or subject heading
- Keep the letter as concise and courteous as you can
- Use subheadings or paragraph numbering if these are consistent with your organization's standard layout and will improve clarity
- Check that the content is correct.

**Review your learning**

Check your understanding of this chapter by completing the following:

1  What is the ABC of communication?

2  What is the difference between formal and informal feedback?

3  List five factors to consider when deciding on the suitability of the communication medium?

4  What do the 5Cs of communication stand for?

5  What are the significance of cultural differences in non-verbal communication?

6  Why is email not necessarily an appropriate medium for transmitting confidential information?

**Theory to practice**

**Apply this chapter to your own experience by answering the following:**

1  What are the levels of knowledge and experience, language skills and confidence of the different members of your team?

2  How does this affect the way you communicate with them?

3  How satisfied are you that you use the most suitable communications media?

4  What improvements could you make?

5  How do you obtain feedback from your team?

6  How good a listener are you, and how can you improve?

# 8 Communicating at work

In the previous chapter we looked at the principles of effective communication stressing the importance to you as a manager. In this chapter we look at different communication situations that you are likely to encounter in the workplace from business report writing to conducting meetings in the most cost-effective way.

## Business report writing

Business reports are written:

- To provide a comprehensive survey of external events
- To provide a comprehensive survey of internal developments or performance
- As a basis for consultation
- As a basis for discussion.

By definition therefore reports are long, contain a lot of information and present challenges related to structure and organization.

These comments are not meant to put you off. Instead, they are intended as a warning that writing business reports demands time, effort and discipline. But it can be made a lot easier if you follow a standard routine. Again, the creation of an effective report starts with answering some fundamental questions. You should not be surprised that these are similar to those which relate to writing an effective letter.

# What is the purpose of the report?

As with a letter, a report may be intended to inform, persuade or influence. A report to inform will emphasize facts and evidence. A report to persuade or influence will emphasize justifications and benefits. In the latter case, the more revolutionary the report's proposals, the better the justifications will need to be.

**Who will read the report?**

This question takes us back to the issue of individual needs, again linked to the purpose of the report. A regular report, like one on team achievement or a management update, can be relatively short and is likely to consist of facts and figures with a brief commentary. Its readers will have seen previous reports of the same kind and will not necessarily pay it a great deal of attention. A one-off report on the other hand is likely to address a significant issue. It may well be controversial and the subject may be unfamiliar to its readers. A report of this kind will require far more background, explanation and, probably, evidence from external sources.

**Guidelines for presentation of business reports**

If your organization has no standard format for presenting and assembling reports you may find the following information provides a useful starting point, based on an analysis of what is logical from the reader's viewpoint.

*Title page*

Obvious but necessary! If your readers receive lots of reports, they want to be able to find the relevant one without difficulty.

*Contents page*

This helps readers to find their way around the report quickly and easily. Long reports may need to be divided into sections and sub-sections – and remember to number the pages!

*Summary*

It is preferable to put the summary at the beginning of the report, but write it last otherwise you will not know what you are summarizing. This will give your reader an idea of what your report is about. By definition a summary is short. It should never be more than one page, preferably less. Highlight the main points of your report but leave the detail contained with the main sections of the report.

### Introduction

Explains the purpose of the report and how the information in it was obtained.

### Main body of the report

Break up the main body of the report by using headings and numbering to make the report easier to follow. This section of the report should contain facts and figures, the evidence will be from internal or external sources and contain current or historical information. Analyse the evidence, arranging it logically. Avoid interpretation or conclusions in this section.

### Conclusions

Your conclusions must be based on the evidence. Avoid the temptation to make conclusions that are unsupported.

### Recommendations

The recommendations should flow from your conclusion and should specify a logical series of actions arising from the situation described in the report. Use the SMART principle when formulating your recommendations and ensure that the organization has the budget, resources and flexibility to deliver them.

### Appendices or annexes

These will contain source material such as graphs and tables.

Before distributing the report, check the content. Ensure that the report actually meets its intended purpose; the evidence supports the conclusions; the recommendations are practical; the content is presented in a logical order; the structure meets your organization's requirements and the grammar and spelling are correct.

# Formal interviews with team members

Formal interviews with your team members will be for the purpose of:

- Task briefing
- Performance reviews
- Discipline.

There are, of course, significant differences between those three purposes but the basic interview structure remains the same. The interview process has three stages:

- Before the interview
- During the interview
- After the interview.

### Before the interview

As preparation, you should:

- Decide what you want from the interview and how relaxed it should be
- Work out how long it needs to last in order to achieve your objective
- Assemble the necessary information and any relevant paperwork
- Plan the interview itself; the sequence in which you will cover points; when you will talk and when you will ask questions; what you will say and the questions you will ask
- Book and arrange the room.

The standard points about the need for privacy, avoiding distractions and interruptions apply. How you arrange the room will depend on whether it is to be a relaxed exchange of views (when comfortable chairs and no barriers between you and your team member will be most effective) or whether, as in the case of a disciplinary interview, you want to create a more formal environment.

### During the interview

There are three stages to the interview itself. Opening the interview will involve setting the scene and explaining its objective and structure. The purpose of the interview will determine whether you create a relaxed atmosphere in which the opening stage is friendly and starts with a general chat or whether it is better to get straight down to the matter in hand.

The main part of the interview should follow a logical sequence and combine statements, questions and, obviously, listening. The balance between you and your team members' inputs to the conversation will depend on your team members' personality (confidence, experience and so on), and on the purpose of the interview. As we suggested earlier, asking questions and encouraging your team members to talk is essential to effective communication. But, typically, task briefings will make you the main speaker; performance reviews should involve most input from your team members; and disciplinary interviews fit somewhere in the middle.

Remember to:

- Maintain control by asking relevant questions to bring your team members back to your agenda
- Use body language that is consistent with your message and the purpose of the interview
- Manage the time.

Closing the interview will involve summarizing what has been discussed and confirming the actions you and your team members will take, usually with objectives and deadlines. Remember to take notes and to inform your own manager of any aspect of the interview he or she needs to know about.


### After the interview

Complete any relevant paperwork. Take any action you have agreed during the interview. Monitor your team members' action and performance.


# Informal conversations with team members

By definition, the content of informal conversations is difficult to predict, particularly if they are initiated by your team members. If a team member says to you:

'Can I have a word?', or

'Have you heard about …?', or

'Do you know what's happening with …?'

you cannot be sure what will come next. When that happens, try to establish what your team member wants to discuss. Then make a judgement as to whether you have the necessary information to deal with the subject. If you do not, give yourself some research or thinking time. Arrange a later time to meet, or simply reply along the lines of:

'I'm rather busy at the moment, can I get back to you in an hour?'

Remember to keep the arrangement and use the time to get the information or ideas together.

Informal conversations you initiate yourself are rather easier to prepare for. They are essential aspects of:

- Managing by walking about
- Checking on morale
- Monitoring progress
- Identifying problems
- Identifying individual needs and motivation
- Knowing and gaining the respect of your team.

Since any communication has a purpose, it helps to work out a series of provisional questions to which you want answers or the information you want to send. The conversation may not go quite as you planned, but the preparation you have done will give you some structure to follow and help to ensure that you achieve your objectives.

## Briefing your manager

There will be many occasions when you need to brief your manager. For example, this may be:

- as part of a formal review of your own performance
- to provide an update on your team's performance
- to propose a change or improvement.

To give an effective briefing, you will need to bring together techniques we cover elsewhere in this book. We can summarize these techniques in the form of four questions:

## 1 What do I want from this briefing?

Start by establishing the purpose – are you wanting to inform, persuade or influence? To gain promotion, development or a pay increase? To give a positive impression of your team? To make changes or improvements? To solve a problem? To provide an update?

## 2 What does my manager want from this briefing?

In some situations your manager will want a quick, brief, factual summary. In others, your manager will expect a longer explanation of ideas, opinions and attitudes. It is likely to be ineffective if you go into a briefing with objectives that are widely different from those of your manager. As far as possible, try to ensure that:

- You raise the issues you want to discuss at a time when your manager is prepared to deal with them
- The briefing is long enough to do them justice
- Your manager knows the issues and can prepare for them
- You know your manager's expectations from a particular briefing
- You match your objectives to those expectations.

## 3 What information does my manager need?

In the case of regular progress updates or reviews of performance against targets, your manager is likely to be content with a concise statement of facts and figures, with a brief explanation of problem areas and your plans to resolve them. But remember that managers do not welcome surprises, so make sure your information is also complete and correct.

If your objectives for the briefing are more far-reaching (gaining permission or seeking development opportunities, for example), you will need to give thought to the benefits these will bring for your manager.

If you are presenting ideas or opinions, remember that they should be justified by evidence as well as the anticipated benefits.

### 4 How should I present the information?

Face-to-face communication is often better if supported by written backup. Indeed, your organization may require regular performance updates in writing. Even if it does not, facts and figures are easier to understand and remember if they are presented in the form of tables, charts, graphs or diagrams. Your briefing will then be limited to explanation and discussion of the documents in front of you both.

Proposals for change need time for consideration. So prepare a discussion paper and let your manager have it in advance, so that the briefing can then focus on the implications of your suggestions and possible alternatives to them.

## Making presentations

Increasingly organizations are requiring staff to make formal presentations. These may, for example, take the form of briefings or be part of the selection process. Many managers find making a formal presentation a daunting process so careful planning and following some simple steps will both reduce the fear and risk of failure.

The steps are as follows:

- Decide the purpose of the presentation
- Decide the content
- Plan the structure
- Make notes
- Prepare support material
- Practise your presentation
- Observe the audience.

### Decide the purpose

The first step is to decide what you want to achieve from your presentation. Decide on your objectives. For example, is your presentation simply giving information or are you trying to sell an idea?

### Decide the content

Work out what you will need to say in order to achieve your purpose. A factual briefing will be limited to 'must knows'. A persuasive briefing may include 'should knows' and 'could knows'.

### Plan the structure

Arrange your content into a logical sequence. Guidelines for a structure are:

*Tell them what you are going to tell them*: i.e., this is your introduction – it should contain a statement of the purpose of your presentation with a bullet point summary of the content.

*Tell them*: this is the main body of the briefing, presenting the content in a logical order; you may, for example, present your investigation, findings and recommendations for improvement.

*Tell them what you have told them*: in other words, summarize the main points from your presentation. Make your conclusion positive and forward-looking. Stress benefits and give your presentation a clearly recognizable finish.

### Make notes

Limit your notes to headings and bullet-points. Write them in capitals so you can read them easily, or cards which will be less obvious and distracting. Avoid writing your briefing out in full and then reading it word for word! However, you will be most nervous at the start, so write out your introductory sentence in full – and also write in full any points, facts or figures you need to quote exactly. You may find it useful to use colours to highlight points and to record cross-references to support materials.

### Prepare support materials

These may be handouts or fact sheets you want to distribute after the presentation. Or visual aids in the form of overhead projector acetates, prepared flipcharts or a Powerpoint presentation. Make sure that visual aids are big and clear. And remember when using handouts that people will expect to read them when you give them out so give them at the end of your presentation otherwise they will read the handout and not listen to your presentation.

### Practise your presentation

Some speakers rehearse in front of a mirror, others will use a tape recorder. Make sure you know how to use any equipment like an overhead projector. Listen to your own words – do any sound clumsy or unclear? Check your timing – but bear in mind that questions and discussions will always make your actual briefing longer than your rehearsal.

### Observe the audience

When giving your briefing, maintain eye contact. Watch body language to judge reaction and understanding. Remember, too, to match your facial expression and gestures to the objectives you want to achieve. Show enthusiasm and smile. Use hand gestures to clarify and emphasize points. Avoid the temptation to fiddle with papers, a pen, jewellery, or change in your pocket. Any of these will distract your audience and your message will be lost.

**Insight**

> You are preparing to make a formal presentation to your team on next month's output targets. They are higher than last month's, which the team succeeded in meeting, but it was a struggle.

**What objectives will you want your presentation to achieve?**

**What content will you include to achieve them?**

You need to communicate the targets, but will also need to encourage your team and convince them that the targets are achievable. The briefing will need to include a factual statement of the targets but you would be well advised to present an analysis of your team's performance against past targets (assuming that they have had a past history of success in meeting them) and convincing evidence that the new targets are not excessively higher than those they have already met (if this is the case). If you have any encouraging news about, for example, extra staff or other resources, you should of course include this as your presentation needs to be a motivator for the team.

## Managing effective meetings

We often bemoan the time taken up in our working day by meetings, viewing them as time wasters and ineffective. As a manager you probably spend up to 60 per cent of your time involved in meetings of one type or another so it is essential that you are able to both manage and contribute to meetings in a timely and cost-effective manner.

Potentially meetings have the capacity to:

- Improve team knowledge
- Improve team performance
- Improve team commitment
- Assist in planning
- Assist in problem-solving and decision-making but only if all those involved understand and fulfil their roles, participate and the meeting is effective and productive.

Meetings can be an extremely effective way of exchanging information but they also have the potential, as we have identified, to be time-consuming, unnecessary and unproductive. So when planning a meeting, ask yourself the following questions:

Is this meeting really necessary?

What would be the outcome if the meeting were not held?

Once you are satisfied that the meeting is necessary, you need to ensure that you maximize its efficiency and effectiveness. You can do this through planning; decide who should attend, when and where it should take place, give notification and prepare an agenda.

Of course you are likely to be involved in both formal and informal meetings. Formal meetings tend to be called in advance, follow formal procedures, are structured with an agenda, require decisions to be taken and actions agreed. Minutes of the meeting record the discussions and the agreed actions.

Informal meetings are as the word suggests, less formal; they may take place in the canteen, a corridor, an office. As they are often spontaneous, it is unlikely that there would be an agenda or minutes, but you may decide to compile action notes following the discussion.

### Contributing to meetings

It is likely that you undertake a variety of roles in different meetings. In your team meetings, for example, you will have the role of chairperson, you may be a participant in senior management meetings, you may have the role of note-taker in committee meetings. Whatever the role, it is about taking responsibility for how the meeting performs and the results achieved. This means sharing responsibility for any actions taken, being cooperative with other members and having common goals.

We can now look at the role of participant, note-taker and chairperson in turn.

*The role of participant*

As a participant you may be called to meetings because you have relevant knowledge, skills or experience to contribute. These may not be directly related to the topics on the agenda, but the chairperson has decided that they could be relevant and valuable.

In consequence, as a participant you should prepare for a meeting by:

- Studying the agenda and identifying the topics to which you could contribute
- Carrying out any necessary preparatory reading (including background papers enclosed with the agenda) and research to assemble the information related to those topics
- Of course, arriving on time contributes to the effectiveness of the meeting. In fact, some minutes now list members' arrival times, so that late-comers can be identified.

During the meeting, you should:

- Ensure that you contribute relevant knowledge and experience
- Express support for or disagreement with others' points, but objectively and with justification
- Avoid irrelevant points and going off on a tangent
- Take note of actions you have agreed to carry out.

After the meeting, you should:

- Take the actions you have agreed at the meeting, without waiting for the minutes, which might be late.

*The role of note-taker*

In some circumstances the role of note-taker is limited to the task of taking minutes. However, the role can be made more satisfying and more productive by extending it to include:

- Consulting with the chairperson to agree the content of the agenda, then preparing it and sending it out

- Booking the location
- Notifying members of the date, time and location of the meeting
- Taking apologies for absence
- Arranging the room – seating plans, notepads, refreshments and so on
- Supporting the chairperson by monitoring time and checking all agenda items have been fully covered
- Clarifying actions agreed
- Drafting minutes and checking them with the chair for accuracy and completeness
- Circulating minutes
- Following up actions, if asked to do so by the chairperson.

# Chairing meetings

The majority of meetings that you are likely to chair are more informal meetings with your team. Nevertheless, as with other forms of communication, these meetings will need to have a clear purpose and structure. They should result in actions and should involve and obtain feedback from the participants.

To meet all these criteria, as chairperson you should:

*Decide on the objectives the meeting is to achieve*

This could be a single objective, or different ones for each item on the agenda. Some items may be for information only, others will need discussion and agreement of actions to be taken.

*Design the structure*

Basically, this means organizing the agenda. If the meeting is intended to make decisions on related issues, make sure the items are in a logical sequence so that a decision is taken before issues that depend on its outcome are taken.

*Design who should attend*

To be cost-effective, meetings should only involve people who have a relevant contribution to make. Equally, make sure you include everyone who can affect the decisions to be taken and the resulting actions.

### Manage the time

Ensure the meeting starts on time. Discourage unproductive discussions. Spend more time on key agenda issues and less time on unimportant topics – you may find it useful to specify how much time is allocated to each topic on the agenda.

Open the meeting by explaining its purpose, rules and anticipated finishing time.

### Involve everyone

Ensure everyone has an opportunity to contribute to the meeting. Observe for any attendees who are not participating and bring them into the discussion.

### Discourage domination

The chairperson needs to control the meeting to ensure that those with the loudest voice or biggest ego do not take over.

### Control the meeting

Keep to time. Stick to the agenda. Assert your authority without overpowering the members.

### Clarify, summarize and confirm

Make sure everyone understands the discussions taking place, arguments being put forward, actions that have been proposed. Confirm the agreed actions.

**Review your learning**

Check your understanding of this chapter by completing the following:

1 What should you do before a formal interview with one of your team members?

2 What are the four questions you should ask when planning to brief your manager?

3 When preparing to make a presentation what steps should you follow?

| **Theory to practice** | Apply this chapter to your own experience by answering the following: |
|---|---|

1 How effective are the formal interviews you hold with your team, what aspects could you change to make them more effective?

2 What steps do you need to take to improve your presentation skills?

3 What meetings do you attend? How could you improve your contribution?

4 What will you now do differently when chairing team meetings?

# 9 Leading and delegating

Is management the same as leadership? Are leaders born or made?

Does being a good manager mean you will also be an effective leader?

The following chapter attempts to answer these questions.

## Managers and leaders

The management task, as we have described it, involves the effective use of resources, including people, to achieve desired results. Therefore, managers are responsible for:

- Plant, equipment and machinery
- Quality
- Output volumes
- Costs
- Short-term and long-term planning
- Some investment decisions.

Many of these responsibilities relate to objects – such as equipment, money and physical production. Others are related to administration – the processes of planning, organization, co-ordinating and controlling, in order to deliver output requirements and meet quality standards. As we have seen, these are all essential, not only to the manager's job but also to the survival and success of the organization as a whole.

INTRODUCING MANAGEMENT

However, they tell us little about the people side of management. This is where leadership comes in. Leadership is to do with:

- Inspiring and motivating people
- Making them feel good about themselves, their work and the organization
- Encouraging their participation and involvement
- Helping them to grow and develop.

People within the organization are a manager's most important resource so these are clearly essential activities. That means that an effective manager has to be an effective leader too. But does it work the other way round? Is a good leader necessarily a good manager?

**Case Study**

Alice was the national sales manager of a specialist publishing company. Her sales team loved her. The atmosphere in a room seemed to warm when she walked into it. She knew all her team well – their family situations, their aspirations, their strengths and weaknesses. Her own sales skills meant that if she accompanied one of her team on a client visit, her presence guaranteed a major order.

Unfortunately Alice became ill and had to take extended leave. During her absence the office manager took over some of Alice's duties, in particular some of the paperwork. She found that:

- Alice had regularly authorized extra discount for new customers so that some sales had been made at a loss.
- She had been in the habit of passing her team's expense claims for payment without checking them.
- Some looked extremely doubtful.
- She had promised her team bigger and better cars when they became due for renewal, even though the company had taken a policy decision to move to more economical models.

**Was Alice a good leader?**

**Was she a good manager?**

Alice appears to have had the personality and popularity of a leader. She was interested in her team, supported and helped them. But she also made false promises to them and took several actions which, whilst increasing her popularity, threatened the business. She seems to have been flawed as a leader but was definitely poor as a manager.

In the next part of this chapter we shall explore various ways of looking at leadership. There are of course differences between them. However, as you read through you should find a number of common threads, to which we shall return later.

## The qualities approach to leadership

This is the traditional view of leadership and comes closest to the idea that leaders are born not made. Countless research projects have been undertaken to identify the ten or twenty or more qualities that make an effective leader. As you would expect, the resulting lists vary – and the longer the lists, the more variety there is in them! Nevertheless, there is reasonable agreement that leadership benefits from the following qualities:

- Decisiveness – the willingness and ability to take decisions, including difficult ones.

- Integrity – having and being known to have a set of personal values which you apply consistently.

- Enthusiasm and commitment – energy, effort and a clear belief in the value of your own work and that of your team.

- Fairness – treating other people even-handedly, without favouritism.

- Interest in people – a genuine liking for people, wanting to help and support them.

- Communication skills – particularly face-to-face, listening and speaking.

- Reliability – consistently delivering what you have promised.

- Confidence – inspiring trust both from and in your team.

- Open-mindedness – a willingness to try new ideas.

- Forward-looking – considering and planning for the future.

# Are leaders born or made?

The list of qualities above may be fairly daunting! In fact, in the past it has been pretty difficult finding enough people with these management qualities, to the extent that people have been referred to as 'born leaders', which somehow implies that leadership is an inherited quality. However, the reality is more promising. If you look through the list again, you will find that most, if not all, of the qualities are demonstrated in normal day-to-day life – taking difficult decisions, for example, or listening carefully, or keeping promises. All of these are learnable skills – things we can all do if only we recognize why they are important and know how to apply them. That is why the qualities approach to leadership, though old, is not out of date. We are suggesting that leadership skills can be learned and managers can be trained to develop them, although the rider to that view is as Adair (1989) suggests:

*The common sense conclusion ... is that leadership potential can be developed, but it does have to be there in the first place.*

# Situational leadership

Many of us will have encountered, if not heard of, company-sponsored team-building exercises. Imagine the situation. The Managing Director along with the Sales Manager and her team are stranded on an island in the middle of the Outer Hebrides. Together they have to build a shelter for the night and cook their food armed solely with cotton wool and a box of matches.

**Would you expect the Managing Director to be the leader in this situation?**

**Is the Managing Director necessarily going to be the most qualified to lead this team?**

The Managing Director may lead this team and be successful, but it is equally likely that someone else from the team will have superior experience and skill, and will therefore lead the group in cooking the food and building a shelter. The leadership here is situational.

There are two ways of interpreting situational leadership. The negative view is that, as different situations demand different strengths and leadership styles, it is impossible for any manager to be an effective leader in all of them. The more positive view contains two elements:

- That managers should be prepared to allow members of their team to take the lead when the situation demands their particular strengths.
- That managers should ensure they have the expertise to command the respect of their team.

Which brings us to the topic of a manager's power.

## Power and authority

In today's work environment we will normally only accept the authority of our leader if we believe it comes from a valid source. French and Raven (1968) argued that there are five possible bases of power:

- Charismatic power – stemming from personality and personal magnetism
- Legitimate power – deriving from the leader's position in the organization
- Expert power – based on the leader's technical knowledge or expertise
- Reward power – the ability to reward subordinates with pay, promotion, praise or recognition
- Coercive power – based on the leader's ability to punish.

Our judgement will in all cases be influenced by the:

- Culture we come from
- Environment we are used to
- Colleagues we work with (their age, experience and job maturity).

The validity of each of those power sources will depend on the situation.

## Functional leadership

Our final approach to leadership is the brainchild of one man, John Adair. Adair's approach goes under two titles. The first – functional leadership – refers to the fact that Adair sees a leader as fulfilling three functions:

- Achieving the task
- Building and maintaining the team
- Developing the individual.

The second title – action-centred leadership – emphasizes his belief that leadership involves a series of actions which can be learned.

Functional or action-centred leadership is usually presented as three overlapping circles, as in Figure 9.1. The fact that the circles over-lap indicates that the role of the leader is to address all three groups of needs.

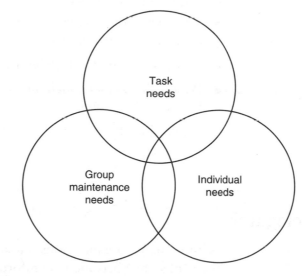

*Figure 9.1*

However, the separate, non-overlapping areas also indicate that there are times when the leader should focus entirely on only one or two groups of needs. The overlaps between the different circles also indicate that, for example, meeting team needs contributes to meeting individual needs, and meeting individual needs helps achieve the task.

# Management *vs.* leadership – is there a difference?

So can we conclude that management and leadership are synonymous? We should all agree that they are not! We can all think of excellent managers who are reasonably ordinary when it comes to leadership. On the other hand, we may also know inspired leaders who have the ability to create confidence in others but who lack good management skills!

## Common leadership themes

The various approaches to leadership described above do, of course, have differences in emphasis. Nevertheless, they tend to have common themes. They all seek to identify what leaders do and how they do it, and answer by saying:

- Leadership is about getting things done.
- Effective leaders have to be able to analyse situations and make appropriate decisions.
- Leaders need to develop the trust and confidence of their team.
- Personality is not enough on its own, the ability to lead requires leaders to be knowledgeable in the particular area.
- Leadership skills can be learned.
- Leaders are made, not born.

## Why delegate?

Within many organizations middle managers are finding that their jobs have become uncomfortably big. There is too much to do and not enough time to do it. There is just too much for one person.

How do you cope?

**Case Study**

Jim Ryan is the operations manager in a large warehouse, which stores and distributes a range of products throughout the UK and abroad. He has worked his way up through the company having started as a warehouse operative. Jim has always set high standards for himself and his staff and expects the warehouse to be clean and tidy at all times. He has three shift managers and twelve team leaders reporting to him. Although the shift managers are very experienced Jim insists on checking each loaded trailer before it leaves the warehouse. As he walks around the warehouse he continually checks on people's work and can often be found sweeping the warehouse floor. Jim complains that he works extremely long hours and that he often gets behind with essential paperwork. Jim justifies his approach by saying: 'If I want a good job doing then I have to do it myself.'

**How would you advise Jim?**

It would be difficult to fault Jim either for his high standards or for his dedication. But it is worth examining the effects of his approach, both on him and on his staff.

Jim is in a senior management position. Managers achieve results through people, so his approach means he is not making effective use of the people resources available to him. That is why he is too busy. And, despite his high standards, the harder he works, the more likely it is that he will overlook something essential, or rush a task and make a mistake.

As for Jim's staff, his standards no doubt mean that they do the basic jobs he gives them superbly well. But there is a limit to how much job satisfaction they will get from these mundane tasks alone. In terms of the principles of motivation we looked at in the previous chapter, they have neither the chance to learn and develop, nor make use of their full potential. This is likely to lead to boredom, frustration and dissatisfaction. Finally, although it is clearly not Jim's intention, he is blocking his staff's promotion opportunities because they are not learning the higher-level skills needed for the next job up the promotion ladder.

We can therefore say that effective delegation:

- Helps managers to make the most productive use of their own time
- Avoids managerial overload
- Improves their team's job satisfaction
- Develops team members knowledge and skills.

101

# Delegation or abdication?

We have just said that delegation has to be effective to deliver these results. So what makes for effective delegation? Let us start with a definition:

> **Delegation involves giving a member of your team the *responsibility* for part of your job and the *authority* to carry it out, but you retain overall *control* and *accountability*.**

The words in *italics* from that definition are the central elements of effective delegation.

Giving *responsibility* involves ensuring that the team member knows just what is required of them and the standards expected.

Giving *authority* means allowing the decision-making freedom to carry out the task and either providing the necessary resources or making sure your team has enough delegated power to gain access to them.

Retaining *control* involves avoiding two contrasting mistakes. The first is that of 'dumping' the task, walking away and forgetting about it. The second is that of appearing to delegate but staying so close to your team that they feel you are sitting on their shoulder. Control means setting-up a mechanism (regular reviews, perhaps, or progress reports) so that you can monitor what is happening without stifling initiative.

Retaining *accountability* is a key principle of delegation. You can delegate responsibility and authority but accountability stays with you. In other words, if the task goes wrong you are not entitled to shrug your shoulders and simply blame your team. And if it goes well, you have a right to some of the praise – although it is good management practice to pass it on to your team and tell others who actually did the work.

# What to delegate

Some aspects of a manager's job should not be delegated. These include:

- Confidential matters which relate to other members of the team.
- Activities that go to the heart of a manager's job, like setting performance standards or staff discipline.

- Tasks you have been specifically asked to do yourself.
- Work that combines high urgency and high importance to the point where it is too risky and would take too long if delegated.

Nevertheless, those exceptions should leave significant scope for delegation. The sorts of tasks that can usefully be delegated are these.

### Specialist, technical tasks

As you are promoted up the organizational hierarchy you will become increasingly distant from the technical content of your original job. You will become more focused on larger matters of managing people, resources, outputs, costs and standards. Consequently your staff will need to be more competent at the technical tasks and delegating to them will maintain and enhance that competence.

### Development tasks

Delegation is also an important source of training and development, as long as you strike a balance between giving authority and retaining control. In order to take on a new task, your team will need access to information, advice and possibly training. It is your responsibility to make sure that these resources are available to them. Equally, you will need to supervise quality and progress more frequently than you might otherwise do – and make yourself available to answer questions and discuss options and concerns.

### Important but non-urgent tasks

These are ideal to develop your teams' skills. They give your team the opportunity to learn new skills and grow personally. The fact that they are non-urgent gives you time to brief the team and monitor their work, and also allows the task to take longer if it is carried out by inexperienced members of the team.

### Bonus tasks

Few things damage a manager's reputation with staff more seriously than delegating all the mundane, tedious tasks and holding on to all of the interesting work like attending exhibitions, visiting clients or being elected to project teams. Of course any, or all of these, may require specialist knowledge or experience but careful selection from your team can ensure these requirements are met and delegating such tasks will contribute to your reputation for integrity as a leader.

### Routine tasks

These are the kinds of work that may spring naturally to mind when you think about delegation. Remember though to avoid the trap that Jim in our Case Study fell into. Delegating does not just mean passing on all your boring work to someone else! It also means delegating the specialist, development, important and bonus tasks we have just described.

**Insight**

Suzanne has studied the principles of delegation. With a relatively inexperienced team, she has been careful to delegate important non-urgent tasks so that they have the chance to develop. She also delegates much of her interesting work. Unfortunately she finds her time taken up with extended briefings, progress monitoring and review meetings. She is also doing more routine, mundane work than before she was promoted.

### What has Suzanne done wrong?

Suzanne's problem seems to stem not so much from a wrong application of the principles of delegation, but more from a failure to combine them with good practice in organizing work and managing people. It is likely that she will enjoy her own job more and develop her people better if she:

- Remembers that it is perfectly allowable to delegate routine tasks.

- Identifies the different levels of experience, ability and confidence her individual staff members are bound to have and avoids the attempt to develop them all at the same rate.

- Improves the balance of what she delegates, to whom and when.

- Recognizes that, as a manager, her right to enjoy her own job is as great as her duty to motivate and develop her staff.

# How to delegate

So far, we have assumed your team would welcome the power to make delegated decisions. You are comfortable delegating decision-making and empowering your team.

However those assumptions do not apply to every manager. Douglas McGregor (1957) described two very different attitudes amongst managers. He called them 'Theory X' and 'Theory Y'.

Managers who believed in Theory X held the attitude that workers:

- Dislike work and responsibility and prefer to be told what to do
- Work for money, not the desire to do a good job
- Need close supervision and control in order to achieve the objectives of the organization.

Managers who believed in Theory Y on the other hand held the attitude that workers:

- Are only passive or resistant because the organization has made them so
- Are keen to develop, to accept responsibility and to support the organization's goals if encouraged to do so
- Have the potential to think for themselves and be creative but are rarely given the chance to do so.

Not surprisingly, McGregor argued that Theory X managers received Theory X responses from their staff and vice versa. He concluded:

*Delegation is not an effective way of exercising management by control. Participation becomes a farce when it is applied as a sales gimmick or a device for kidding people into thinking they are important. Only the management that has confidence in human capacities and is itself directed towards organizational objectives rather than towards the preservation of personal power can grasp the implications of this emerging theory. Such management will find and apply successfully other innovative ideas as we move slowly towards the full implementation of a Theory like Y.*

**Do you agree with him?**

Could it be that your attitudes are themselves causing the behaviour you experience from others?

McGregor suggests that there is a 'wrong way' and a 'right way' of managing people. Unfortunately it is not so clear-cut.

Tannenbaum and Schmidt, two American psychologists, developed a decision-making model. The relevance of this model – which they call the 'continuum of leadership behaviour' – to delegation stems from the fact that your approach to decision-making will depend on the urgency of the decision and the maturity of your team. If your team lacks skill and experience, you will need to give specific and detailed instructions, allowing little freedom for them to contribute. The more skilled, experienced and knowledgeable they are, the more you should seek their ideas and suggestions until you reach the 'joins' end of the continuum where you can simply explain the desired results and leave your team to decide how to achieve them.

| Tells | Sells | Tests | Consults | Joins |
|---|---|---|---|---|
| Manager makes decision and announces it. | Manager 'sells' decision. | Manager presents tentative decision, asks for comments. | Manager presents problem, gets suggestions, makes decision. | Manager asks group to make decision, within defined limits. |

*Authority of manager* / *Freedom of subordinates*

*Figure 9.2*

Extending these ideas, it is obvious that, whilst you will need to closely monitor, supervise and control an inexperienced team, it will be possible and desirable to give a mature, capable team much more freedom.

## Delegation, training and you

As you were reading about the principles of effective delegation, you may have been concentrating on your responsibilities towards your team. In that case, you will have recognized that:

> Regardless of maturity, all of your team need to be carefully briefed about what they are to achieve; standards; time-scales; available resources; and limits of their authority.

When tasks are delegated, the manager should monitor progress and be available to give advice and guidance. In the case of familiar tasks and competent staff, monitoring can be less frequent, and less detailed. Guidance will be less necessary. With new tasks or less competent staff, the opposite applies.

How does your manager delegate to you? After all, managers should expect to be treated in the same way. That means that YOU should be seeking the same development opportunities as we have been recommending you should give to your own team.

The following checklist contains questions which you as a manager should be asking about your own development:

- What are the key areas of knowledge, skill and experience that I need for my job?

- How confident am I about my ability in each of them?

- If I cannot answer that question by myself, which of my colleagues (including my manager) would I consult?

- What does that analysis say about my strengths and weaknesses?

- What action is my manager taking to build on my strengths? (For example, delegating more demanding tasks; involving me in project teams; arranging formal training; giving me greater understanding of the department's work.)

- Are these actions sufficient?

- If not, what more should I be asking for?

- What are the mechanisms for asking? (For example, the appraisal process, regular performance reviews, informal discussions.)

| **Review your learning** | Check your understanding of this chapter by completing the following: |

1 'Managers must be leaders, leaders must be managers'. What are your views about this statement?

2 Allowing members of the team to take the lead on occasions is an aspect of _ _ _ _ leadership.

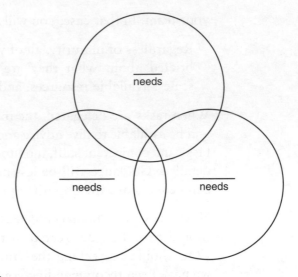

*Figure 9.3*

3  Complete Figure 9.3.

4  List five benefits of effective delegation.

5  Which of Tannenbaum-Schmidt's leadership styles would you use with a member of staff who was proficient at a task?

<table>
<tr><td>**Theory to practice**</td><td>**Apply this chapter to your own experience by answering the following:**</td></tr>
</table>

1  Compare your own leadership qualities with those listed on **p. 96**. Which qualities and their associated behaviours need developing? Draw up an action plan, with the help of your line manager, of how you will go about developing these qualities over the next three months.

2  Which power bases apply to your situation and why?

3  What kinds of tasks do you currently delegate? And what kinds do you think you should delegate more of?

4  Are your attitudes to staff Theory X or Theory Y? What are their implications for delegation?

5  Using Tannenbaum-Schmidt's continuum, how could you improve your delegation?

# 10   Motivating

| Chapter Objectives | • *What is motivation?* |
|---|---|
| | • *Why is motivation so important?* |
| | • *What motivates people?* |

In the previous chapter we looked at the qualities of leadership and the skills of management. One of the key aspects of being a successful manager is the ability to motivate people so that they are willing to work effectively to meet the organizational objectives. In this chapter we will attempt to define motivation, introduce some of the theories of motivation and look at some of the problems you may encounter as a manager in trying to motivate your staff.

**So what is motivation?**

Motivation is:

*the art of helping people to focus their minds and energies on doing their work as effectively as possible.*
Veniard (2004)

As a manager you need to understand what motivates your staff both as individuals and as a team and to create a conducive environment in the workplace in which the conditions, behaviours and attitudes enable people to be sufficiently motivated to perform.

## The basics of motivation

The remainder of this chapter examines a range of motivation theories. All of them start from two basic principles:

• That all people are different

• That people's work must be structured according to what is important to them.

**PROVIDING DIRECTION**

**Case Study**

> Amy Brown is an intelligent young woman who enjoys working with people. She found school boring and left with minimum qualifications. She is starting a job in the local branch of an estate agent. The branch has a front office (dealing with customers) and a back office (administrative) functions.
>
> It is Amy's first day, and although excited about the prospect of the job she is feeling rather overwhelmed at starting work.
>
> As the Branch Manager, how would you introduce her to her new job, in order to maintain and, if possible, increase her enthusiasm for it?

Can you remember how you felt when you started your first job? You probably felt the same as Amy:

- Insecure
- Unsure what to do
- Vulnerable
- Surrounded by strangers
- Unsure of the work environment.

However, Amy is intelligent and therefore she will potentially learn quickly. She also relates well to people.

As her manager, you might have decided to start her in the front office, to make best use of her people skills. But, in order for her to operate effectively and to avoid making her feel more unsure, she will need to understand the:

- Products
- Systems
- Paperwork.

That means she will need some introductory or induction training before she starts, to boost her confidence. She is also new to the branch and knows nobody so she would also benefit from the chance to meet colleagues, not just to say 'hello', but also to find out something about each of them and their roles and responsibilities within the branch.

We have said nothing about pay or promotion. That is deliberate. We can assume that Amy would not have accepted the job if the pay were not adequate. And, at the moment, she is likely to be more concerned with short-term survival than with long-term advancement!

The case study has highlighted the following factors relevant to motivation:

- Security
- Relationships with colleagues
- Training
- Confidence in doing a good job
- Pay
- Promotion.

All these factors are more or less important to different people. And each one is relevant at some points of an individual's career, but less so at others. You will find them cropping up repeatedly in the motivation theories which follow. The skill is recognizing which ones are significant to a particular individual at a particular time.

# Maslow's Hierarchy of Needs

Abraham Maslow published his theory of a 'Hierarchy of Needs' in 1943. One way of understanding his theory is by putting yourself in the position of a survivor from a shipwreck.

**Insight**

> Your ship sank several hours ago. Since then you have been swimming in a rough sea, supporting yourself on a piece of wreckage and swallowing unpleasant amounts of salt water. You see a desert island and manage to swim to the shore.

**What will be your first priority when you land?**

**And your second priority?**

**Your third priority?**

Maslow's theory suggests that we seek to satisfy five levels of motivational need. He argued that someone would not seek to satisfy a need until more basic needs had been satisfied – hence he called it 'a hierarchy of needs'. We can show Maslow's hierarchy as a kind of pyramid.

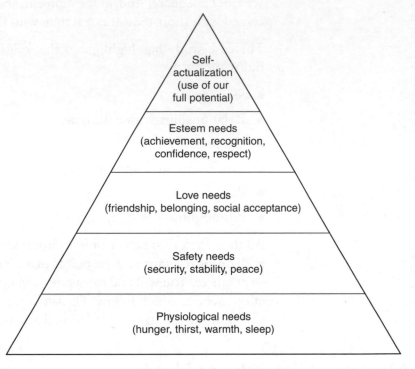

*Figure 10.1*

If we apply Maslow's theory to our desert island, we can assume that:

- Landing wet, cold, hungry, thirsty and exhausted, our survivor's first priority will be food, drink, a fire and sleep. These will be so important, says Maslow, that our survivor will risk personal safety, by fighting wild animals, for example, or venturing into the unknown, in order to achieve them.

- Our survivor's second priority, according to Maslow, will be shelter, a hut, perhaps, or a cave to meet safety and security needs.

- After a while, though, our survivor will start to feel lonely. So, in Maslow's terms, the third priority will be companionship, a group of other people to belong to.

The use of this analogy works less well for the top two levels of Maslow's hierarchy. So we can translate his ideas back into work terms. In that context, Maslow is suggesting that:

- We will accept danger, loneliness and a boring job in order to earn enough to buy food and drink.

- When those needs are met, we will treat personal and job security as priorities.

- Friendly and supportive colleagues become important at the next level.

- Beyond that, the knowledge that the worker is doing a worthwhile job (self-confidence, self-respect) and praise from others (recognition) are the greatest needs.

- Finally, we will seek a job that makes the fullest use of all we are capable of.

Most, if not all, of us will be able to identify with the five elements that make up Maslow's theory of motivation. In fact, they provide recurrent themes in the various theories that follow. However, later psychologists and probably our own experiences have disagreed with the theory that one level of need does not come into play until the lower level has been satisfied. For example:

- How to explain an artist who is prepared to starve in order to produce a masterpiece?

- What about a police officer prepared to risk his or her life in order to protect members of the public?

- And, more personally, if you had no money to buy food, would you no longer be interested in respect and affection from your family?

Many people satisfy the higher order needs of esteem and self-actualization outside of the workplace, for example, through their leisure activities.

Although we can see the limitations in Maslow's theory, as indeed he recognized himself, it nevertheless serves as a starting point in understanding motivation. It also provides a valuable explanation of what people look for from their work.

# Herzberg: motivators and hygiene factors

Frederick Herzberg's ideas have had a huge influence on the way motivation theory is considered and taught. They stem from his book *The Motivation to Work*, published in 1959.

Herzberg's research resulted in the discovery that there were two distinct categories of factors that influenced people's satisfaction with their work. He called one category maintenance or 'hygiene needs'. In this category he placed:

- Company policy and administration
- Supervision
- Salary
- Interpersonal relations
- Working conditions.

When these needs deteriorate below an acceptable level the employee will become dissatisfied. However, if they are adequately met they are not sufficient in themselves to provide motivation to work.

Herzberg called his second category 'motivators'. These were:

- Achievement
- Recognition
- The work itself
- Responsibility
- Advancement.

Herzberg found that these were the things that made people put more effort in. More importantly, the more of them people got, the more motivated they became.

The message Herzberg was trying to send was that employees should be motivated by the job and not through the use of the carrot and stick.

Later writers have called the job satisfiers 'intrinsic' factors and the dissatisfiers 'extrinsic' factors. In other words, if you as a manager give your staff a sense of achievement, recognition for success, satisfying and responsible work and promotion based on results, they will put in extra effort because they find their work motivating. On the other hand, enlightened company policy, effective supervision, high salaries, a friendly atmosphere and a comfortable workplace will stop people complaining – but will not make them work any harder!

Maslow and Herzberg use different terms, but it is worth noting that Herzberg's hygiene factors are similar to the factors contained in the first three levels of Maslow's hierarchy, while his motivators appear in the top two levels of the pyramid.

# Expectancy theory

The two theories we have examined so far present a reasonably clear picture of what people want from work and what motivates them to try even harder. But that is only part of the story. Consider the following situation:

**Insight**

> Your team has been struggling to achieve their targets. Sometimes they succeed. More often they fail. You offer them £1 million each if they can double their output next month.

**How much extra effort will they put in?**

Your team will almost certainly ask two questions:

- Based on history, how possible is it for us to double our output?
- If we do, how likely are you as manager to deliver the money?

The most probable answers to these questions are that it would be impossible to double the output, and you could not find the money anyway. As a result, it is most unlikely that your team will try any harder when the target is unrealistic and the reward is almost certain not to appear.

Of course, the Insight assumes that money is a motivator. And, as we have seen, that may not be the case. However it does provide a good example of expectancy theory.

The Expectancy theory of Victor Vroom (*Work and Motivation*, 1964) suggests that people will only put in effort if they are confident that:

- Effort will result in the required performance
- Performance will lead to the promised (or expected) reward
- The reward is of a nature that people want.

These ideas work best as a diagram (Figure 10.2), which indicates that:

- Motivation results in effort
- Effort results in performance
- Performance results in reward
- Reward results in motivation.

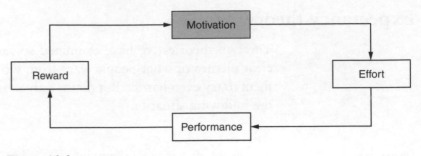

*Figure 10.2*

But as our Insight indicated, there is no point in the manager asking for performance that is not achievable; promising unrealistic rewards is unproductive.

Our experience affects what we expect in the future. In most cases we expect that history will repeat itself:

I do this, then that happens.

**Insight**

> Richard has been told by his manager several times in the past three years that good performance will result in promotion. His performance has been consistently good but there is no sign of a better job. Richard's manager has asked him to take on a special project, with the promise of a promotion if he succeeds.

**How likely is Richard to take on the project?**

One tends to think it will be highly unlikely! Richard's experience should have told him that his manager's promises are meaningless.

This chapter has provided an introduction to a subject that has much wider implications than have been covered so far. It has not given answers to several questions:

- What constitutes adequate supervision?
- How can a manager make jobs more satisfying?
- What makes relationships with colleagues work?
- How can I raise the performance levels of my team?

We will answer these questions in later chapters.

INTRODUCING MANAGEMENT

116

Check your understanding of this chapter by completing the following:

1 What do we mean by the term motivation?

2 What are the five levels of motivational need described by Maslow?

3 Which of the following are motivators and which are hygiene needs as described by Herzberg?

- Salary
- Opportunity for promotion
- Responsibility
- Status
- Working conditions
- Supervision
- Sense of achievement

4 Draw a diagram to represent expectancy theory.

5 Why is it important for managers to honour their promises?

Apply this chapter to your own experience by answering the following:

1 What are the factors that motivate you at work?

2 What are the factors that motivate the individual members of your team?

3 What are the main things which dissatisfy them?

4 How could you reduce these dissatisfiers?

5 How will you use your understanding of the theories of motivation to improve your own performance, and that of your team?

**PROVIDING DIRECTION**

# 11 Developing productive work relationships

**Chapter Objectives**

- *How do I manage conflict?*

As we show in subsequent chapters, one of the requirements of you as a manager is to build and develop the team so that the organizational objectives are successfully met. We suggest that effective teams know, understand and are committed to their objectives. They respect and support each other, have complementary skills and fundamentally need to cooperate and work together.

As the manager the way you behave affects the way other people in the team behave. So it is essential for you to review the way both you and the individuals within your team relate to each other – in other words, you need to focus on the interpersonal relationships within the team.

## Interpersonal relationships

In Section 1 we said that 'management is about getting the best out of people to achieve objectives'. As a manager you are judged by the performance of your team.

*Harmonious working relationships and good teamwork help make for a high level of staff morale and work performance.*
Mullins (2002)

All members of the team need to be able to form good working relationships, and as the manager you need to:

- Form good relationships with your team members and colleagues
- Encourage the development of productive working relationships.

This means valuing each individual member within the team, behaving appropriately, showing respect, recognizing and acknowledging contributions from individuals and the team as a whole.

A climate of openness and trust will help to foster good working relationships and strengthen the team abilities through cooperation and mutual support.

You can do this through regular open communication with the team, encouraging individual development, involving everyone in decisions as appropriate.

The capacity to form good relationships is dependent upon the effectiveness of an individual's interpersonal skills. We tend to use these skills subconsciously, without much thought or analysing what is involved. Being aware of what is involved and striving to refine and improve these skills can only bring benefit to you as a manager, the team and the organization as a whole.

# Managing conflict in teams

As we will all have experienced at some time, however, not all working relationships are productive. Inevitably we will experience sources of frustration and conflict in our working lives.

Our instinctive first reaction is that conflict is negative and destructive – to be avoided if possible and dealt with firmly if it does arise. However, within the stages of team development, we see that:

- Conflict is a natural, even inevitable, part of the storming stage of team development.

- In effective teams, members share ideas openly. This will often lead to disagreement, which will be resolved through discussion and debate.

So we can say that conflict, at least in the form of disagreement and debate, is a sign of a healthy team. Of course that does not mean that all conflict is healthy. Table 11.1 differentiates between productive and destructive conflict.

In the main, productive conflict centres on the task and ways of tackling it. It results in debate, leading to agreement on the best way forward. Destructive conflict is between individuals. It results in bad working relationships and poor performance from both the team and individuals.

119

**Table 11.1**

| Productive conflict | Destructive conflict |
| --- | --- |
| Argument and debate to resolve problems and find improvements | Personal antagonism between members |
| Disagreement over the exact nature of tasks and objectives | Physical violence |
| Conflicting expressions of real feelings | Refusal to cooperate |
| | Lack of mutual support |
| | Bottled-up dislike or resentment |

Both kinds of conflict can arise from similar causes. It is the way the leader deals with it which differs. Those causes are:

*Lack of information or understanding*

Debate over tasks, objectives and priorities arises from lack of clarity. This may be because they have not been properly explained or alternatively because they have not yet been fully defined. Personal antagonism or resentment often arises because one team member believes another is being treated more favourably.

*Seemingly impossible or incompatible objectives*

Disagreement over the task and rejection of the leader may be caused by individual and team objectives that appear unachievable. Resentment towards other members may result if they appear to be working in opposition to the rest of the team.

*Failure to follow team norms, principles or procedures*

Most often the cause of destructive conflict, this involves members of the team failing to meet its standards or follow agreed working practices. Nevertheless, it can also lead to a constructive review of those standards and practices with the intention of making them more appropriate.

*Latent hostility*

One team member may harbour dislike or resentment of another. This may be caused by something personal outside work; a past working relationship that went sour; a fundamental difference in personality, attitude or outlook. That hostility will be kept in check until a minor incident brings it to the surface. On the productive side, feelings can then be expressed and the issue resolved. On the destructive side, it may lead to a shouting-match or even physical violence.

Conflict amongst team members has the potential to be very costly to an organization; trying to resolve it can be time-consuming. Managers often avoid dealing with issues such as personality problems, shy away from giving feedback and difficult situations:

*managing conflict ..., is very difficult, and a lot of managers shy away from it if they can't find support in the organization.*
Hope (2005)

However, your role as a manager involves identifying the signs and potential sources of conflict in the workplace, understanding the causes and being able to take the appropriate action to resolve it. Several techniques are available to you when dealing with conflict. Not all are suitable for every situation. The skill is in selecting those that address the causes and are relevant to the individuals, the team and the environment. Here is a menu of techniques which seem to work:

### Communicate clearly and openly

Misunderstanding and disagreement can often be avoided if you ensure the team knows as much as you do about the task, its objectives and standards. Make sure you explain in such a way that people understand properly.

### Encourage discussion

Give your team plenty of opportunity to debate issues, particularly at the start of a project when there are signs of disagreement or lack of clarity. Allow as much scope as possible for the team to establish its own objectives, standards, norms and working methods.

### Focus on the task

Keep conflict productive by preventing disagreement degenerating into criticism of the person.

### Show respect and fairness

Be seen to pay equal attention to everyone's ideas and suggestions. Avoid any sign of discrimination or favouritism.

### Contribute without dominating

Explain your own view clearly and carefully. If you disagree, say so. But be prepared to back off if the team has a preferred solution that is different from your own.

All of these techniques rest on the assumption that it will be possible to involve the team in reaching solutions and decisions that will resolve the conflict. But what if that is not possible? Here are three fallback techniques to use in extreme cases:

### Be prepared to take the initiative

Remember that an effective manager will be willing to take hard decisions. If team members fail to agree, they will expect you to decide on action yourself. They may not always like it, but you will gain more respect by taking a decision that is unpopular than by leaving the conflict unresolved.

### Know the rules

In most cases, serious conflict may need to be dealt with through disciplinary action. Be sure you know your organization's procedure and the law – and be ready to follow them promptly and accurately. This is likely to involve keeping written records at each stage of the procedure, informing the staff involved of their misdemeanour and their rights, and allowing them to be accompanied by a colleague or union representative at formal hearings.

### Consult your manager

If matters are getting out of control or look likely to do so, make sure your manager knows about it. Ask for advice and clarify your own limits of authority so that you know at what point you should pass responsibility to your manager.

# Outcomes of conflict

There are three potential outcomes of conflict:

*Win–lose* – one side gains what they want but at the expense of the other side

*Lose–lose* – neither side gains, both sides lose equally

*Win–win* – both sides feel they have gained equally. This is the outcome you strive to achieve.

**Review your learning**

Check your understanding of this chapter by completing the following:

1 Give four reasons why conflict may arise.

2 What is the difference between productive and destructive conflict?

3 List four techniques you can use to manage conflict.

**Theory to practice**

Apply this chapter to your own experience by answering the following:

1 How effective are you in managing conflict within your team? What could you do to improve?

2 Think of a recent occasion when a significant conflict or disagreement arose within your team:

- What steps did you take to resolve the conflict?

- How successful were you?

3 Do your team members all have access to the same information? If not why not?

4 How can you ensure that your team members do not interpret information differently?

PROVIDING DIRECTION

# Resource bank

## References

Adair, J. (1983) *Effective Leadership*, Gower

Adair, J. (1989) *Great Leaders*, Talbot Adair Press

Argyle, M. (1969) *Social Interactions*, Methuen

French, J. R. P. and Raven, B. (1968) *Group Dynamics Research & Theory*, Harper & Row

Goleman, D. (1999) *Working with Emotional Intelligence*, Bloomsbury

Halpin, N. (2005) WorkLifeBalanceCentre.org.uk; accessed November 2005

Herzberg, F. (1959) *The Motivation to Work*, Wiley

Hope, K. (2005) 'The fear factor', *People Management*, May, pp. 16–17

HSE Management Standards for Work-related Stress

Incomes Data Services, Diversity at Work No. 6 (December 2004)

Leech, C. (2004) *Developing Personal Potential*, Elsevier

Leech, C. (2005) *Positive Recruitment and Retention*, Elsevier

Maslow, A. (1943) 'A theory of human motivation', *Psychological Review*, 50, pp. 370–396

McGregor, D. (1957) *The Human Side of Enterprise*, MIT Press

Mullins, L. (2002) *Management and Organizational Behaviour*, FT Prentice Hall

Oldfield, H. (2005) 'E-mail etiquette', *Edge* (Institute of Leadership and Management Journal), March

Tannenbaum, R. and Schmidt, W. H. (1973) 'How to choose a leadership pattern', *Harvard Business Review*, May/June

Vroom, V. (1964) *Work and Motivation*, Wiley

## Additional reading

Barker, A. (1997) *How to Hold Better Meetings*, Kogan Page

Covey, S. (1989) *The Seven Habits of Highly Effective People*, Simon & Schuster

Covey, S. (2006) *The 8th Habit: From Effectiveness to Greatness*, Simon & Schuster

*Edge* (Institute of Leadership and Management Journal)

Honey, P. (2005) *Valuing Diversity*, Peter Honey Publications

*Introducing and Managing Flexible Working: Guidance for Managers and Supervisors.* Equal Opportunities Commission

Murdock, A. and Scutt, C. (2003) *Personal Effectiveness*, Elsevier

# Website addresses

**www.cipd.co.uk**
Chartered Institute of Personnel & Development – HR and development including information on employment legislation, surveys and best practice guides

**www.cre.gov.uk**
Council for Racial Equality

**www.drc.org.uk**
Disability Rights Commission – information on legal framework and good practice

**www.dti.gov.uk**
Government department for trade and industry

**www.efa.org.uk**
The Employers Forum on Age – publications and relevant legislation

**www.eoc.org.uk**
Equal Opportunities Commission

**www.hse.gov.uk**
Health and Safety Executive – source of legal, statistical and good practice information

**www.worklifebalancecentre.org**
Centre for information, research and publications on achieving work/life balance

**www.venworks.co.uk**
Management trainer (Veniard)

# Section 3 People and Performance

- *What makes an effective team?*
- *How do I build a team?*
- *How do I effectively review the performance of a team?*
- *What are the processes involved in training and development?*
- *How do I manage under-performance?*
- *What makes change successful?*
- *How should I solve problems?*
- *How do I make decisions?*
- *How do I select the right person?*

# 12 Managing teams

| Chapter Objectives | • *What makes an effective team?* |
|---|---|
| | • *How do I build a team?* |

Most people, when asked to think of a team, will typically come up with an example from sport – a football team, perhaps, or cricket or hockey. It may not be famous, it may not be playing very well, but, in their minds, it is still a team. Ask them for an explanation of what makes that group of sports people a team though and they will find the question a lot more difficult to answer. So that is where we shall start.

## What is a team?

Workplaces are full of teams, so what makes some teams effective whilst others are not?

In effective teams members:

- Share a common purpose
- Are interdependent
- Respect each other
- Are selected
- Have commitment.

All the members of a team should have a common purpose – they should be working towards common objectives. The individuals in a team that is not working well will have few objectives in common.

The members of a team will depend on each other. For example, an advertising team will be made up of account managers, media planners, media buyers, art director, copywriter, account planners and more. Each will bring a particular set of skills and the team will not be able to function properly unless each makes his or her contribution. The members of a team who do not interact will not work effectively.

Team members should respect each other. They should carry that respect to the point where they also care for and support each other. In ineffective teams individuals are likely to know very little and care little about each other.

Members of a team are brought together deliberately. Selection should be on the basis of skills and knowledge. As a manager you need to put effort into seeking and finding people who, together, have the ability to achieve the team's objectives.

Finally, a team is made up of members who are committed, both to each other and to achieving their common purpose. A group that lacks mutual respect and common objectives will not reap the benefits of team working.

You will certainly have been the member of a team at some point – a sports team, work team, a project team or perhaps a team of volunteers. You may well have been thinking that not all the criteria we have been describing applied to your experience. That should not be surprising. Our descriptions relate to effective teams, working well together. When one or more of these criteria is missing, the so-called team is no more than a group of individuals who happen to be in the same place at the same time.

## Building a team

*When you start managing any team of people, sit down with them and thrash out a set of standards and rules by which everyone has to abide. Once you get this buy-in, everyone can concentrate on moving the business forward without fear of disruption.* (Clive Woodward – former England Rugby Union coach)

So far, we have said nothing about teams having a leader. Of course, sports teams usually have a captain, a coach or a manager who leads them. In the work environment this would always have been the case in the past. There are exceptions, however. De-layering (removing layers of management) and empowerment (giving people the responsibility and authority to make decisions for themselves) have led increasingly to the formation of self-managed teams, teams the role of the leader is similar when a new member is introduced into an existing team.

In the same way as with a totally new team, the new member:

*Forming*      will need to understand the task and the objectives to be achieved; will need information and resources; may feel anxious and insecure.

*Storming*      may experience rejection by, or conflict with, other members of the team; may decide that moving into the team was a mistake.

*Norming*      will need to be integrated with other members; will be establishing what team membership involves.

*Performing*      and, finally, will become a fully productive member of the team.

Now apply Tuckman's team-building model to the following situation.

**Case Study**

Alya has just taken James, a school-leaver, into her call centre team. On James's first day, Alya introduced him briefly to the other members of the team, ran through details of start and finish time, meal breaks, how his salary would be paid and the basic emergency procedures, following the company's induction checklist.

Initially, James appeared to be settling into the role, then after about a week the problems started to arise. Other members of the team complained that the 'new boy' was much too slow at his job and was continually interrupting them to ask for help. His clothes were too casual to meet the company standards and he was not responding to callers in the proper way. Alya took James to one side for a quick chat to point out what he was doing wrong.

After another week, James came to tell Alya that he was leaving. He explained that 'it was an awful job, nobody talked to him or helped him, he was stupid to have taken the job in the first place'. Alya accepted his resignation.

Applying Tuckman's model to this situation, what would you have done differently?

How effective is the company's induction procedure?

The information in the Case Study suggests that:

Alya should have been more careful at the start to explain how James was to do his job and the standards expected of him. As a minimum this should have included the company dress code and the protocols for dealing with customers. In other words, she rushed the forming stage.

Other members of the call centre team did not accept James. They may have resented his arrival, or simply felt uncomfortable with a stranger. Alya could have prevented this, not only by spending more time on the introductions, but also by involving them in James's basic training. Such actions would have helped the forming stage, but also reduced the rejection and resentment that are part of storming.

James's resignation was an emotional response; partly to the treatment he had received and partly to the isolation, lack of support and personal incompetence he was feeling. These are all typical of the storming stage if it is not managed effectively. Alya could have lessened these negative effects by paying more attention to the forming stage, but even now it is not too late. Accepting James's resignation is simply accepting defeat. Alya could alternatively sympathize, acknowledge his criticisms and work with the whole team to integrate James properly this time.

As for the company's induction procedure, it appears that this consists of no more than a checklist. It would be far more effective if it took account of the human side of joining a team!

## Effective and ineffective teams

We have already suggested that effective teams:

- Know, understand and are committed to their objectives
- Respect and support each other
- Have complementary skills
- Cooperate and work together.

From the performing stage of Tuckman's team-building model, we can add that effective teams also:

- Monitor their own performance
- Remain focused on task objectives
- Solve their own problems.

Douglas McGregor extended these characteristics and contrasted them with the performance of ineffective teams, as shown in Table 12.1.

We have already said that effective teams should be made up of people with balanced, complementary skills. The obvious application of that is to technical skills. After all, in a road-laying team, there would be no point in having a member who could pour the tarmac if no one knew how to drive the roller! However, Meredith Belbin, a Cambridge psychologist, has extended the idea

**Table 12.1**

| Effective teams | Ineffective teams |
| --- | --- |
| Informed, relaxed atmosphere | Bored or tense atmosphere |
| Much relevant discussion with a high degree of participation | Discussion dominated by one or two people and often irrelevant |
| Team objective understood and commitment to it obtained | No clear common objective |
| Members listen to each other | Members tend not to listen to each other |
| Conflict is not avoided but brought out into the open and dealt with constructively | Conflict is either avoided or allowed to develop into open warfare |
| Most decisions are reached by general consensus | Simple majorities are seen as sufficient basis for group decisions which the remainder have to accept |
| Ideas are expressed freely and openly | Feelings are kept hidden and criticism is embarrassing |
| Leadership is not always with the formal leader but tends to be shared openly | Leadership is provided by the formal leader |
| The team examines its own progress and behaviour | The team avoids any discussion about its own behaviour |
| Low staff turnover and absenteeism | High staff turnover and absenteeism |

of complementary skills to a more general consideration of effective team working.

Belbin and a team of researchers studied the behaviour of managers across the world. The managers undertook a variety of psychometric tests and were placed in varying team situations. Their personality

**Table 12.2**

| Role | Contribution | Allowable weaknesses |
|---|---|---|
| Co-ordinator | Mature, confident, a good chairperson. Sets the agenda. Delegates well. | Can be seen as manipulative. Delegates personal work. |
| Shaper | Challenging, dynamic, thrives on pressure. Has the drive and courage to overcome obstacles. | Can provoke others. Hurts people's feelings. |
| Team worker | Co-operative, mild, perceptive, diplomatic. Listens, builds, calms the waters. | Indecisive in crunch situations. Can be easily influenced. |
| Plant | Creative, imaginative, unorthodox. Solves difficult problems. | Ignores practical details. Too absorbed to communicate. |
| Implementer | Disciplined, reliable, conservative, efficient. Turns ideas into practical actions. | Somewhat inflexible. Slow to respond to new possibilities. |
| Completer | Painstaking, conscientious, anxious. Searches out errors and omissions. Delivers on time. | Inclined to worry. Reluctant to delegate. Can be a nit-picker. |
| Monitor–Evaluator | Sober, strategic, discerning. Sees all options – judges objectively. | Lacks drive and ability to inspire others. Overly critical. |
| Resource–Investigator | Extrovert, enthusiastic, communicative. Links team to outside world. Develops contacts. | Over optimistic. Loses interest once initial enthusiasm has passed. |
| Specialist | Single-minded, dedicated. Provides knowledge and skills in short supply. | Contributes on only a narrow front. Dwells on technicalities. Overlooks the 'big picture'. |

(Adapted from R. M. Belbin, *Team Roles at Work*, Butterworth-Heinemann, 1993.)

traits, intellectual styles and behaviours were assessed by the researchers. From the research Belbin identified nine team roles each of which embodies a function that is essential to team effectiveness. Of course, not all teams have nine members, so in smaller teams members will have to take on more than one function for the team to be effective. Belbin's team roles, with a description of the contribution each makes to the team and the probable weaknesses each brings, are shown in Table 12.2.

Now apply Belbin's team roles to the following situation.

**Case Study**

> The technical project team of Ducati Motor Group has been working for 18 months on the problem of how to develop a diesel engine that will provide better performance than an equivalent petrol engine, reduce environmental damage whilst retaining the fuel economy associated with diesel. To date, the team has produced six alternative designs, three of which run on either petrol or liquefied gas. Two of the remainder are impossible to put into production. One looks promising but the team is too busy looking for better ideas to take it further.

**Which roles are missing from the team?**

The team seems to be well supplied with innovators (which explains the unorthodox ideas). However, they appear to lack a co-ordinator who would have reminded them that their task was nothing to do with petrol or gas engines. A shaper might have helped to avoid or overcome the production problems, supported by some specialist input. And an implementer would have turned their promising design into a practical prototype.

So far we have concentrated on what makes a team effective. Two final principles help to explain why teams are sometimes ineffective.

The first reflects a corruption of our earlier point that, in effective teams, members care for and support each other. Blake and Mouton (1961) suggested that teams show varying degrees of:

- Concern for people
- Concern for production.

Their theory is best represented by way of the grid in Figure 12.2.

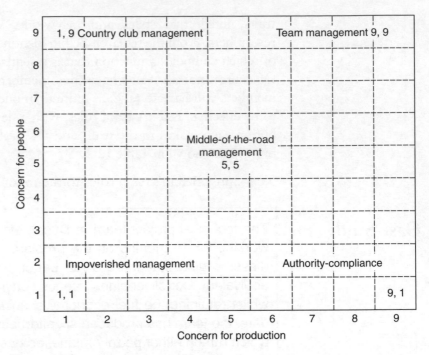

*Figure 12.2*

Although expressed in management terms, the attitudes indicated at the five marked points of the grid are equally applicable to team thinking.

### 1,1 Impoverished management

*Attitude*: The work group expend the minimum of effort on the work in hand. They do just enough to keep their job.

### 9,1 Authority-compliance

*Attitude*: The team focus on efficiency in operations in such a way that human elements interfere to a minimum degree. Output is all that matters. There is minimal social contact.

### 5,5 Middle-of-the-road management

*Attitude:* Adequate organization performance is possible through balancing the need for morale and the need for output, i.e. moderate attention to both people and output.

### 1,9 Country club management

*Attitude*: Attention to the needs of people for satisfying relationships in work. This leads to a comfortable, friendly atmosphere and work tempo, i.e. keep people happy. Output is unimportant.

### 9,9 Team management

*Attitude*: Work is accomplished by committed people; interdependent on each other, with a 'common stake' in the organization. This leads to relationships of trust and respect, i.e. maintain an equally strong emphasis on task and human requirements and both output and people will benefit.

'Country club management' is the corruption of the idea that team members should care for and support each other. It is distorted to the point where the team spends so much of its time and effort looking after its members that nothing else is achieved.

'Team management' of course presents an alternative way of describing effective team working.

Another distortion of an idea that underpins effective teams is that of 'group think'. Effective teams are confident, committed and largely self-reliant. Taken to an extreme though, these positive characteristics turn into a set of attitudes that can be summarized as:

- Nothing can possibly go wrong
- We always know best
- Anything we do is infallible
- Nothing outside the team affects or concerns us.

Of course, these are extremes. However, it is interesting to note that many major organizations in both the public and private sectors deliberately split up teams after they have been operating effectively for a time, specifically to avoid the onset of 'group think'.

**Review your learning**

**Check your understanding of this chapter by completing the following:**

1  Explain the five criteria which define a team.

2  What are the five stages in team development?

3 According to Belbin, what contribution is made to the team by the:

- Co-ordinator?

- Innovator?

- Monitor–evaluator?

4 Explain 'group think'. Why can it present problems?

**Theory to practice**

Apply this chapter to your own experience by answering the following:

1 How effective is your team in achieving its objectives?

2 What are the signs of ineffectiveness in your team? How can you improve the effectiveness?

3 Which stage of development has your team reached? How suitable is your behaviour to that stage and why?

4 Using Belbin's team roles as a benchmark, identify the contribution individual members make to the team. Look at the overall strengths within your team, which are the areas that require development?

5 Which of Blake and Mouton's five descriptions best fits your team? What might you do to improve its effectiveness?

# 13 Improving performance

**Chapter Objectives**
- *How do I effectively review the performance of a team?*
- *What are the processes involved in training and development?*

In an ideal world:

- The workforce would remain unchanged
- All staff members would consistently achieve the standards and targets required of them
- Work objectives would stay the same
- Nothing outside the organization would change
- Nobody would have any ambition to gain promotion, extend their experience or move elsewhere
- Staff would neither grow older, nor retire.

Of course such a world is unrealistic – and the manager's job would be extremely simple, but very boring!

Reality is very different:

- Experienced staff are promoted, retire or resign
- Staff fail to perform
- Task requirements change
- Existing products and services are no longer demanded
- New expectations arise
- Job content changes as a result of new technology, increased competition or changes to company culture.

All of this may seem obvious. But it provides the background to this chapter which deals with the topics of performance review and training and development.

# Performance review

Elsewhere, we have explored the need for staff to know the:

- Volume of output required of them
- Standards to be achieved
- Behaviour expected.

Understanding these is achieved formally through induction, regular briefing, target-setting and performance reviews. We shall return to the last topic later. However, there are normally significant gaps of time between these events. Induction happens once only. Briefings take place at best weekly, usually less often. Targets are set and performance reviewed twice a year at best (once a year is more normal; sometimes not at all).

As a result, formal performance assessment is not enough. That does not mean it is irrelevant. On the contrary, most organizations depend on setting and monitoring objectives and performance standards in order to co-ordinate their activities and develop their staff. But the formality of these processes can get in the way. They cannot replace what is often known as 'management by walking about'.

This style of management means:

- Getting to know your team
- Finding out how they are getting on
- Identifying their problems and concerns
- Praising their successes
- Being approachable and available for your team, and
- Can contribute to the formal assessment of team performance.

Performance review is a regular event that takes place in the majority of organizations. It involves the manager and team member sitting down together in order to review:

- The extent to which the team member has achieved the objectives set for the last period
- The team member's ambitions for the future
- Development needs to achieve those ambitions
- Objectives for the coming period.

In addition to this, in some organizations, performance review or appraisal is also designed to:

- Determine future pay awards.

It is probably obvious that these two sets of objectives are contradictory. The first set requires team members to be open about failures, under-performance and future needs. The second set concentrates on how well the team member has done and the rewards potential arising from that performance.

In order to deal with that contradiction, many organizations separate performance assessment into two stages:

- The first deals with training and development needs
- The second addresses performance against standards and objectives.

Nevertheless, even with a gap of time between the two stages, it is still likely that team members will be reluctant to accept past failures in loss of pay or disciplinary action. That is why it is so important for managers to know how well their staff is doing on a day-to-day informal basis.

**Case Study**

> Andrew is conducting a performance review with Richard, a member of his staff, whose main responsibility is to maintain and update a computer database of customers. Andrew has noticed on several occasions when using the database that records are either incomplete or inaccurate. He raises this point with Richard, who claims that the records Andrew has looked at must have been entered by his predecessor, and that any inaccuracies must have been caused by incorrect information from the customers themselves. The discussion degenerates into a 'Yes I did – No you didn't' argument.

**How might Andrew have avoided this situation?**

**Why do you think Richard is behaving defensively?**

Andrew appears to be basing his judgements on second-hand evidence rather than factual information: the records he has looked at. He seems unable to justify them from personal observation of Richard's work. Consequently, he cannot tell whether:

- The missing information and inaccuracies resulted from someone else

- Richard has a careless attitude
- He has a training need (does he know what information should be included on a customer record or have the mistakes crept in because Richard is not using the software properly?).

In summary, Andrew does not know enough about how Richard does his job to appraise his performance effectively.

Of course, one way of dealing with this lack of knowledge would be to get Richard to talk honestly about his work during the review. But he is not prepared to do this. The most likely explanation is that he fears a report that identifies weaknesses will have a negative effect on pay, job security or promotion. This may be the case or he may simply not understand the organization's appraisal philosophy. Whatever the reason, Richard clearly does not trust Andrew sufficiently for the interview to succeed.

There are several reasons why a performance review system may fail:

- Staff may distrust the intention behind it
- Staff or managers, or both, may not understand it well enough to use it well
- One or both sides are ill prepared
- The paperwork is so complicated that it becomes simply an exercise in form filling
- The process is rushed, either by the manager to get it out of the way, or by the organization setting unrealistic deadlines for completion
- Different managers apply different standards
- Managers show bias in favour of staff they like.

Some of these problems arise from the way the system is designed or administered. You are unlikely to be in a position to influence either of these although some organizations with a culture of consultation do regularly ask their managers and staff to comment on the effectiveness of the system and to suggest improvements. If the system you operate is imperfect (and few are totally faultless) the only advice is to get to know it well enough to make the best use of it, despite the imperfections.

The majority of the problems, however, occur because either managers or staff, or both, do not put enough time or energy into making the system work. This is what should happen.

### Before the review

Allow time for you and your team to prepare. Some systems include a preparation sheet, others a log for managers and team members to complete independently during the year. Even if your organization does not have these, it is helpful for both parties to make notes of the strengths and areas for improvement, with examples of past events to support them, potential training needs and how they could be met. Staff should also record short-term and long-term personal objectives and career plans. A fortnight should be long enough for this preparation.

Set aside a formal time for the meeting and advise your team members. Be realistic about the length of time required. This will vary according to the individual and the complexity of the system, but it is advisable to make a judgement on the time your longest meeting will take and allocate the same amount for each of them. This is particularly important if members of your team work closely together, to avoid them jumping to conclusions about the nature of the meeting, based on the time allocated. It is also rarely successful to fill a whole day with reviews. You will find them exhausting and will be unable to give of your best in later ones. It is a good idea to conduct just one meeting in a morning and one in an afternoon, to give yourself breaks from them by doing other work.

Book a private room for the meeting. Make sure it is arranged informally, ideally with easy chairs. At the very least avoid being separated by a desk and make sure you will not be interrupted.

### During the review

- Explain the purpose and structure of the review
- Encourage staff to talk more than you do by asking questions and listening to the answers
- Avoid generalizations about strengths and weaknesses. Be specific and quote examples
- Focus on behaviour not personality

- Agree performance, training and development objectives and how they will be met
- Maintain a relaxed and convivial atmosphere.

### After the review

- Complete the paperwork while the interview is still fresh in your mind
- Arrange any training or development activities you have agreed
- Monitor progress.

Remember that formal performance review only succeeds if it is supported by regular informal feedback.

Performance reviews are one way of giving feedback to your staff. In fact, staff often say that they are the only opportunity they get to find out from their managers how well they are doing! Of course, managers who act in this way are running counter to the principles of effective performance assessment, which should be an ongoing, day-by-day process. As you would expect, the same applies to giving feedback.

Feedback involves informing your staff of their performance against the standards required of them. Unfortunately, it is a process with which many of us feel uncomfortable. This is especially true of managers, particularly if they have established friendly, working relationships with their team. And, at least in the UK, giving praise for good performance does not come naturally, either!

Nevertheless, giving feedback is an essential part of improving performance. As you will have gathered, much of this chapter is as relevant to you as it is to you as a manager. So ask yourself these questions:

**How insecure would you feel if your manager never told you if your work was good, bad or indifferent?**

**What chance would you have to build on your strengths and overcome your weaknesses?**

**How could you decide what your future career plans should be?**

Your team members will feel the same way. We often find giving feedback uncomfortable; this is because:

- It seems too personal
- Negative feedback feels like an attack
- We are reluctant to let our emotions show.

These concerns are because the feedback is ineffective; giving effective feedback significantly reduces these problems. Effective feedback focuses on behaviour and performance, not the person.

Consider the following two statements:

*There, you've done it again. I don't think you've got it in you to ever get this right.*

*Could you adjust the margins to 2 centimetres on each side please. It will look better as it will be in line with our standard format.*

**Which of these two is more effective feedback?**

**What are the differences between them?**

The first statement sounds exasperated, rude and aggressive. It makes a personal attack on the listener, gives no detail about the error and no suggestions for improvement.

The second statement is assertive but supportive. It gives specific guidance for improvement and explains the need for it.

Table 13.1 summarizes the differences between effective and ineffective feedback.

**Table 13.1**

| Effective feedback | Ineffective feedback |
| --- | --- |
| Is supportive and constructive | Is aggressive and critical |
| Is specific | Makes broad generalizations |
| Suggests improvements for the future | Focuses on past failures |
| Looks for solutions | Allocates blame |
| Addresses behaviour | Attacks the person |

*Effective feedback*

- Shows respect – it assumes that performance can be improved and that the staff member wants to improve. It values the person.

- Is immediate – this is why feedback is ongoing. That allows you to address weaknesses when they arise and the staff member will be in the right frame of mind to deal with them.

- Is limited – staff performance may show scope for several improvements. Effective feedback is restricted to a limited number of priorities, to avoid overwhelming them.

- Puts the improvement into context – it explains the need and stresses the benefits.

- Is two-way – it allows the staff member to explain what went wrong and, where possible, involves the person in suggesting alternatives.

# Approaches to training and development

The people within our organizations are a crucial resource and an essential part of the role of the manager is to develop individual members of staff as well as the team as a whole.

So is there a difference between training and development?

**Training** is a short-term systematic process, which improves and develops the knowledge, skills and attitudes of employees to meet the current and the future needs of the business.

**Development** is a longer-term process, which enables individuals and organizations, through time, to reach their full potential.

Training brings a number of benefits to an organization; it is a process that can:

- Improve current skills: Training can be used to achieve and maintain performance ensuring high-quality work from your team. It can be used, for example, to improve poor performance and reduce accidents and absenteeism.

- Increase range of skills: It provides people with the opportunity to develop their potential.

- Develop future skills: Training is the key to ensuring that people are prepared for the changing demands of the workplace, for example, new technologies and working practices.

Overall, training can increase the commitment, confidence and motivation of staff, which can be directly linked to the success of the organization not only in its ability to change, but also in increasing its competitiveness in the market place. However, it is important to stress that training for training's sake will not bring about these benefits. It needs to be part of the overall culture of the organization and be relevant to the needs and objectives of the business.

The aim of development is to improve an individual's overall knowledge and confidence and so broaden their opportunities for career progression. This may result in transfer to a specialist department and/or a management position within the company. Table 13.2 includes possible development methods. A word of caution – some companies are reluctant to encourage development, as they fear it will encourage staff to think about moving on!

# A systematic approach to training

Training is an investment in people and, as with any investment, there are costs attached to it. So it is important to gain the maximum benefit, and to ensure that it does not become a wasteful expense, by taking a planned and systematic approach to managing the training.

There are simple steps in this process:

1   Identify the training needs – what are the current skills, knowledge, attitudes and behaviours?

2   Next identify what future skills, knowledge, attitudes and behaviours are required to move the business forward.

The difference between points 1 and 2 is often referred to as the 'learning gap'.

1   Design and plan the appropriate training to meet the 'gap' (Table 13.2 gives you suggestions for possible methods).

2   Deliver the training.

3   Validate the training to determine if it has been successful in achieving its aims and review how the learning will be applied in the workplace.

4   Evaluate the training in terms of the cost compared with the financial benefit gained by the improved performance of the staff. Examples of this may include a reduction in accidents, fewer customer complaints and increased productivity.

**Table 13.2**

| Training and development method | Description |
| --- | --- |
| Formal courses | The traditional 'classroom' based approach usually involves presentations, case studies or practical exercises. Can be residential, delivered on company premises or non-residential. Can be costly to the organization but usually popular with delegates if well designed and relevant to their job roles. |
| Open or distance learning | Usually text based, such as the Pergamon Flexible Learning Super Series. Designed to be used in the workplace, they contain case studies, examples and activities to reinforce learning. |
| e-learning | Learning via communications technology. Learning materials are delivered online, reducing costs and increasing access. |
| Demonstration | Skills are demonstrated by the trainer and then practised by the learner. |
| 'Sitting with Nellie' | A form of on-job training where the learner is trained by an experienced colleague. Can be effective if the colleague has the skills and ability to transfer knowledge but can result in the transfer of bad habits. |
| Coaching | One-to-one training by a colleague or manager to pass on skills and knowledge, answer questions and review work. |
| Projects | Involvement in company and/or department projects provides an opportunity to address a work-related problem or issue. Develops company knowledge, decision-making and presentation skills. |
| Secondments | The staff member is transferred to a different position on a temporary basis to gain new knowledge, skills and experience. |
| Job rotation | Giving people the opportunity to work in other sections or departments. Care should be taken to match the learning needs to the job. |
| Visits or working with other companies | Exposure through visits or working with other organizations provides an effective way of broadening perspectives and benchmarking work practices. |

**Review your learning**

Check your understanding of this chapter by completing the following:

1 List the benefits to your team of you managing by walking about.

2 List five of the reasons why a performance review system may fail.

3 What makes feedback effective?

4  Explain the difference between training and development?

5  What is the 'learning gap'?

<table>
<tr><td>

**Theory to practice**

</td><td>

**Apply this chapter to your own experience by answering the following:**

1  How could you improve your contribution as manager to the performance review process?

2  What changes are taking place in your organization that will lead to training needs for your staff?

3  Of the training methods listed in this chapter, which might be worth exploring as possibilities for your staff?

4  How effectively does your organization evaluate training? How could it be improved?

5  Which of your staff have the potential to develop? How could you help them do so?

6  What more could you do to develop yourself?

</td></tr>
</table>

# 14 Discipline and grievance

There will be times as a manager when problems arise with members of your team that may, for example, be affecting their performance. You will find that an informal discussion with the individual is often all that is required. ACAS (Advisory, Conciliation and Arbitration Service), refers to this process as *counselling* and suggests that using this process can be an effective way of improving performance without the need for disciplinary action. During a counselling session your role as the manager is to determine the cause of the problem and look at ways of assisting the individual to improve their performance. A note of caution – you should ensure that a counselling session does not turn into a disciplinary interview as this may deny the individual certain rights and you may find yourself not adhering to procedure.

As an effective manager you are likely to have few disciplinary problems with your staff. You will be aware of problems, issues, potential conflict before they arise and will have taken steps to resolve them.

Nevertheless, there will be occasions when you are required to take a firmer stance with a member of your team and use the disciplinary process to improve performance. Many managers shy away from disciplining staff for fear of making themselves unpopular or because they are not fully aware of the correct procedures.

An organization's disciplinary procedure often conjures up pictures of punishment and ultimate dismissal. However, these are false. Instead, an organization's disciplinary procedure is intended to address under-performance by providing a means of bringing it to the required standard.

INTRODUCING MANAGEMENT

Disciplinary and grievance procedures provide a clear and transparent framework to deal with difficulties that may arise for both the employer and the employee. Having procedures in place ensures that everybody is treated in a fair and consistent way and compliant with legislation. Well-written procedures ensure that everyone in the organization knows what is expected of them and what they can expect in return.

Details of the procedures must form part of an employees 'contract of employment', be in writing, accessible, known and understood by all employees.

In order to achieve that, a disciplinary procedure should ensure that:

- People know what they should do and to what standard.
- If they fail to meet the standard, they should be given the opportunity to improve.
- The organization should help by providing any training, support or guidance needed.

Each organization determines its own discipline and grievance policy and procedure but should follow the ACAS Code of Practice which ensures that organizations comply with the relevant employment legislation.

Whilst organizations are able to adapt the Code of Practice to reflect the needs of their particular situation, ACAS sets out advice on what constitutes a good disciplinary procedure.

Procedures should, for example:

- Be in writing
- State who they apply to
- Be non-discriminatory
- Allow for information to be kept confidential
- Allow employees to appeal against a decision
- Require management to investigate fully before any disciplinary action is taken.

Detailed information is available from the ACAS website: www.acas.org.uk.

Companies use a three-stage process, as advised by ACAS, which is made up first by a verbal warning, and followed by two written warnings.

Each warning should specify:

- In what ways performance has been inadequate
- The nature of the improvement required
- The time allowed to make that improvement.

There will be a time-gap after each warning, varying from a few weeks to several months, depending on the nature of the work, the help to be provided and what the courts describe as 'the principle of reasonableness'. In other words, taking account of the improvement necessary, how long should it reasonably be expected to take?

Viewed in this way discipline becomes an extension of the holistic process of standard-setting, performance review, training and development rather than simply punitive.

**Case Study**

> Paul is a difficult man and he is often late for his job at the warehouse. Ian, his team leader, has just been promoted to his first management position. He would ideally like to get rid of Paul, whom he sees as disruptive and a bad influence.

### What advice could you give to Ian?

We can understand Ian's frustration but he should focus on the need to identify specific issues, for example poor time-keeping or attitude. First, Ian should tackle the issue of poor time-keeping. Assuming that Paul is required to commence work at a clearly stated time, Ian needs to ascertain from Paul reasons for his lateness, e.g. family or transport problems, whilst restating the time Paul should be available for work.

Ian could then discuss Paul's attitude, again restating the company's expectation in terms of behaviour from its employees.

These do not appear to be training issues so Ian would be advised to give Paul a specific period, e.g. two weeks, to improve both his time-keeping and/or attitude. Following this period, Ian should review the situation with Paul.

As a manager you should view disciplining staff members as a last resort. However, should the need arise, you should ensure that you fully understand your role and legal responsibilities in the disciplinary process, what authority you have for taking action and any likely pitfalls. You should know your company's policies and procedures and should be trained and supported to carry out disciplinary interviews with your team. At this point it is necessary to understand that failure to follow the procedure correctly could result in a breach of contract and/or you facing disciplinary action! Use your HR department for advice and guidance as appropriate.

# Common mistakes managers make

Because managers sometimes shy away from their responsibilities when it comes to discipline procedures, mistakes can occur:

### Not seeking help

Just because you are the manager does not mean that you will always have all the answers. When it comes to discipline you must get support and advice. Consult with your line manager, colleagues, the HR manager.

### Not checking the organizations rules and procedure

Ignorance is no excuse! You should know your organization's rules and procedures, check them. Relying on your memory is not sufficient.

### Not keeping records

You should keep notes to ensure you have accurate records complying with your organization's procedures. You cannot claim to have warned someone for persistent offending if you have no written record of events.

### Acting hastily

Always take time to prepare and make decisions having consulted with the appropriate personnel. Snap decisions are dangerous.

### Acting inconsistently

You should always act fairly and consistently. Reprimanding one employee for lateness whilst turning a 'blind eye' on another team member who is continually late is not acceptable practice. It can lead to accusations of harassment or favouritism.

### Prejudice

Keep an open mind. Make sure you obtain all the evidence and facts before you make a judgement.

### Avoiding issues

Deal with incidents of, for example, underperformance, as they occur. Trying to avoid issues or problems because you are worried about being unpopular can make the situation worse as employees can claim that they were not given fair warning about their performance.

Failing to comply with internal procedures, or failing to carry out a proper investigation or not acting reasonably, could mean that the case is taken to an employment tribunal.

## Dealing with grievances

It is important that grievances from employees are dealt with in the same robust way as discipline issues. You should also remember that what may seem insignificant to you may be a serious problem for one of your team members.

Resolving problems and issues effectively helps maintain harmonious working preventing resentment and dissatisfaction amongst the workforce.

*A grievance procedure enables individual employees to raise concerns, problems or complaints with management about their employment. It should allow for both an informal and formal approach.*
ACAS

### Handling grievances informally

You should encourage your team to discuss day-to-day issues on an informal basis with you. This might be in team meetings or as you are walking about or during informal review sessions. This will enable them to raise their concerns and for you to respond to them as appropriate.

### Handling grievances formally

There will be occasions when an informal approach does not resolve an issue and the matter has to be raised formally through the grievance procedure.

The grievance procedure should allow for an employee's grievance to be heard fairly and objectively and all employees should know the procedure and the formal route open to them, this should include:

- How and with whom they should raise the issue
- Who next to appeal to if not satisfied
- Time limits for each stage
- The right to be accompanied by a fellow worker or trade union representative.

## Statutory grievance and disciplinary procedures

In October 2004 it became a legal requirement for all organizations to have disciplinary and grievance procedures in place. The statutory procedures set out a minimum standard that must be followed by all employers and employees.

This chapter has shown the importance of seeking to resolve issues and problems informally as they arise. This helps to maintain harmonious working and limits disruption to work.

Nevertheless, the discipline and grievance procedures are essential when the informal routes have not been effective; they provide a framework for ensuring that people are treated fairly and consistently and are part of the overall process of ensuring a productive working environment.

**Review your learning**

Check your understanding of this chapter by completing the following:

1 What does ACAS stand for?

2 List four examples that constitute a good disciplinary procedure.

3 Give three common mistakes managers make in the disciplinary process.

4 How can you handle grievances informally?

**Theory to practice**

Apply this chapter to your own experience by answering the following:

1 What is your organization's grievance procedure?

- What are the stages?
- What is your role in the procedure?

2 How do you ensure that your team knows the standards expected of them?

3 How do you ensure that your team members are able to discuss problems with you?

4 What measures do you use to monitor poor performance?

# 15 Managing change

| Chapter Objectives | • *What makes change successful?* |
|---|---|

*The journey of change that one has embarked upon is a permanent one – there is no final destination.*
Taylor (1994)

Change can be exciting, challenging, stimulating; it can also be frightening, threatening and unsettling. However, as we saw in Section 1, change in the external world is something organizations often have no choice or control over. In order to survive in dynamic business environments, organizations have to be prepared to constantly evaluate what they do, making and implementing appropriate changes.

So why are some people excited, challenged and stimulated by change while others feel frightened, threatened and unsettled? If change is inevitable how can you as a manager ensure your team is positive about changes that you or the organization may need to implement?

The success of any change is dependent upon not only the way it is implemented but also determined by the staff within the organization. Their ability to respond and have a sense of ownership is also critical to successful change.

One of the fundamental issues for a manager is to create an environment whereby staff are able to make sense of the changes surrounding them. There is plenty of evidence to show that people dislike and resist change if it is simply imposed on them, without explanation or consultation.

By contrast, people will be more positive about change if they are:

- Informed about the reasons for it
- Helped to understand the benefits that should result
- Involved in planning and designing the change

**PEOPLE AND PERFORMANCE**

- Encouraged afterwards to recognize what they have gained from it.

The rest of this chapter develops these suggestions in more detail and offers some practical techniques for achieving them.

# The change process

There has always been a need to manage change and there are numerous books and articles on the subject of change. One contributor to this literature was Kurt Lewin, who made a significant contribution to our understanding. Although many writers have developed his original model further, it provides a useful starting point in our understanding of the change process.

Lewin started his analysis of change by presenting a diagram (Figure 15.1) that showed why change does not take place easily.

*Figure 15.1*
*'Force field analysis'*

Lewin's argument was that situations remain constant when they are subject to two sets of equal and opposite forces: driving forces and restraining forces.

**Case Study**

Atlas Engineering manufactures sub-assemblies which are bought by a small number of customers making domestic appliances. Atlas operates a rigorous but traditional quality control system. One of its main customers has now insisted that all suppliers must have ISO 9002 registration. Atlas recognizes that failure to obtain ISO 9002 will result in a major loss of business straight away and, potentially, a decline in reputation and further lost business in future if other customers introduce similar requirements. On the other hand, to achieve ISO 9002, the firm will need to develop quality assurance procedures, may need to revise its operating methods and will experience disruption, cost and lost output if this goes ahead.

**Draw a force field diagram showing Atlas's situation**

Without expanding the information given, the diagram would probably look something like the one in Figure 15.2.

*Figure 15.2*

Whether Atlas now decides to go for ISO 9002 will depend on whether the management team decides that the driving forces in favour are stronger or weaker than the restraining forces against.

Although a force field diagram is a helpful way of visualizing change, Lewin goes a lot further. First, he presents two types of strategy for achieving change.

A *push* strategy involves making the driving forces stronger. In our example, this would happen if:

- More pressure was added to the existing forces, perhaps by another customer demanding ISO 9002 now.

- Additional driving forces were introduced, for example, if the Managing Director expressed his support for the initiative.

'*Push*' strategies have the best chance of success when restraining forces are practical or financial. They are far less likely to work when the restraining forces are people's attitudes or concerns.

Under these circumstances, if the driving forces get stronger, the restraining forces will push back harder and nothing will change.

Lewin's second strategy is a '*pull*' strategy, which involves reducing the pressure of the restraining forces. In our example, this might be done by:

- Reducing the likely level of disruption

- Finding ways of lowering the costs

- Bringing down potential lost production.

In most cases the pressures against change have a strong human element. Lewin strongly recommends a '*pull*' strategy in these cases.

Successful change, Lewin argued, involves three stages:

### Unfreezing

For change to take place, the old ways have to be unfrozen and the need for change accepted. To achieve this requires consulting with people, making them aware of the risks of not changing, the benefits of change, explanation and involvement. These are the themes of the next part of this chapter.

### Changing

The second stage is a process of finding alternatives, defining and allocating responsibilities, implementing and troubleshooting. These are central activities in the 'implementing change' part of this chapter.

### Refreezing

When changes have been made, they are still not established. People will feel tentative about them, problems will arise and it is possible that things will slip back. At the refreezing stage, it is important to highlight the successes, reward those involved and deal positively and effectively with any snags. These topics are covered in the final part of this chapter.

You may well be thinking that the change processes that you have experienced have not followed the neat, logical process that Lewin suggested. His theory belongs to the 'planned' change approach. Other writers suggest that change in organizations seldom occurs as a linear process and that to be able to effectively manage change processes it is important to acknowledge the unpredictable nature of change. This is referred to as 'emergent' change.

As Burnes (1996) suggests

*successful change is less dependent on detailed plans and projections than on reaching an understanding of the complexity of the issues concerned and identifying the range of available options.*

# Shaping attitudes to change

At the beginning of this chapter we stated that people often feel frightened, threatened and unsettled by change and these emotions can lead to strong resistance to change that you as a manager may want, or need to implement.

*change is neither sought after nor welcomed. It is disruptive and intrusive. It upsets the balance.*
Strebel (1996)

Strebel suggested that managers frequently misjudge the effect of change on employees.

Resistance to change often results from a combination of:

*Fear of the unknown*

People do not necessarily understand the implications of change and feel more comfortable with past routines (however unsatisfactory they may have been).

*Fear of loss*

Change may involve: loss of status; loss of income; loss of job. These fears may be unfounded but will still be present.

*Ambiguity*

People will wonder: what the change will involve; whether they will be able to cope; what the consequences may be.

*Insecurity*

We tend to fear the worst! Not knowing what will happen leads to the assumption that the worst may happen.

*Loss of control*

When people believe that change will mean they will have to sacrifice control over their own work, responsibilities or destinies, change will be unwelcome.

Of course change may, in reality, result in:

- Better working practices
- A more comfortable environment

- Greater rewards
- More satisfying work
- A more secure future.

But – and this is the significant point – the less people know, the more anxious they will feel and the more resistant to change they will be.

From the perspective of the manager, the process of shaping people's attitudes so that they accept the need for change requires action in three key areas:

### Information

Most of the reasons listed for resistance to change result from a lack of knowledge or lack of understanding – and a consequent belief that the worst will happen. Communication is crucial.

### Consultation

Consultation is the opposite of imposed change and encourages people to feel that they are still in control of the process.

### Enthusiasm

If the manager appears to lack belief or confidence in the proposed change, it is unlikely that the team will feel any more committed. But it goes further than that. To develop enthusiasm in team members will also involve providing them with the necessary knowledge and skills to cope effectively with the change.

It is worth looking at each of these three processes in a little more detail.

*Information* answers the questions:

- What is going to happen?
- Why is it going to happen?
- When and how will it happen?
- What will the consequences be?
- How will I benefit?

If the change has already been decided and planned in detail, the team will have little influence over the 'what', 'when' and 'how'.

More often though change decisions are taken in broad terms and it is left to those closer to the work to decide how they will be implemented. Under those circumstances, team members will feel more in control and less insecure, because they will be able to determine how to make changes more effective and less disruptive.

The reasons, consequences and benefits though are a different matter. As a manager, if you announce that a change is taking place but cannot explain why or what will happen as a result, you will generate greater fear and anxiety than if you had waited until you had the information to hand.

Consider the following situation:

**Case Study**

> Rumours of a merger had been rife in the office for weeks. Finally the senior management team circulated an email confirming that merger terms had been agreed. Many of the workforce had read the news in the local evening paper the night before. Rashid, the office manager, called his team together to announce that the two operations were to be merged in three month's time. He was bombarded with questions:
>
> Will we lose our jobs?
>
> Will there be redundancies?
>
> Will our jobs change?
>
> Will we be paid more or less?
>
> Rashid was not able to answer the questions.

**What should Rashid have done differently?**

Rashid has done no more than confirm what his team could have read in the papers yesterday. It is easy to understand his wish to keep them informed but there was really no point in holding a formal meeting until he knew enough to answer his team's questions. He should have kept his team informed, as much as he had the authority to do, through the process   this would have helped to prevent rumours and misunderstanding occurring.

*Consultation* has been a central theme of other chapters in this book. As far as change is concerned, your approach to consultation will vary according to the amount of freedom delegated to you in implementing it.

As we have pointed out elsewhere, lack of consultation is bad practice, resulting in dissatisfied and insecure staff and, usually, the imposition of systems that do not work as well as if they had been designed by those responsible for implementing them. Nevertheless, if change is to be imposed, the best you can do is to attempt to gain a little more flexibility by making representations to your own manager. Failing that, you will need to use all your skills of leadership and persuasion to convince your team.

One of these skills will be your ability to demonstrate and provoke *enthusiasm*. The first step is to make sure that you find out enough about the proposed change to understand properly why it is essential, the consequences of not changing and how your team will benefit. You will then be in a better position to gain their commitment.

## Implementing change

The implementation process of change involves both logistic and people considerations.

The process of managing resources to achieve results is covered elsewhere in this book and is just as relevant here. We can summarize its relevance to change by pointing out that implementing change requires:

- Clear objectives for the change
- An action plan with deadlines
- Milestones and responsibilities
- Resources and a budget
- A system for monitoring achievement against the objectives, deadlines and budget.

The people side of implementation involves:

- Individual and team briefings related to tasks, standards and output
- Training to accommodate job changes
- Regular communication
- Continual checking on progress, problems, concerns and complaints.

Beyond these activities, it may also require:

- Decisions on promotion and transfer
- A critical examination of the structure of your team
- The design of new working methods
- New definitions of your own and your team members' responsibilities.

# Consolidating change

This is an important part of the process and enables organizations to answer the following questions:

- How well did it work?
- What further action is necessary?
- How are people feeling?
- What can we learn for the future?

The first aspect is to review the outcome of the change. Change activities are not always totally successful. Once up and running there are bound to be:

- Aspects overlooked or forgotten
- Opportunities for improvement.

If change is to be accepted, people will need to see evidence of its success. The more action is taken to smooth any remaining rough edges, the more persuasive that success will be.

The second aspect is to confirm ownership of the change. Some people will need further help to gain the new knowledge and skills required. Otherwise they will lose confidence and try to return to their old ways. Work teams may have been separated. New teams will need to be built, following the techniques we explored in the chapter on team-building. Pay schemes will need to reflect new work demands. But it also means ensuring that performance receives praise and that, for example, review systems are revised to incorporate new objectives arising from the change. Communication needs to be ongoing.

The final aspect is evaluation of the change. It is in place, it has worked and people will have learned some valuable lessons – some of them painful. Evaluation means working out what can be learned from those lessons and recording them so that they can be applied to the next change activity that comes along.

**Review your learning**

Check your understanding of this chapter by completing the following:

1 How can people be more positive about change?

2 What are the differences between push and pull strategies?

3 List five reasons for resistance to change.

4 What are the three actions that will help to consolidate change?

**Theory of practice**

Apply this chapter to your own experience by answering the following:

1 Identify a change taking place in your organization at the moment. How do the people involved feel about it? Why is that?

2 Think of a change you would like to make to improve your operation. What restraining forces would you face? What could you do to lessen them?

3 What mechanisms do you use to inform and consult with your team? How could they be improved?

4 How much do you know about the reasons for the changes taking place in your organization? How could you find out more?

5 How effective is your organization generally in managing change? How could it improve?

# 16    Solving problems and making decisions

| Chapter Objectives | • *How should I solve problems?* |
|---|---|
| | • *How do I make decisions?* |

An essential skill of a manager is effective decision-making. A considerable part of your working day will involve you making decisions. Depending on the nature of your job, some of these decisions will be more or less important.

*Making decisions and bearing the responsibility for them is one of the cornerstones of the manager's job.*
Cooke and Slack (1991)

You may be finding that increasingly you are under pressure to make more complex decisions in reduced time-scales. So it is vital that you understand the processes involved in solving problems and making decisions.

*Managers spend their time choosing between alternative courses of action on the basis of the information available to them at the time; in other words, making decisions.*
Dixon (2003)

In broad terms, solving problems and making decisions are two stages in the same process.

- Solving problems answers the question 'What is wrong?'
- Taking decisions answers the question 'How do I fix it?'

However, this is not always the case. Sometimes the problem is so obvious that its solving does not involve any real decision-making at all. The analysis leads directly to the solution.

Decisions can also be linked to a search for a better way of doing things, even if there is nothing really wrong with the current way.

**PEOPLE AND PERFORMANCE**

Nevertheless, we can most usefully picture the process as a single cycle, although the relative importance of each stage will differ according to:

- The nature of the situation, issue or problem to be addressed
- Whether the issue has operational, tactical or strategic significance, which will determine who is involved in the process
- The complexity of the issue
- The extent of the choice of alternative actions
- The predictability of the outcome
- The levels of cost and risk
- The time-scales involved.

## A problem-solving and decision-making model

There are eleven stages in the process of problem-solving and decision-making. The first five relate to problem analysis. Six relate to decision-making. Each stage is expressed in the form of a question (see Figure 16.1). We shall look briefly at each stage.

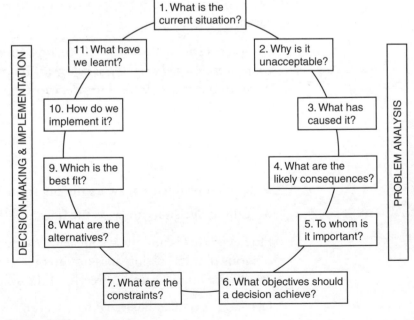

*Figure 16.1*

*1   What is the current situation?*

What is the gap between where we are and where we want to be?

*2   Why is it unacceptable?*

This covers a range of issues, for example high cost to the organization, loss of production, too many accidents.

*3   What has caused it?*

An analysis of when the problem occurs, how often, under what circumstances and where, enables the problem to be isolated. Possible causes can be identified and each one assessed to see whether it is the likely cause.

*4   What are the likely consequences?*

Answering this question identifies both the urgency with which the problem needs to be solved, or whether the problem is big enough to warrant corrective action.

*5   To whom is it important?*

Someone owns the problem. Someone will have to authorize action. Someone will have to take the action.

*6   What objectives should a decision achieve?*

These are formed from the identification of the current situation and why it is unacceptable.

*7   What are the constraints?*

These relate to costs, resources and time-scales.

*8   What are the alternatives?*

This is the stage when a range of alternatives are produced.

*9   Which is the best fit?*

All the various alternatives are compared with the objectives the decision should achieve to enable the one that comes closest – the best fit – to be chosen.

### 10 *How do we implement it?*

Implementing a decision uses the same techniques as project management. It requires an action plan, an analysis of necessary resources, budget and time, briefing and communication, monitoring and control.

### 11 *What have we learnt?*

The final stage, as with any project, is to review the success of the decision, make any final changes to cope with unforeseen snags and draw conclusions that can be applied to the implementation of future decisions.

## Problem analysis

The stages of problem analysis identify:

- The true nature of the problem
- Whether it is serious enough to justify the effort, time and cost needed to put it right
- Whether the people involved are appropriate and have the authority to make changes.

## Problem definition

Identifying the nature of the problem may seem an obvious first step. But, surprisingly often, organizations are content to deal with the 'present problem' and do not look closely enough to find the underlying cause. As a result, the actions they take do not address the root of the problem. Let us look at this example.

**Insight**

Petra's team has been complaining for a long time about the poor pay they get. But other teams in the same department are not complaining to the same extent, although no one is ever totally satisfied with their pay.

**If it were possible to award Petra's team a pay rise, do you think this would get rid of the real problem?**

The clue in this Insight is the fact that Petra's team seems to be the only one really unhappy about their pay. That probably raised suspicions in your mind. It is clear that there is something else going on.

Two techniques will help to identify the real problem. The first is to keep on asking 'why?' until you reach the root of the problem.

- *Why are Petra's team complaining about their pay?*

  Because they are generally fed up with their jobs.

- *Why are the jobs boring?*

  Because they are undemanding and routine.

- *Why are the jobs routine?*

  Because that is what the procedures dictate.

- *Why are the procedures that way?*

  Because they have never been challenged.

This brief set of questions and answers has redefined the problem. It is no longer: 'How to find a practical way of paying Petra's team more.' Instead, it has become: *'How to redesign their jobs so that they remain efficient while increasing job satisfaction.'*

The 'why' technique assumes that a solution has been found to the problem, then asks what extra benefits would come from the solution. In the case of Petra's team, higher pay should make them more satisfied, so the issue is one of satisfaction rather than pay.

Our second technique is designed to come up with a precise description of the problem by establishing the circumstances under which it does and does not occur. Table 16.1 shows this.

**Table 16.1**

| | |
| --- | --- |
| When does the problem occur? | When does it not occur? |
| Where does it occur? | Where does it not occur? |
| Who is involved? | Who is not involved? |
| In what conditions does the problem occur? | In what conditions does the problem not occur? |

Both techniques depend on accurate information being available. Problems can also be categorized according to whether they are:

- Deviation problems
- Potential problems
- Improvement problems.

# Identifying causes

Identifying the causes of problems is seen as critical by analysts and problem-solvers. A useful technique is the Ishikawa diagram, also known as the cause–effect or fishbone diagram. This technique was originally developed and used in the field of quality management but is now recognized for its wider application in problem-solving and decision-making.

You start by drawing the head and backbone of a fish, with a summary of the effect of the problem written into the head (Figure 16.2).

*Figure 16.2*

You then draw in a framework of potential causes as the main bones leading from the backbone (Figure 16.3). Standard headings are:

People, Environment, Methods, Plant, Equipment, Materials

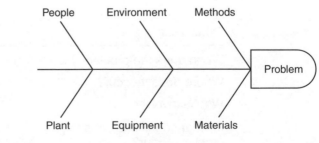

*Figure 16.3*

The next stage is to apply creative thinking to the headings using the prompts:

What, where, when, why, who, how?

For example:

- How does the environment contribute to this problem?
- Why are materials not of the required standard?
- Who are the people involved?
- What is wrong with the equipment?

The answers to these questions provide smaller bones which you can add to each of the six main bones, resulting finally in a diagram that will look something like Figure 16.4, which is an analysis of the causes of late deliveries in a particular postal region.

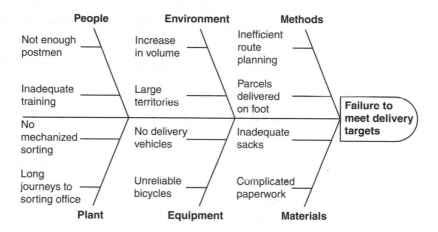

*Figure 16.4*

# Consequences

An analysis of future consequences should take both a short-term and a longer-term view. For the short-term, it is important to know what the problem is costing now in terms of productivity, standards and staff motivation. And then to compare these with the costs of resolving it. In the longer term, product or service changes, reorganization or a planned investment programme may indicate that it would be better to live with the problem until a larger initiative in the future resolves it. In other words, doing nothing is a perfectly valid response to a problem, provided you have made a conscious and reasoned decision to ignore it. Again, information is important – current costs, improvement costs, future plans and their impact.

# People

An identification of the people involved, or likely to be involved, in the problem is the last stage in problem analysis. They will fall into three categories:

### Problem-owners

These are the people most affected by the problem; those who must be sufficiently inconvenienced or dissatisfied to want to resolve it. If this is you, ask yourself:

- Do I care enough to take action?
- What autonomy and resources do I have to act?
- What are the limits to the action I can take?

### Authority-holders

Answers to those questions may reveal that you need to seek support, permission or approval from someone higher up the organization. In that case, ask yourself: the problem may be important to me, but is it sufficiently important to my line managers for them to authorize the necessary action, resources and expenditure?

### Implementers

These are the people who will take the action to resolve the problem. That is likely to be the members of your team. Ask yourself:

Do they understand the nature of the problem, its objectives and the benefits the solution will bring to them? Will you involve them in designing the solution? Have they the necessary skills and resources to implement the solution and make it successful?

Now bring the stages of problem analysis together by tackling this situation:

**Insight**

> National targets have been introduced to reduce class sizes in primary schools. In response, Wellbourne School has recruited a new teacher, Lizzie Matthews, who will be teaching her class in a disused Portakabin on the school playground. Unfortunately the classroom is cold, damp, draughty and generally in need of refurbishment.

**What information will Lizzie need about this problem before considering what to do about it?**

Looking at the current situation, Lizzie's problem is that her new classroom does meet the standards in school classrooms and there is a gap between what she has and what she would like.

It is unacceptable because her own comfort and her pupils' motivation to learn will be affected by the conditions.

The ultimate cause of the problem was, indirectly, the new national targets. But Lizzie cannot influence those and, in any case, the intention behind them was positive. More immediately, the cause was the school's decision to make use of available resources to achieve the target. However, Lizzie may want to find out:

- What is the deadline for achieving the target?
- Was this a unanimous decision by the school governors or influenced by a few?
- Is any money available for refurbishment?

The short-term consequences will involve discomfort and reduced learning. Lizzie can calculate roughly what it would cost to put the classroom right, so she will need to find some way of costing the current disadvantages, in order to make a comparison.

For the longer-term, she will need to know:

- Is there investment planned to upgrade the classroom? If so, when will this happen?
- Does the school have any plans for new permanent buildings?

- Is there any intention for her class to move into a permanent classroom in the existing school?
- Is the increase in pupil numbers likely to continue?

As far as people are concerned, the problem-owners are Lizzie and her pupils; the authority-holders are the headteacher and the governors, who will need to authorize the work and the expenditure; the implementers will be mainly outside contractors. Although Lizzie and her class may be affected, Lizzie needs to decide:

- Is she willing to cause a fuss in the first months of her new job?
- Will parents take practical action by supporting her?
- Are the authority-holders more concerned about meeting the targets, protecting their budget or improving conditions?
- Will she and her class cope with any disruption?

As you can see, consideration of the five questions contained in problem analysis is essential in identifying:

- The real issue to be addressed
- Whether it is worth dealing with
- The people whose support is required and whether they will give it.

Only when you have this information will you be able to decide if you should take the issue further. If you do, you will have a firm basis for deciding on the action to be taken.

# Decision-making and implementation

### Setting objectives

An important step in the decision-making process is the clarification and setting of objectives. These will obviously vary according to the situation you and your team face at any one time. Objectives of the decision need to be clear, unambiguous, agreed and understood by everyone concerned. Without this clarification you will be in danger of embarking on a journey with little knowledge of where it is leading and therefore will have difficulty knowing if you have arrived! As a manager you need to be able to make a judgement as to whether a particular decision that was made was effective or not.

### Identifying constraints

This involves a thorough analysis of all the factors that are involved in the decision that may limit the scope. The following questions may help you in the process:

- How long have I got before this decision must be fully implemented?
- What staff can I use to put it in place?
- Do they have the necessary skills and experience to enable the decision to work?
- How much budget do I have?
- What will be the impact on other teams/departments of this decision?

This process recognizes the importance of working within the constraints of an organization. We often need to be creative in identifying ways of working with these constraints and generating alternatives.

### Generating alternatives

This is an important stage in the process and involves considering all possible alternatives. This is the stage where creating ideas and involving other people will benefit you in several ways:

- The more people, the more ideas
- Involve colleagues and managers and learn from their experience
- Involve your team, who may well have a better understanding, as they are closer to the issues
- Involving them is also likely to increase their ownership and commitment to ensuring successful implementation.

The culture of your organization together with the nature of the problem will determine how creative you can be in generating ideas. The more unstructured a situation is increases the need for a creative approach. There are a number of techniques that enable individuals and groups to creatively generate ideas. It is worth noting that rarely are important or critical decisions made by one person. The focus with any of the techniques is to ensure that all ideas, even those that are apparently unworkable or off-the-wall, are considered equally.

### Evaluating the alternatives

Finding the best fit involves two steps:

First, discarding from your list of alternatives those which are irrelevant, clearly unworkable, illegal or at odds with the values of the organization.

Then, making a careful, objective comparison between each on the basis of the objectives you have set for your decision and the constraints under which it must operate. You will be choosing the best alternative on the basis of which alternative addresses most of the problem with the least cost, upheaval and disruption.

# Implementing the decision

This stage makes use of a number of techniques that apply to project management, managing change and continuous improvement. In summary, it involves:

- An action plan, perhaps in the form of a flow-chart or critical path analysis
- A calculation of required resources, costs, time-scales, milestones and deadlines
- Identifying and allocating responsibilities
- Communicating reasons, standards and targets
- Designing and installing some form of control loop to monitor progress and initiate remedial action
- Carrying out a risk analysis
- Formulating contingency plans in case something goes wrong.

Strictly there are two steps in this stage. The first is the plan, the second is the implementation. Even when you plan how to carry out your decision, you could still find that:

- Detailed calculations show your decision does not fit the constraints
- Your plan needs more resources than you have
- The plan is too risky.

Careful planning, by highlighting issues like these, will avoid the plan collapsing when you try to implement it. That will allow you to revise your plan to make it achievable. As a last resort, you might even decide that, as we mentioned earlier, the current situation is preferable to a high-risk plan to deal with it.

# Review and evaluation

It involves:

- A final check on how successfully the decision has been implemented
- Action to deal with any remaining snags
- Learning and noting lessons, which can be applied to the implementation of future decisions.

**Check your understanding of this chapter by completing the following:**

1 What are the eleven questions in the problem-solving and decision-making model?

2 Which are the two techniques that help to identify the real problem?

3 What is the Ishikawa diagram also known as?

4 Why do you need to set objectives in the decision-making process?

5 Why is it useful to involve team members when generating alternatives?

**Apply this chapter to your own experience by answering the following:**

1 Think of a problem you faced recently. What more could you have done to establish its root cause?

2 Who would you consult for ideas on solving:

- A people problem?
- A quality problem?
- A budget problem?

3 How careful are you to evaluate the success of your decisions? What more could you do?

4 What problem-solving and decision-making techniques does your organization use? How can the process be improved?

**PEOPLE AND PERFORMANCE**

# 17 Recruiting to the team

| Chapter Objectives | • *How do I select the right person?* |
|---|---|

People leave organizations for numerous reasons, for example, promotion, relocation, financial incentives, dissatisfaction. Staff turnover is a cost to organizations in terms of recruitment costs and staff morale and motivation.

In the UK the overall employee turnover is 16.1%. CIPD (2005) figures show that levels vary from region to region and between industry sectors. The highest levels of employee turnover (50% in some cases) are in retail, hotel, restaurant and call centre environments. The lowest levels are in the Civil Service, fire and police services.

As a manager your challenge is to: maintain performance, lead and develop your team, create an environment where the individual feels valued thereby contributing to the overall levels of staff retention. In this chapter we briefly look at the main aspects of the recruitment and selection process. In the Resource Bank at the end of the section you will find suggested additional reading and references which will provide you with more detailed information.

Hutchinson and Purcell (2003) highlighted through their research how the behaviour of first-line managers directly related to the levels of commitment, motivation and satisfaction among employees. They found that a poor relationship with a line manager was frequently given as a reason for leaving an organization.

As a manager you will be monitoring your team's performance, absenteeism and retention. However, should a member of your team leave then it is good practice to conduct an 'exit interview'. This enables you to identify and discuss their reasons for leaving and you will be able to determine whether these are within or outside of your control. For example, if the reason is because of dissatisfaction with the job because of work allocation, or conflict in the team, then these are issues that are within your control to change, and you should have identified these prior to the individual leaving! Promotion and relocation are likely to be factors outside of your control. You should remember though that exit interviews are not always reliable; in many instances individuals are reluctant to criticize their manager, colleagues or the organization – particularly if they are wanting a reference for their new job!

Recruiting a new employee costs an organization in terms of the recruitment and selection process, costs of covering the vacancy and the training of the new employee, so it is important to get it right.

*Recruiting the best possible candidate for any vacancy takes time and effort – and a lot of thought. But choosing the right person for the job first time round makes a manager's life a lot simpler.*
Veniard (2004)

As a manager you will be expected to contribute to the process of recruiting staff to your team. You may not be involved in every stage of the process, for example advertising the vacancy, but you still need to be clear about what the post entails and the type of person you are looking for.

## Starting the recruitment process

The amount of involvement you have with the recruitment process will vary with the organization. In some organizations the process is controlled through the Human Resource department with minimal involvement from the managers. Ideally you will work in partnership with the HR department in the recruitment and selection of the right individual for your team.

## Is there a vacancy?

The first stage when a vacancy arises is to review your actual requirements. For example, do you need to replace the individual? Can the work be reallocated within the team? Could you create an opportunity for a secondment from another department? Could you employ someone on a temporary basis?

Once you have decided that the vacancy does need to be filled the next stage is to analyse the job, defining exactly what is needed and critically looking at the job to determine ways to make it more effective.

# The job description

Having analysed the post you are then in a position to write the job description which sets out the main responsibilities of the job. The job description should be clear and accurate. Many organizations have a standard format for writing them, and include:

- Job title
- Main purpose of the job
- Responsibilities of the job
- Who the job holder is responsible to and for
- Conditions of employment
- Performance measures.

# Person specification

The next stage is to write the person specification – this sets out the skills, knowledge and experience, the qualifications and personal qualities required to do the job. This can be subdivided into *essential*, for example a specific qualification is required, or *desirable*, relating to a technical skill that can be offered as part of the induction process.

Throughout the whole process you should ensure that you comply with all the relevant legislation that prevents discrimination.

It is illegal to discriminate against individuals at work on the basis of:

- Gender
- Race
- Disability
- Sexual orientation
- Religion or belief
- Age.

Relevant legislation includes:

Equal Pay Act 1970 (Amendment) Regulations 2003

Sex Discrimination Act 1975 (Amendment) Regulations 2005

Race Relations Act 1976

Disability Discrimination Act 1995

Employment Equality Regulations 2003

# Attracting applicants and drawing up a shortlist

Your organization will have its own policies and procedures for advertising a job vacancy both internally and externally. External methods can be through advertising in trade journals, local and national newspapers, on the Web, in job centres or through an external recruitment agency. The nature of the post will determine the most appropriate method.

Once you have received the applications you are then able to draw up a list of suitable candidates, having assessed them against the job description and person specification.

# Selection methods

There are a wide range of methods by which you can determine whether or not an individual is suitable to fill the vacancy. These include:

- One-to-one interviews
- Panel interviews
- Assessment centres
- Numeracy and literacy tests
- Personality questionnaires
- Psychometric tests
- Online tests.

The method used will again be determined by company policy and practice together with the nature of the job. There is a cost associated with all of these methods so it is important that the appropriate method is used. Of equal importance is that those involved in the selection process should have been trained and have the necessary skills to, for example, interview or run assessment centres.

# Making an offer

Once the decision has been made the successful candidate is notified. This is often done by telephone but must be followed by a formal offer in writing together with the terms and conditions of employment.

Unsuccessful candidates should also be informed promptly. This is common courtesy and many organizations give feedback to unsuccessful candidates.

We said at the start of this chapter that staff turnover and recruitment are costly to organizations so retaining staff begins at the process of welcoming a new employee to your team. You should plan a suitable induction programme for your new member of the team. The first impression that a new employee has of an organization has a significant impact on how long they stay. The Case Study in Chapter 12 showed the importance of appropriately inducting a new employee.

*One in five new employees leave after less than six months.* (Source: CIPD)

The purpose of induction is to enable the new employee to:

● Get to know the organization
● Learn about their own work/team environment
● Adjust to their new workplace.

You will be able to use the tools and techniques discussed elsewhere in this book for managing and reviewing the performance of your new team member, agreeing and setting achievable objectives, and identifying development opportunities. Using Tuckman's model (Chapter 12) will also help you to minimize the impact a new member may have on the overall performance of your team.

**Review your learning**

Check your understanding of this chapter by completing the following:

1 What should a job description specify?

2 What should a person specification include?

3 Give three selection methods.

4 What is the purpose of an induction programme?

**Theory to practice**

Apply this chapter to your own experience by answering the following:

1 Review the job descriptions of your team. Do they accurately reflect the work they are doing? If not, update them with advice from your line manager and the HR department.

2 What steps can you take to improve your knowledge of the relevant legislation?

3 How does your organization induct new employees? What involvement do you have? What improvements can you make to the process?

# Resource bank

## References

Belbin, M. (1984) *Management Teams: Why They Succeed or Fail*, Elsevier

Blake, R. and Mouton, J. (1961) *The Managerial Grid*, Gulf Publishers

Burnes, B. (1996) *Managing Change: A Strategic Approach to Organizational Dynamics*, Pitman

CIPD (2005) Recruitment, retention and turnover 2005. Survey Report, London

Cooke, S. and Slack, N. (1991) *Making Management Decisions*, Prentice Hall

Dixon, R. (2003) *The Management Task*, Butterworth-Heinemann

Hutchinson, S. and Purcell, J. (2003) *Bringing Policies to Life: The Vital Role of Front Line Managers in People Management*, CIPD

Lewin, K. (1951) *Field Theory in Social Science*, Harper & Row

Strebel, P. (1996) 'Why do employees resist change?', *Harvard Business Review*, May/June, pp. 86–92

Taylor, B. (1994) *Successful Change Strategies*, Director Books

Tuckman, B. W. (1965) *Psychological Bulletin*, 63, pp. 384–399

## Website addresses

**www.acas.org.uk**
Advisory, arbitration and conciliation service – source of advice, publications and legislation

**www.cipd.co.uk**
Chartered Institute of Personnel and Development – information, publications, survey reports on recruitment and selection

**www.cre.gov.uk**
Commission for Racial Equality – anti-discriminatory advice

**www.drc.org.uk**
Disability Rights Commission – information, legislation and employment rights

**www.eoc.org.uk**
Equal Opportunities Commission – good practice and legal information

**www.venworks. co.uk**
Training information (Veniard)

PEOPLE AND PERFORMANCE

# Section 4  Effective Resource Management

- *What are the best ways of controlling costs?*
- *How do I get the best from my resources?*
- *How are inputs transformed into outputs?*
- *What management information do I need?*
- *How should I store and record information so that it is readily accessible?*
- *What financial information do I need?*
- *How can I use the budget process to monitor performance?*

# 18 Managing and controlling costs and resources

| Chapter Objectives | • *What are the best ways of controlling costs?* |
| | • *How do I get the best from my resources?* |

Monitoring and controlling costs and getting the best from your resources are a key task for you as a manager. Managing costs and resources is a six-stage process:

- Knowing what you want to achieve
- Identifying the quality and quantity of inputs needed to achieve it
- Setting standards for measurement
- Monitoring performance against them
- Taking corrective action if necessary
- Comparing results with plans.

This chapter will provide a brief explanation of each of these six stages, describing in more detail some techniques that are specific to controlling costs and resources. We will also consider inventory/ stock as a resource and some of the associated quality issues.

## The control process

### Knowing what you want to achieve

We have already stressed that effective control depends on being able to compare actual performance with plans expressed in quantified terms. But we have also pointed out that quantified plans are reflections of qualitative judgements. In other words, they start with general aims like:

- To satisfy customer demand
- To improve productivity
- To reduce costs.

Then they are quantified by being refined into numerical or financial values like:

- To achieve sales of £3.2 million
- To increase output from 1,200 units to 1,400 units per machine per week
- To make savings of £150,000 in energy costs this year compared with last year.

These quantified targets will, ideally, be agreed with you then issued to you formally as:

- Individual objectives
- Team objectives
- Departmental budgets
- Team budgets.

### Identifying input quality and quantity

The objectives and budgets set through the annual planning process are not usually detailed enough for the day-to-day control of costs and resources which will be your primary responsibility. In order to carry out that responsibility, you will need quantified statements of, for example:

- Machine hours
- Labour hours
- Raw material volumes
- Output targets.

These are relatively straightforward to calculate. The question of input quality is more complicated. For example:

- You know the number of labour hours required for a particular job. But what skills and experience will your team need in order to complete the job to the required standard?
- You know how much raw materials you need. But of what quality must it be to meet your output and waste targets?

As mentioned earlier, you can only exercise control if you can compare numbers. To do that, you will need a specification for each of the inputs required to achieve your outputs. The exact form of each specification will vary according to the nature of the input.

The specification for people may include the successful completion of a skills training programme, specific professional qualifications or so many hours', months' or years' experience.

Materials specifications will probably involve statements of, for example, purity, size, tolerances, durability, breaking strain and so on.

Even production equipment and machines may have quality specifications related to maximum outputs available, reliability and maintenance requirements.

**Case Study**

> James is a cabin steward for an airline running services between London Heathrow and Paris Charles de Gaulle airports. James serves passengers a light meal during the flight. The meal is prepared and packed on trays by an outside catering firm. The aircraft has 150 seats for passengers and storage space for 160 meals. The airline has recently changed to a cheaper catering firm. Of the meals they supply, 8% are found to be missing some of the food – this is usually either the bread roll or the fruit.

**What impact will this have on James's ability to feed his passengers?**

An 8% failure rate means that if 160 meals are loaded on to the aircraft, 13 of them will be rejected by the passengers. If the aircraft is not full, the airline can adjust by loading more meals than passengers flying. But if the plane is full, three passengers will not be fed. For James this problem is not just about having sufficient meals to meet demand but also about meeting customer expectation; delivering poor customer service can prove costly to an organization.

### Setting standards

These relate to both inputs, as we have described, and outputs. The standards need to:

- Measure both quality and quantity
- Reflect the complexity of the process which creates the output.

For example, producing ball-bearings is a quick, one-stage process which will need simple standards frequently applied. Building a multi-storey office block on the other hand is a long process with multiple stages. Useful standards will break the process down into individual stages and probably sub-stages as well. But the standards are likely to be applied less often than for ball-bearings.

One approach that is often used for repetitive processes is based on standard performance rates. Often called 'standard costing' it involves:

- An analysis of an individual task, job or product, normally by work study measurements
- The quantity of inputs required (materials, time, energy)
- The costs of those inputs.

These result in standards of measurement that can be used as a basis for job or product costing and pricing.

### Monitoring performance

We have described the principles of performance monitoring elsewhere. Here, it is worth noting the variety of monitoring systems and documents available to you:

- Timesheets
- Overtime statements
- Reject rates
- Customer complaints and letters of praise
- Purchase invoices
- Sales invoices
- Budget statements
- Goods received notes
- Standard performance rates
- Standard costings.

### Taking corrective action

In Chapter 22 we introduce the idea of controllable and non-controllable variances. We suggest the importance of differentiating between them:

- Variances you can control
- Variances your line manager can control – or at least influence
- Variances outside your organization's control.

Similar considerations apply to the process of controlling costs and resources.

Costs can be separated into:

- Variable and fixed costs
- Direct and indirect costs
- Overheads.

Variable costs vary directly with the volume of output produced. With a transport fleet, for example, fuel costs will increase directly in line with the number of miles covered. Fixed costs still vary, but less directly. Thus, in our example, the depreciation costs of trucks in the fleet will stay the same, even if they cover no mileage. However, if the distance to be covered continues to increase, it will ultimately be necessary to buy an extra truck and depreciation will go up.

Direct costs are those that can be attributed directly to the output process. In a manufacturing environment, the workers who operate the machines are sources of direct costs. The sales force, on the other hand, is not involved in production. Their salaries are indirect costs. Similarly, the components used in manufacture are direct material costs, whereas the costs of stationery and clearing materials are indirect costs.

Overheads are a form of indirect costs, but even further removed from the production process. For example, an office will typically have reception staff and administrative staff. However, they service all the operations carried out in the office and are therefore overheads. Overheads may relate to:

- Sales and distribution
- Administration
- Heating and lighting
- Office and factory rental.

Typically, you will have more control of variable and direct costs than of the remainder. Therefore, although your budget may charge you a notional rent for the space your team occupies, you are unlikely to be able to control either the rate per square metre or the space for which you are charged.

## Comparing results

This is the final stage of the control process. It involves checking whether the corrective action you have taken has eliminated the variances between plans and performance. On a regular basis, the feedback information you get will come through monthly budgeting control techniques or the more frequent control documents we listed earlier. Improvement or change projects are also, of course, methods of narrowing the gap between actual performance and what you would like to achieve. Their success will need to be compared with the targets and objectives you set for the project at the beginning.

## Case Study

> Swinbourne local council has a training officer who runs induction and sales training programmes from an office and training room at the back of the building. When courses are running, delegates receive free coffee and meals and are given training notes to take away and written activities to complete during the programme.

**What are the training officer's variable costs and fixed costs?**

**What overheads are likely to apply?**

**How would you recommend the training officer controls the inputs and outputs?**

The most obvious variable costs are the delegate's drinks, meals and the handouts given to them. If no delegates attend then these costs are not incurred.

The primary fixed costs will be the training officer's salary, pension and depreciation on equipment used such as an overhead projector.

Overheads will take the form of heating, lighting and possibly a central administrative service used by several functions in the building.

## Managing resources

So far, we have lumped together costs and resources. Strictly, though, managers do not control costs. Costs are no more than a set of financial values applied to the use of resources. So the manager's job is to manage resources in the most cost-effective way.

A complete list of resources used by an organization would include:

- Land
- Buildings
- Finance
- Equipment
- Materials
- Information
- Energy
- Time
- People.

Managers have little control over location. The decision to buy or lease a particular site will probably have been taken a long time ago and relocation decisions are generally taken at the most senior level.

It is much the same with buildings, although you may be able to re-arrange your team's work area to make it more comfortable or efficient. You may also be able to influence how clean it is or the way it is decorated. You will recognize these as a couple of the hygiene factors that Herzberg suggested can dissatisfy people, although getting them better will not make people work any harder.

Finance is a different matter. You probably have no control over actual cash, unless you have access to a small amount of petty cash for incidental expenses. However, you may well be able to:

- Influence investment decisions
- Influence or instruct your team, for example concerning the standard of hotels they use, whether they travel first or second class and so on.

The remaining items on our list are even more under your control and management.

*Managing equipment*

Equipment is used wastefully when it is:

- Inadequately maintained
- Used by people who lack the proper training
- Unsuitable for the purpose
- Insufficient for the purpose.

The results of these kinds of ill-usage are:

- Breakdowns
- Poor quality
- Damage
- Reduced output.

Depending on your situation you may be able to:

- Alter or improve the standard, frequency or nature of maintenance schedules
- Train staff to use equipment properly
- Influence recruitment decisions
- Recommend the acquisition of the right equipment.

In most cases you will do this most successfully by using the persuading and influencing skills we described earlier.

*Managing materials*

In a manufacturing environment, materials will consist of:

- Components
- Raw materials
- Disposable items like lubricants or cleaning stuffs
- Finished goods.

In a retail environment, materials will be:

- Stock lines
- Service items
- Till rolls, order forms, customer information leaflets and so on.

An office-based organization will use:

- Stationery
- Binders
- Computer paper
- Pens, pencils, markers.

All of these will need to be purchased, held in stock and accounted for.

In a later chapter we describe ABC analysis and just-in-time techniques – two approaches to managing stock. Here, we will consider purchasing and security.

*Purchasing* involves:

(a) *Finding the right supplier*: In other words, suppliers who can deliver the right products, at the right time, to the right quality, in the right quantities and at the right price. Tight and accurate product specifications are important here.

(b) *Negotiating terms*: It is often said that 'there is always a cheaper supplier'. But alternatives may be cheaper because the quality is poorer. Negotiating terms is a matter of ensuring what you are getting gives you the best price for the quality you need.

(c) *Ordering goods*: Ordering 'little but often' keeps down the cost of holding stock. But it also increases the administrative costs. ABC analysis can help here, by identifying those high value, low volume items which are costly to hold in stock and therefore justify frequent re-orders.

Effective *security* addresses the issues of external theft, employee theft and employee fraud. It is interesting to note that, in most retail operations, employee theft is a far bigger source of loss than shoplifting. (Retail managers tend to find this fact uncomfortable and therefore put most of their effort into preventing shoplifters, who present the minority of problems.)

For theft to occur requires:

- Something worth stealing
- A thief
- An opportunity
- A means of removal.

The likelihood of theft can be reduced by:

- Limiting knowledge of valuable items (goods or information) to those who need to know
- Careful selection of staff
- Controlling visitor access
- Adequate physical security (locks, bolts, alarms, fences and so on)
- Strict guidelines on what can be removed from premises and when.

### Managing information

As a manager, you depend on information. Your effectiveness will be tied up with, for example:

- Materials specifications
- Production schedules
- Customer orders
- Control information.

We suggested earlier that good information needs to be:

- Relevant
- Accurate
- Timely
- Complete
- Concise.

The essence of managing information is to decide the information you and your team need based on these criteria and compare the information you get with the specification of your ideal requirements.

Then *identify the shortcomings*. Take personal action to address them or find someone else in the organization who can bring what you get in line with what you need.

### Managing energy

We can draw a distinction between physical energy (heat, light, power) and human energy in the shape of effort. Managing physical energy will involve you reminding staff to switch off unused equipment and unnecessary lighting; checking for examples of waste; looking for and recommending ways of improving energy waste.

Improving the use of human activity can be undertaken through performance review, training and motivation – encouragement and finding more effective ways of doing things.

### Managing time

The time taken to complete a job is a measure of efficiency. You can manage time by:

- Monitoring staff attendance records
- Assessing and addressing machine and staff productivity

- Revising operating methods
- Reviewing production and maintaining schedules.

Time is a precious resource that vast numbers of managers complain they do not have enough of! We have therefore, deliberately included managing time in this chapter. You should apply the same principles to managing your time as you do to other resources.

We have probably all, at some time or another, attended a time management course, often resulting in disappointing results. Improving the management of one's time cannot be achieved on a quick fix basis. It requires a systematic and planned approach with small step changes and realistic goals. But managing your time does not start with planning, it actually starts with information. You need to understand, for example, how your time is used and misused, how much of your time is actually spent on unplanned, unproductive activities, how many times you are interrupted and why.

How much of your time is lost through the following?

- Failure to define priorities – resulting in important tasks being neglected or hurried.

- Procrastinating – so that you have to work late to complete those monthly reports.

- Inefficient delegation – remember Jim in our Case Study in Chapter 9?

- Attending meetings – meetings are a potentially costly activity, particularly if they are not really necessary.

Spending time analysing (this is productive) how your time is wasted and lost can be extremely beneficial in enabling you to make better use of this precious resource in the future.

Mullins (2002) suggests that the essentials of good time management include:

*Clear objectives, careful forward planning, the definition of priorities and action; and the ability to delegate successfully.*

### Managing people

In the same way as you manage and control equipment, materials and information you need to manage people. However, people are a unique and special resource and managing them is not simply a control process! As we have shown you in previous chapters, getting the best from your team means knowing your people, treating and valuing them as individuals as well as understanding what motivates them. Nonetheless, they still need to be productive in the most efficient and effective way as possible.

Your role involves getting the best possible results from people by:

- Making sure you know what you require from them (output standards, quality, quantity and so on).
- Communicating those requirements to them.
- Agreeing and providing them with methods of measuring actual against required performance.
- Encouraging them to seek reasons for any shortfalls.
- Involving them in finding solutions.
- Providing or arranging help in implementing them (which may be in the form of training, additional or more suitable resources).

In other words, it involves applying a minor but important variation of the control process with which we started this chapter.

### Review your learning

**Check your understanding of this chapter by completing the following:**

1   Give three examples of quantified statements needed for day-to-day control.

2   Standard performance rates are:

- Hourly payment rates for a particular job
- Measures of the inputs used on a job under normal circumstances
- Output quantities expected from a member of staff under normal circumstances
- Output volumes which must be achieved before a bonus is earned.

(*Tick one*)

3   Explain the difference between variable and fixed costs.

4   List three examples of poor time management.

Apply this chapter to your own experience by answering the following:

1 How much attention do you pay to the quality specifications needed for your inputs? What more could you do?

2 What performance monitoring documents do you see regularly? Which performance standards do they relate to?

3 List the costs charged to you in your budget. Which can you control?

4 How does your organization carry out purchasing? If you do not know, how could you find out?

5 How can you and your team reduce costs?

6 What changes could you introduce which would make your team/department more cost-efficient?

# 19 Changing inputs into outputs

**Chapter Objectives**

● *How are inputs transformed into outputs?*

An organization exists to satisfy the needs of its customers or consumers; this is the case whether it is a manufacturing company, a retailer, a school or even a hospital.

Customers or consumers are the recipients of the products or services of that organization. In Section 1 of this book we introduced the idea that managers are responsible, among other things, for transforming inputs into the products and services that people want.

The transformation of inputs into outputs is at the heart of the organization – the operation – of the organization, and operations management is the responsibility of all managers.

*Operations management is the business function that manages that part of a business that transforms raw materials and human inputs into goods and services of higher value.*
Denzler (2004)

This definition suggests that value is added through the transformation process. We introduced the principle of added value earlier. It is worth re-emphasizing that:

● All products and services cost money
● Customers will only pay for things they value
● All organizations have customers.

Every function in an organization costs money. All organizations receive limited revenue in the form of prices paid by customers, budgets or subsidies from local or national government. Consequently any organization will work hard to ensure that it makes the most effective use of the revenue it receives. That means that any function must be able to justify its existence on the basis of the value it adds to the products and services provided by the organization it serves.

As economies become increasingly dependent on international trade and therefore need to compete with other countries, so the importance of adding value becomes more obvious.

So where does operations management fit into this big economic picture? Earlier references to inputs, transformation and customers hint at the answer to this question:

- All organizations have customers
- Customers will only pay for things they value
- Organizations exist to add value by transforming inputs into products and services that customers want
- Every function contributes to that transformation process.

Therefore the role of operations management is to ensure that every function in an organization adds as much value as it can, making the most efficient and effective use of the resources at its disposal:

*a business is really a set of processes, each of which has inputs, outputs and structure. Each process has a job to do and each should be measured on how effective it is in achieving the desired outcomes.* Denzler (2004)

Outputs are what go on to the next link in the supply chain. That next link may be the final customer or an internal customer in the organization. However, outputs do not necessarily bring added value.

**Insight**

> The Production Unit of a drinks manufacturer takes cost and output data for each production line and uses them to prepare information which is intended to show the team leaders of each line how well their operations are performing. However, the resulting information is bulky, difficult to analyse and leaves the reader to work out comparisons.

Figure 19.1 illustrates the fundamental of operations management:

*Figure 19.1*

**What are the inputs, transformation and outputs of this process?**

**Do you think it adds value?**

The inputs to this process are the cost and output data produced by each line. In theory these are then transformed into management information which represents the output. However, to be useful management information should present easily identifiable comparisons – with previous performance, for example, with budgets and between lines.

The insight suggests that individual team leaders might do better to compare the raw data and make their own comparisons. The process certainly produces outputs but appears to add little or no value.

Inputs consist of the resources used in a process: consumable resources, like raw materials, time, energy, budget and renewable resources, like premises, machinery, tools and expertise. Outputs should ideally be the products and services that customers want – in the right place and at the right time.

Transformation is the process of changing inputs into outputs. However, since operations are every manager's responsibility it is not possible to give a simple definition of what that change involves. You will get a feel for the transformation process by answering the following questions:

**What transformation takes place when:**

1  A retailer buys a box of chocolate bars from the cash and carry warehouse and displays them on his shelves?

2  A dentist drills and fills your tooth?

3  A gardener cuts your lawn?

4  A bricklayer mixes cement?

5  A florist buys flowers from the market and displays them as bunches in her shop?

6  Your local garage repairs your noisy exhaust?

Transformation may involve a change in:

● Form

● Content

● Location

- Presentation
- Efficiency.

So in our questions:

- Question 1 involves changes in form (single bars not a whole box) and location.

- Question 2 may involve a change in form or content but certainly involves a change in efficiency!

- Question 3 involves a change in presentation.

- Question 4 involves a change in both form and content (a combination of water, sand and cement).

- Question 5 involves a change in form (single flowers to bunches) and location and presentation.

- Question 6 involves a change in efficiency (and possibly content if the repair required, for example, results in a new exhaust).

# Economy, efficiency, effectiveness

Added value is not an absolute. Of course it is relatively easy for customers, both internal and external, to decide that a product or service adds value at all. Over time they may come to the realization that they can happily do without it completely.

However, this is an unusual situation. Consider these two insights.

**Insight**

> Barnett Fabrications buys sheet steel which they use as a major component in the manufacture of industrial shelving units. The price of steel from their current supplier is making the units too expensive to compete with those of other manufacturers.

**Can the company do without this component completely?**

**If not what option could they consider?**

**Insight**

> Wexford Local Authority provides a weekly refuse collection service to local traders. The collection is currently carried out by staff employed by the local authority. The local traders are complaining about the prices charged for the service.

**Can the traders do without the service completely?**

**What could the local authority do to reduce the price?**

Sheet steel is obviously an essential component for Barnett Fabrications – no steel means no product. However, they are not permanently tied to their current supplier. A relatively simple alternative would be to find another supplier able to provide sheet steel of a suitable specification at a lower price.

Wexford's local traders are unlikely to be able to do without refuse collection completely. But the local authority charges separately for it so there appears to be nothing stopping them from taking their business elsewhere. They might choose to:

- Form a cooperative to buy the service from a commercial provider.
- Or even make individual arrangements so that each store is serviced by a different refuse collection business.
- Or else band together to recruit their own refuse collectors.

The local authority could choose to withdraw the service but it would lose a valuable source of income and could create an environmental problem. Less extreme alternatives would be to reduce the cost of the service by:

- Raising the productivity of its existing refuse collectors
- Finding a commercial provider who could offer the same service for less.

Either approach would then allow it to reduce the price of the service whilst maintaining its income.

Implied in these insights are three concepts which are central to the process of operations management and adding value.

*Economy* is the term used to describe how cheaply inputs can be bought. By finding a supplier of the sheet steel at a lower price, Barnett Fabrications would be improving the economy of its purchasing. So would Wexford's local traders if they found a commercial provider prepared to offer a cheaper deal.

*Efficiency* relates inputs to outputs. Increased efficiency comes from achieving greater outputs using the same or fewer resources. This is what Wexford Local Authority would be doing by improving the productivity of its existing refuse collectors. Other ways of increasing efficiency include:

- Reducing waste
- Increasing production speed
- Making more efficient use of equipment and machinery
- Introducing equipment and machinery which is better suited to the job
- Improving staff capability through better training, instruction or management.

*Effectiveness* describes the extent to which outputs achieve the objectives set for them. That means the extent to which outputs satisfy the needs and wants of the next customer in the supply chain. The closer outputs come to meeting their needs, the more customers will value them.

However, improving effectiveness does not necessarily mean providing a better product or service. The emphasis here is on achieving a match between outputs and customer needs. The next insight illustrates this point.

**Insight**

> Weston Couriers offers a delivery service to local businesses. It guarantees collection and delivery within 4 hours in a 50 mile radius of its depot and charges a premium price for the service. However, many of its customers actually want packages delivered outside the 50 mile radius and are content for this to take up to 24 hours. The customers also complain about paying a premium price for non-urgent deliveries.

**What are the customers' needs and wants?**

**How could Weston Couriers improve its effectiveness?**

The problem for Weston Couriers is that they are providing a fast, guaranteed service at a high price to customers who, in many cases, actually want a cheaper, slower service.

Contradictory as it may seem, the company could improve its effectiveness most easily by lowering its standards, thereby reducing its input costs so that it can offer lower prices. In everyday language, this would result in a service of poorer quality but in the terms of quality management the quality would actually improve because it would be a closer match with customers' needs.

Both in this chapter and earlier in the book, we have stressed that quality means meeting customer needs (the Total Quality message). In Chapter 24 we shall describe various ways of finding out what those needs are.

In many cases, managers and staff alike are perfectly aware that the economy and efficiency of their operations are not as good as they might be and that their outputs do not fully meet customer requirements. They also have a good idea of what is going wrong and, perhaps even more importantly, what should be done about it. This is totally consistent with the idea of delegated decision-making we mentioned earlier.

The practice of quality improvement therefore involves both you and your team looking continually for ways of improving operating methods.

## Review your learning

Check your understanding of this chapter by completing the following:

1  Give a definition of operations

2  What do the terms

- Economy

- Efficiency

- Effectiveness

mean?

3  What does added value mean?

## Theory to practice

Apply this chapter to your own experience by answering the following:

1  Describe the inputs you use, the transformations and outputs for which you are responsible.

2  Who are the customers (internal and external) in the next link in your supply chain?

3 How economical are the inputs you use? What improvements could you make?

4 How efficient is your transformation process? What improvements could you make?

5 How effective are your outputs? What improvements could you make?

6 What more could you do to involve your team in quality improvement?

# 20  Information management

| Chapter Objectives | • *What management information do I need?* |
|---|---|
| | • *How should I store and record information so that it is readily accessible?* |

Managers:

- Make plans
- Respond to external factors
- Manage change
- Control resources
- Manage budgets
- Make improvements
- Solve problems
- Make decisions.

There is considerable variety in these responsibilities. Nevertheless, they have at least one thing in common:

> None of them can be done effectively without accurate, timely and relevant information.

For example:

- *Plans* are pointless if you never know whether you are achieving them.
- You cannot *respond to external factors* if you do not know how they are changing.
- How can you *manage change* or make improvements if you have no way of knowing when they are necessary?
- *Controlling resources* and *managing budgets* depends on knowing how effectively and efficiently they are being used.
- You cannot *solve problems* unless you know they exist.

- *Decisions* can only be effective if you know what they are required to achieve and whether they have succeeded.

Decision-making is a central part of management – and good information is essential to effective decision-making. We can categorize the uses of information into that required before, during and after the event. The uses are shown in Figure 20.1.

| Used for: | Planning | Monitoring and control | Review and evaluation |
|---|---|---|---|
| Information: | Before the event | During the event | After the event |

*Figure 20.1*

We also need to differentiate between quantitative and qualitative information:

- Quantitative information can be measured and expressed as numbers (and normally relates to facts and figures).
- Qualitative information is difficult to quantify and normally deals with feelings, attitudes and opinions.
- Quantitative information is easy to compare and analyse into patterns and trends.
- Qualitative information is messier and more difficult to formalize. Even so, it is a mistake to overlook qualitative information, because it is often the only guide to human factors like staff motivation or customer satisfaction.

# Data, information and good information

We said just now that effective decisions depend on good information. But what is good information? To answer that question, we need to explore the difference between data and information and then examine what makes information good.

### Data

Data are raw facts, figures, expressions of attitudes or opinion. They (the word data is technically plural) are the raw material from which information is derived.

**Insight**

> You are told that your team's output last week was 132 units. You are asked if you are satisfied with that performance.

**What more would you need to know before you could answer the question?**

The fact that your team produced 132 units is only data. It may be accurate. It may be worth remembering. But it tells you nothing.

For it to be useful, you need to be able to compare it with something. So, if you are told that the output of 132 units was 98% of target and 7 units higher than last week, the figures start to tell you something.

**Information**

Information is data that have been processed and analysed to make them useful. It provides answers to questions and is a basis for decisions.

However, not all information is good. Consider the following situation:

**Case Study**

> Greg receives information about his team's output on a monthly basis. It comes in the form of actual output compared with targets and previous months' performance. It is now November and Greg has just received output information for his team's performance in September. It shows a performance of 98% against target. However, the team is paid a bonus for achieving this target. They tell Greg that their own informed records show that in September they achieved 103% of target. Additionally Greg's performance is assessed on his team's output compared with that of other teams.

**Why is September's output not good information?**

To be good, information must meet the following criteria. It must be:

- *Relevant* – in other words, it must tell you what you need to know.

- *Accurate* – it must be true and reliable.

216

- *Timely* – it must arrive soon enough for you to be able to make decisions based on it.

- *Complete* – it must also tell you all you need to know.

- *Concise* – but without drowning you in unnecessary detail!

In our case study, the information is relevant (it is valuable for monitoring and control) but not complete (no comparisons with other teams). It is neither reliable nor timely. Because Greg's team is telling him something different about output (which should be accurate because it is based on data gathered at the point of production), either they are wrong or the information is. Greg does not know which, so can rely on neither. The information also arrives too late for him to take any corrective action for two months. That is too long to wait before correcting under-performance.

# Formal and informal information

Good information may be either formal or informal. Formal information is recorded and accessible via a recognized system (management accounts, perhaps, or a goods received record, or an analysis of timesheets or MIS). Informal information is like the output claims made by the team in our last Case Study – comments made in passing, not recorded, and irregular.

Both types of information have strengths and weaknesses. A summary of these is given in Figure 20.2.

| Formal information | Informal information |
|---|---|
| Should be accurate and reliable | May be subjective and biased |
| Available easily (regularly or on demand) | Depends on having the right contacts |
| Processed for you | Requires you to draw your own conclusions |
| Content dictated by the system | Allows you to ask what you want to know |
| Deals best with facts and figures | Gives access to opinions, feelings, attitudes |
| Shows trends and patterns | One-off |

*Figure 20.2*

On the face of it, the comparison is weighted in favour of formal information. In reality, the two types are complementary. Both are essential because each tells you things the other cannot.

# Collecting information

Good information is relevant – it tells you what you need to know. As a result, the first priorities in collecting information are:

- Deciding what information you need
- Identifying suitable sources.

### Needs and sources of information

The manager's responsibilities listed at the start of the chapter imply that you will spend most of your time dealing with the day-to-day running of your operation. As a result, the information most relevant to you is likely to deal with relatively short-term, internal matters. However, managers at all levels should have an understanding of, for example, external factors, how they are affecting customers, local competition and developments in technology. So it would be a mistake to overlook external sources of information, such as:

- Government statistic
- Industry statistics
- Specialist reports
- Newspaper, radio and TV reports
- Trade magazines
- Experts' comments.

Most of the information you need will be required to support tactical decisions. By definition, these will be frequent, implemented straight away and of limited long-term impact. In a well-run organization that information should be readily available from formal, internal systems. It may be from different sources.

### Local information

In other words, this means information generated in your section by your team. It may be derived from production counts, quality checks, materials stocks or attendance records. You will certainly have easy access to it, although how good it is may depend on the quality of the system that produces it. Nevertheless, you should have some influence over its relevance, accuracy, timeliness, completion and conciseness.

### Remote information

This information will be produced elsewhere in your organization – for example, future demand from internal customers, maintenance schedules, materials deliveries. Whether you get the information you need when you need it and in the form you need, will depend both on your relationship with other teams and the flexibility of the information systems they operate.

### Central information

This is normally information based on data coming from different parts of the organization, collected, processed and analysed at a central point, then distributed. It is likely to be more complete than any other information available to you, but may be late, irrelevant and contain too much detail. Of all the internal information systems available to you, this is likely to be the most difficult to change. Doing so will almost certainly involve representation through your manager, because of the inevitable impact of changes both on the rest of the organization and the department which collates and processes the information.

Not all the information you require will be tactical though. With the advent of delegated decision-making, you may be involved in longer-term planning of your team's operation, or in improvement or change projects. These will be less frequent and sometimes one-off. They may mean that you need:

- External information
- Access to central information you do not usually see
- Informal, internal information.

In the first two cases, finding the sources of information may involve you in some research into what is available in your organization. In the last case, you will probably need to create your own.

Most organizations have more information than their managers realize. Ask yourself:

- Does my organization have a central resource library?

- Where are the archives kept and how do I gain access to them?

- What happens to trade and professional journals? Are they stored, if so where?

- Who are the best people to ask for: personnel information, financial information, sales records, customer and competitor information, production information, environmental trends?

There is no set way of doing this. It is a matter of finding out by asking your manager, asking colleagues and the relevant departments, such as accounts or marketing.

Informal, internal information will come from none of those sources. You will need to set up:

- Interviews and discussions

- Questionnaires

- Telephone conversations

- Lunchtime chats

- Checklists.

The results of this research will start off as data. To turn it into information you will need first to record it in a consistent way (on a manual system or PC) and secondly to look for trends, patterns and comparisons. In this way you are creating a system and turning informal into formal information.

## Storing and retrieving information

Most organizations appear to be overflowing with information. Actually, that appearance is deceptive. In reality most organizations are full of data that are often difficult to access, are dispersed and are often held in a form that contains too much irrelevant detail, is too incomplete and has not been processed in any way. It hardly counts as information, let alone good information.

**Insight**

Tom has been asked to undertake a development project which will involve making recommendations on how to improve customer satisfaction. As part of the project, he has decided to compare the number of customer complaints with numbers of customers, turnover and profit for the last five years.

The customer service department keeps details of complaints for two years. They are then transferred into off-site storage. Sales keep records of existing customers. Past customer records are only available from invoices, which are held by accounts for three years and then copied on to microfiche and archived in another part of the building.

Turnover and expenditure for the year to date are held by finance. They do not calculate a reliable profit figure until the year-end. Previous years' turnover and profit figures are contained in the published accounts, which are held by the company secretary.

**What will Tom need to do to turn all this data into information?**

He will need to visit five separate departments plus two different storage sites. He will need to extract all the relevant data, estimating this year's profit before analysing and processing it in order to make comparisons.

This situation is not unusual. In fact, it is to be expected. Tom's project is one-off. It would be excessively expensive to make the comparisons he wants to make on a regular basis. Of course, information needs to be accessible but there is no point in producing it just in case someone may possibly want it at some unspecified time in the future. And who knows what form they might want it in anyway!

Nevertheless, all organizations need to keep a huge volume of both data and information. Some of it is needed on a day-to-day basis. Some of it is needed as a historical record, and some is required by law – in the UK that applies particularly to personnel records, details of contracts and company financial accounts.

# Information systems

The development of information and communication technology over the past few decades has had a significant impact on organizations. Organizations can now process and transmit information globally with relative ease. Despite this, information that is used by businesses continues to be processed both by internal computer systems and by manual systems. The important point, however, is not so much which system is used but, does the system meet the wide range of information needs across the organization? Information systems, whether computerized or manual, need to contribute to the whole process of managing information effectively.

To make an effective choice between a manual or a computerized system for a particular purpose will require consideration of the following criteria:

- Number and location of people who will use it
- Ease and speed of access
- Complexity and volume of information
- Processing power required
- Equipment cost
- Input and output costs.

Computerized systems allow information to be held centrally, then called up by individuals on their own computers as required.

Manual systems are only accessible in one place, making them awkward for several people to use. So if the information you use is only relevant to you, a manual system will be fine. If several people use it, particularly if they are dispersed over a sizeable area, computerized systems will be more efficient.

Ease of access and complexity are linked. A simple piece of data or information (like a meeting time you have recorded to save you remembering it) will usually be quicker to check from a diary than if you have to call it up on the computer screen. However, if you need lengthy or complicated information, it should be easier to access from a computer memory, because the computer will help you find it. Which brings us to our next point.

Manual systems are static. They hold the information – you do the job. Computerized systems are usually embedded in equipment that will do processing jobs for you, like analysis, calculations and formatting.

Equipment cost is an obvious consideration. A pocket diary is cheaper than a desk-top computer! Of course, the cost should not be seen in isolation but treated as one factor in a more complex set of criteria.

Input and output costs relate to time, equipment and accuracy. Sending an email to a colleague notifying them of the date, time and venue of a meeting may be a better use of time than making a mental note that you must remember to tell them about the meeting next time you pass their desk.

Manual systems include:

- Card indexes
- Personal notes
- Directories
- Catalogues
- Files.

They may contain telephone numbers, invoices, payment records, personnel records or product specifications.

Computerized information systems have a range of functions that can contribute to the overall operation of an organization. The technological advances continue to impact on industry sectors in different ways. The following list gives some examples:

- *Retail*: EPOS (electronic point-of-sale) systems/terminals ensure speedier customer checkout, monitor sales and many are now linked to suppliers to ensure stocks are replenished.
- *Manufacturing*: CAD (computer-aided design) can be linked to manufacturing processes to improve product time to market. EDI (electronic data interchange) enables speedier and more accurate exchange of data between customers and suppliers.
- *Financial services*: Online and Internet banking has revolutionized the way customers can access accounts, financial information and services from the high street banks and financial institutions.

### Storage devices

These are all ways of recording and holding data or information. Developments in technology means that organizations have a number of choices that can meet their storage requirements.

### Hard disks

These are integral to computers, the data centre of the PC providing permanent storage. All programs and data are stored on the hard disk – the bigger the hard disk, the greater the storage.

### Floppy disks

Can be used to input program files and to store master files. Becoming less common as developments in other forms of media have superseded the floppy disk and less and less computer manufacturers are producing computers with floppy disk drives.

### Optical media

This is another type of storage media, commonly known as the Compact Disc (CD) or Digital Versatile Disc (DVD) – the content is held in digital form and written and read by a laser. This type of media has advantages over other types in that the capacity is greater. One disk holds the equivalent of 500 floppies worth of data and lasts seven times as long as traditional storage data.

### Magnetic tape

Now mainly in the form of high speed 'tape streamers' which are used as backup storage for large amounts of data held on hard disk.

## Insight

Tony is a freelance consultant, close to retirement, who runs presentation skills training courses for a living. His courses have remained largely unchanged for many years but he has a number of regular and satisfied clients. He has deliberately avoided any interest in or understanding of computers. His daughter, Christine, is the computer manager of a large accountancy firm. She has been trying for a long time to persuade Tony to abandon his manual records in favour of a computer-based system, but without success.

Why do you think Christine's experience leads her to favour computers?

Would you recommend Tony to take her advice or not?

Christine's employers process large amounts of data frequently and regularly. They also need to keep abreast of frequent changes in accounting law and have many clients and many employees. The volume and complexity of data and the need for many staff to access central information are sound justifications for a computerized system.

Tony on the other hand uses information in the form of handouts that rarely change. He has relatively few clients and his invoicing and accounting systems are likely to be simple. If he switches to a computer-based system it will take him time to learn, he is likely to make many errors so the cost of learning and equipment, and the aggravation involved do not seem justified.

# Information security

There is a significant need for security in the case of information systems. Effective security is necessary to ensure:

- Confidentiality (particularly related to personnel records, client records and customers' financial details)
- Accuracy (information is not useful if it is not reliable)
- Avoidance of loss.

In the case of computerized systems, there is a further need to avoid:

- Hacking (unauthorized tampering with records or programs, normally from a distance, over a telephone line from another computer)
- Viruses (instructions fed into files or programs which corrupt the data stored on them. These normally enter the system from disks which are themselves infected).

There are a number of ways of securing information, reducing the risk of security breaches.

*Restriction of access through the provision of physical security*

- Limiting access to authorized personnel
- Locks on doors
- Entry detectors and alarms

- Locks on filing cabinets, desks, computers
- Procedures to ensure that all records are securely stored when unattended
- Use of passwords and entry codes for PCs
- Separate passwords/access codes to enter confidential files or change data.

### Division of labour

This can involve:

- Having work checked by someone else before it is confirmed
- Having discrete elements of confidential work done by different people
- Ensuring that the person authorized to commission work is not also allowed to authorize payment (to avoid loss in the form of fraud).

For computer systems, a related technique is to include validation checks into the programs.

### Staff relationships

Staff loyalty and competence reduces the risk. These can be enhanced by careful selection, relevant training and suitable reward.

### Backup

Relevant mainly to the avoidance of loss, backing up computer files by downloading data into a separate storage device is common practice. It is less common with manual systems, although it is worth noting that government departments insist that there should be both a working copy and a file copy of every document.

There is an important piece of legislation, the Data Protection Act 1998, which applies to both manual and computerized personal files and includes private filing systems maintained by managers. The 1998 Act covers all aspects of processing data from its collection, holding, access, use and disclosure to its destruction. The Act was passed to protect individuals who had data or information about them stored on computer. It requires organizations which keep such records to register with the Data Protection

Register. Under the Act processing personal data must comply with the eight enforceable principles of good practice, data must be:

- Fairly and lawfully processed
- Processed for limited purposes
- Adequate, relevant and not excessive
- Accurate
- Not kept longer than necessary
- Processed in accordance with the data subject's rights
- Secure
- Not transferred to other countries without adequate protection.

# Processing information

There are a huge variety of IT applications capable of undertaking various tasks which include word processing, databases, spreadsheets. These different applications enable information to be processed in a timely and appropriate manner.

Increasingly organizations are including IT skills training as part of their overall training requirements for staff. This helps to ensure speed, consistency and efficiency of information-handling.

# Transmitting information

In Section 2 we looked at different techniques for communicating effectively. Face-to-face and written communication are traditional methods of transmitting information. The development of information and communications technology has extended the methods to include:

- Facsimile (fax)
- Email
- Video-conferencing
- Computer networking
- Internet and intranet.

From this list it is important to differentiate between one-way and two-way communication. Faxes, emails, computer networks and the Internet are all one-way. In other words, messages can be transmitted when no one is at the other end, stored and retrieved when the other person arrives. That is one of their major benefits but it also brings drawbacks in that you cannot be sure the message has been received and it is difficult to judge the receiver's reaction to the message.

The transmitter can receive confirmation that the message has arrived in the case of fax and email, but that does not mean it has been either read or understood!

It would be wrong though to underestimate the advantages brought by electronic communication:

- The telephone reduces the delay (and to an extent the cost) of long distance communication.
- Faxes increase the speed of written communication.
- Email addresses the problems of distance and time difference.
- Video-conferencing eliminates travelling time.
- Computer networking improves information transfer between offices and sites and reduces the cost of shared facilities like printers or a common database.
- The Internet makes common database searching for information faster and more convenient.

Nevertheless, it is interesting to note that as electronic communication has led to increasing numbers of people 'teleworking' (working from home or remotely but linked by electronic media), organizations have recognized the need to bring teleworkers together regularly to enjoy the benefits of being in a group. In other words, electronic information transfer solves the practical difficulties, but does not address the human aspects of communication.

## Review your learning

Check your understanding of this chapter by completing the following:

1  Data are. . . . . . . . . . . . . . . . . . . . . . . . . . . . . .

   Information is . . . . . . . . . . . . . . . . . . . . . . . . .

2  List the criteria for good information.

3  What criteria would you use to make a choice between a manual or computerized system?

4  Why was the Data Protection Act 1998 passed?

**Theory to practice**

Apply this chapter to your own experience by answering the following:

1 How good is the management control information you receive?

2 How could it be improved?

3 Where would you find external information in your job?

4 What information systems do you use?

5 Are they the most suitable for the information you need? If not, how could you change them?

6 How secure is the information you use? How could information security be improved?

7 How have the advances in information technology impacted on your organization?

# 21  Financial information and management control

<table>
<tr><td>

**Chapter
Objectives**

</td><td>

● *What financial information do I need?*

</td></tr>
</table>

Earlier in this section we stressed the need for managers to monitor and control the use of resources. We have also pointed out that monitoring and control are dependent on your ability to measure both inputs and outputs.

Consider the situation given in the following insight.

**Insight**

> Julia is in charge of a local council department responsible for refuse collection. It is the time of year when budgets are prepared. Julia is told that in order to improve her team's performance, she can have either a new refuse vehicle or three additional staff.

**What information will Julia need to enable her to make a decision?**

Faced with a straight choice between these two alternatives, Julia will need to know how much extra output she will gain from each, so that she can choose the best.

In most situations, managers are expected to maximize output from minimal inputs. Julia therefore needs to know:

● The cost of the additional inputs such as the extra staff and the dustcart

● The increased volume that will result from each option.

Then she can make a value-for-money decision. But that is only possible if Julia can measure the value of the inputs and the value of the outputs.

However, there are problems associated with giving everything a financial value. Some outputs cannot be given a financial value. How could you put a value on your organization's:

- Customer loyalty?
- Customer satisfaction?
- Staff loyalty?
- Staff morale?
- Management competence?
- Effective leadership?

We accept that these outputs are all important, so how can we quantify them?

Taking customer loyalty as an example: customers cost money to attract. A business that does not retain customers must replenish its customer base in order to maintain sales. Such poor customer loyalty could be costed by calculating the money that would need to be spent to attract new business. On average it costs eight times more to attract new customers than to retain existing ones.

Looking at morale: when morale is high, staff retention is high. There is no reason to leave. However when morale is low employees leave. Such staff turnover can be costed on the basis of the additional cost of advertising, filling vacancies, and training new staff.

Financial information provides us with a common measure of outputs which allows us to make decisions. As well as helping us make decisions, financial information can measure the health of an organization.

Annual financial accounts give a picture of what the organization owns and what it owes, whether it is trading profitably or at a loss, and its ability to continue to finance its operation.

Management accounts provide more detailed and frequent information so that managers can assess past performance early enough to take remedial action. The starting point for this process is the construction of budgets, which we explore further in Chapter 22.

# Financial information and decision-making

We explored the general principles of decision-making earlier. Here we will concentrate on the financial implications of the process, remembering of course that most results of decisions can be translated into financial values.

Financial information helps managers decide upon:

- What to do
- How to do it
- Whether we can afford it.

Financial information is important in decision-making, but taking decisions purely on the basis of financial data does not take into account a large range of non-financial factors.

# What shall we do?

We can use financial information to help answer this question at a strategic level as it affects the organization as a whole. This will result in long-term decisions concerning products, services and markets. Or we can answer it at an operational level resulting in short-term, day-to-day decisions.

At a strategic level organizations need to decide:

- What markets should we operate in?
- What products or services shall we offer?

The answers to these questions will depend upon the attractiveness of different markets, productivity of new products and the return on investment of new products. All of these can be quantified in financial terms.

Strategic decisions such as

- What markets should we attack?
- Which products should we produce?
- What services should we offer?

will benefit from information on:

- The size of the markets in which we currently operate:
  (a) How much do all customers in our markets spend?
  (b) The sales trend: are our sales growing, declining or are they remaining at a constant level?

- The market share in the markets in which we operate:

  (a) Are we the major provider in any of our markets or are we a small operator compared to our major rivals?

- The size of any new markets we might enter:

  (a) Their anticipated growth

  (b) Whether they are dominated by a single supplier, which will make entry difficult, or whether they are served by a lot of small suppliers.

- The performance of our existing products (sales volumes, turnover, profitability):

  (a) Their current trends and forecasted growth

  (b) Predicted performance of proposed new products

  (c) Development, launch and promotion costs

  (d) Investment in new equipment.

You are unlikely at this stage to be involved in decisions at a strategic level. However, it is important to understand the extent to which financial information lies at the heart of them.

At an operational or tactical level, you will still be involved in making financial decisions. As we pointed out earlier, the financial information you will need to help make these decisions will include:

- The cost of inputs
- The value of outputs you are seeking
- The cost of doing nothing.

# The cost of inputs

Costs can be categorized according to how they change with output or time.

### Fixed costs

Remain relatively unchanged regardless of whether output is going up or down. These include costs such as: rents, rates, heating and lighting.

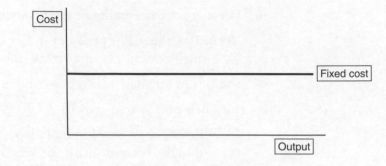

*Figure 21.1*

### Variable costs

Vary directly according to the level of output. These include costs such as: materials used in processes, products, bonuses paid to the sales team. During busy periods the business will incur more variable costs than when it is quiet.

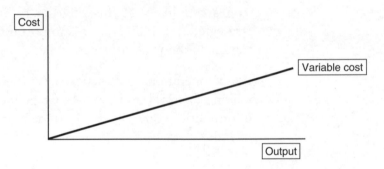

*Figure 21.2*

Of course, no costs are truly fixed; for example, on what basis would the following costs vary?

- Heat and light
- Electricity usage of machinery
- Production line staff

Heat and light will vary according to the time of year. More heat will be required in the winter. This is a fixed cost as it does not vary relative to output.

Electricity usage on machinery may change as a result of more efficient use. This is classed as a fixed cost, again because it does not vary in relation to increases or decrease in output.

Production line staff costs may not vary at all in the short run, if they are salaried. When extra staff are employed the costs will rise in a stepped fashion. This cost is a stepped cost, and has features in common with both fixed and variable costs.

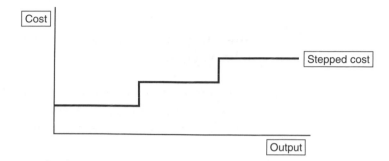

Figure 21.3

# Revenue helps to pay costs

For a company to make profit, its revenue must exceed its costs. Any revenue should at least cover the variable costs of production, for example. Any revenue received on top of this contributes to the payment of the company's fixed costs. This is referred to as the **contribution**. Calculating contribution is useful to you as a manager.

Contribution = Sales value − Variable cost

It is useful because it can be used in break-even analysis. Break-even analysis identifies the output level at which the value of the outputs exactly equals the cost of the inputs, i.e. where our total costs (TC) equal our total revenue (TR).

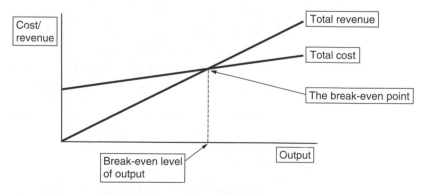

Figure 21.4    Break-even chart

**Insight**

> Product selling price = £25
> Variable costs = £15
> Monthly fixed costs = £500

**How many units of this product will need to be made and sold to break even?**

> Selling price of £25 – variable cost of £15 gives contribution for each unit of £10. £500 fixed costs divided by unit contribution of £10 gives a break-even point of 50.

We can therefore deduce that if we sell less than 50 units we shall make a loss; and that if we sell more than 50 units we shall make a profit. Break-even is very helpful when deciding a price for a product or order. Indeed it can help to decide whether to accept an order at all.

If output volumes have not yet reached break-even point, any orders will be welcome, at any price provided it makes some 'contribution' to the payment of fixed costs.

Operating above break-even point but below full capacity allows you more flexibility. As a result of your fixed costs being covered, you can choose to price an order with nil contribution if necessary. Alternatively you can choose to maximize contribution on orders. This decision may well rest upon how other customers might react if you offered a new customer a special deal.

**Case Study**

> Selling price = £25
> Variable costs = £15
> Monthly fixed costs = £500
> You are currently producing 150 units per month and have the capacity to increase this to 180 units.
>
> A new customer wants to order this product at £23 and buy 20 units a month.
>
> Your current profit is:
>
> Total revenue − Total costs = Profit

Total revenue − (Variable costs + fixed costs)
   = (£25 × 150) − [(£15 × 150) + £500]
   = £1,000

This can be calculated in a much quicker way if we use contribution.

Total contribution − Fixed costs = Profit

(Contribution per unit × Output) − Fixed costs = Profit

(£10 × 150) − £500 = £1,000

The new customer's order would increase your total output to 170 units which is still within your capacity. But each extra unit's contribution towards fixed costs would fall to £8 (Selling price of £23 − £15 Variable costs). That is not a problem. The original 150 units are still contributing £10 each to fixed costs and as long as your original customers don't find out about this new order you won't have to adjust your original price.

Total contribution would then be:

For the first 150 units: £10 × 150 plus for the special order of an extra 20 units: £8 × 20 = £1,500 + £160 = £1,660

Taking away your £500 fixed costs would result in an increased profit of £1,160.

However, what would happen to your profit if ALL your customers demanded the product at £23?

(Contribution per unit × Output) − fixed costs = Profit

(£8 × 170) − £500 = £860

The critical factor which affects your ability to vary prices, is whether your current customers are in a position to find out what prices you charge to your other customers. If they are likely to find out, it is unwise to offer discounts on new or special orders.

This all has most relevance in that you can price yourself more competitively if you have exceeded your break-even point, because you need only cover your variable costs in order to increase profit!

Of course, if you are already producing at full capacity, the only way of increasing output would be by adding extra resources, which would result in a stepped increase in fixed costs.

Break-even is also useful when making decisions about whether the best way to tackle a situation is to do nothing.

**How shall we do it?**

Different actions will require different inputs and create different outputs. The inputs can be costed and outputs forecasted to determine the most cost-effective or profitable solution.

This question again has relevance at both strategic and operational levels. At a strategic level, the decision will depend upon what resources are required and how much will they cost.

How much investment will be needed and where will the money come from? How long will it take to recover the investment? How risky is this course of action?

All of these factors can be quantified, although the third and fourth will be subject to varying levels of uncertainty.

Investment appraisal helps when we are comparing alternative methods of delivering strategic objectives. There are three main forms of investment appraisal:

**The payback period**

This method measures how long it will take to pay back the initial investment cost with revenue, i.e. for revenue to equal investment.

You have the option of investing in two possible ventures: selling beer and selling cigarettes at your social club. You have conducted research and forecast the following revenues and necessary investment.

|  | Cigarettes (10,000) | Beer (20,000) |
|---|---|---|
| Initial investment |  |  |
| Yr 1 cash | 4,000 | 9,000 |
| Yr 2 cash | 5,000 | 9,000 |
| Yr 3 cash | 5,000 | 12,000 |
| Yr 4 cash | 4,000 | 10,000 |

How long does it take to repay your investment on each?

Cigarettes pay back the £10,000 investment after 3 years as does beer.

What are the problems with this form of calculation?

The problems here are that we cannot see which gives us the best return on our investment. All payback does is give us a time-scale of how quickly the investment gives us a return.

*The average rate of return*

This takes the predicted life of the investment and calculates the average annual percentage return on the investment over its whole life. Let us take our earlier example again to see which is best:

|  | Cigarettes (10,000) | Beer (20,000) |
|---|---|---|
| Initial investment | | |
| Yr 1 revenue | 4,000 | 9,000 |
| Yr 2 revenue | 5,000 | 9,000 |
| Yr 3 revenue | 5,000 | 12,000 |
| Yr 4 revenue | 4,000 | 10,000 |
| Total revenue | 18,000 | 40,000 |
| 4 yr profit | 8,000 | 20,000 |
| Average yearly profit | 2,000 | 5,000 |
| As a percentage of our investment | | |
| ARR | 20% | 25% |

Therefore beer is better, because it gives a better average return.

*Net present value*

This method of investment appraisal is calculated in the same way as average rate of return but recognizes that money received in the future will have reduced value at today's prices as a result of inflation. Therefore future revenues are discounted.

These methods are strategic in nature and, at an operational level, your role in deciding on investment decisions is more likely to be based upon knowing:

- How much spare capacity you have
- What the cost of increasing capacity would be

- What additional resources alternative decisions would require
- Whether they are available and how much they would cost
- Which of these various alternative actions would address the situation most cost-effectively.

In an ideal world, extra capacity and additional resources would be freely available, though at a price. In the real world, however, some resources are fixed, and therefore limited. They cannot be increased, either because no more are available or because your organization has, for example, put a block on capital spending.

In these situations you have three choices. You can:

- Buy in from elsewhere
- Choose your action on the basis of resource limitations
- Make a deliberate choice to do nothing because the necessary resources are not available.

The following are brief comments on these three alternatives.

Buying in from elsewhere (often known as the 'make or buy' decision) gives you access to:

- Resources you need on a short-term basis, like temporary staff, consultancy support or extra transport.
- Top-up inputs at busy times. These are acceptable, provided that their cost does not change a profitable product or service into a loss-maker.

## Case Study

Cedar Construction is a small housing developer. For many years it made its own window and door frames, before recognizing that its main expertise lay in building houses rather than woodwork. As a result, it closed down the woodworking facility, made staff redundant and sold the machines. However, it still has the workshop on a long lease, which it cannot terminate before it expires. The workshop rental costs £100,000 per year.

Cedar buys in windows and doors from a specialist company at £100 per unit and purchases 2,000 each year.

What is the time cost of each unit? i.e. what is the real cost of buying in each window when Cedar still has to pay for the lease of the workshop?

To calculate the time cost of each unit, we need to take account of the cost of the redundant in-house workshop. The annual workshop rental of £100,000 should be spread over the 2,000 units bought each year. As a result, the time cost of each unit is:

$$£100 + (£100,000) = £150$$

Choosing your action according to resource limitations involves identifying the 'limiting factor'. This may be:

- Equipment
- Raw materials
- Staff availability
- Expertise.

Tom is production team leader for a company making printed packaging. He has received an urgent order for a simple two-colour job and has two machines which are capable of producing it.

It is 10 am in the morning. The job has to be completed by 4 pm. The job requires 6,000 printing impressions. Machine A is capable of a maximum of 1,000 impressions per hour. Machine B can deliver 1,200 impressions per hour. Machine A costs 5 p per impression. Machine B, which is more up to date and offers higher quality, costs 6 p per impression.

**Which machine should Tom use?**

The answer to this question is both quantitative and qualitative. Both machines have the capacity to complete the job in the time. However, in the case of Machine A, this will only be possible if nothing goes wrong – no snags, no need for adjustments during the print run. Machine A is only likely to be the better choice if the cost of the job makes its higher contribution necessary and if the quality specification can be achieved despite its poorer quality.

You will choose to do nothing if either revenue is exceeded by your costs or your alternatives require resources that are not available to you. Both can be quantified.

**Can we afford it?**

This question can be answered based on:

- A comparison of input costs with available budget
- An investment appraisal
- A comparison of the output value of the project with that of the alternatives.

## Making a case for additional resources

You may be wondering why, as a team leader, for example, do you need to have this knowledge and understanding of costs, contribution and break-even points? You may consider that this is the remit of the finance department in your organization.

Well you would be wrong! Having a basic understanding of finance and financial controls is essential if you are to understand the financial consequences of the decisions you make.

You may need to make a case to your line manager or the senior management team for additional resources. This might for example be for an additional member of staff, it may be a case for employing temporary staff, a new piece of equipment, a training course.

In all of these examples you will need to demonstrate your understanding of the financial implications by identifying:

- The costs of an additional salary, equipment, training
- The availability in the budget (using budgets is covered in Chapter 22)
- What the contribution would be
- The projected profit
- The return on the investment
- The cost to the organization of not having the additional resources.

In other words, you are putting forward a business case based on factual information which you have used to consider the options and justify your request.

Of course, this does not necessarily mean that your request for additional resources will be granted! It may be that even though you can justify the expenditure it does not fit with the organization's overall strategy or that it has implications for other departments which cannot be justified.

**Check your understanding of this chapter by completing the following:**

1 List three uses of financial information.

2 Why is financial information not a complete basis for management decisions?

3 What is the difference between a fixed and a variable cost? Give an example of each.

4 What is meant by the term contribution?

5 Name three financial implications you would need to include to make a case for additional resources.

**Apply this chapter to your own experience by answering the following:**

1 What financial information is available to you?

2 Is it sufficient to enable you to make effective management decisions? If not, how could you gain access to more?

3 How well does your organization measure more subjective factors like customer satisfaction or supplier loyalty? What more could it do?

4 How does your organization make strategic decisions? If you do not know, who could you ask?

5 What do you see as the main limiting factor in your operation?

6 To what extent do you use quantitative analysis when making decisions? What more should you do?

# 22 Preparing and using budgets

| Chapter Objectives | • *How can I use the budget process to monitor performance?* |
|---|---|

A key responsibility for managers is monitoring and controlling performance, as we saw in Chapter 18. We also described the effective system of 'top-down, bottom-up' strategic planning which is commonly used to set performance objectives.

The principles which underpin setting objectives, monitoring and controlling performance apply equally to budgets.

Let us start with some useful definitions:

*A budget is a statement of allocated expenditure and/or income, under specific headings, for a given period.*

*A budget forecast is a statement of expected expenditure and or income, based on the best information available for a given period.*

*A cash flow forecast is a plan or estimate of cash in and cash out, for each item of expense and revenue.*

We all have a household budget, although we might not always think of it in such terms! We usually know for example, the costs of the mortgage, rent, rates, gas and electricity. We also know when these need to be paid and allocate the appropriate amount of our income accordingly. The principles of a business budget are exactly the same as a household budget.

## The process of preparing budgets

All organizations need answers to the following questions:

- What do we want to achieve?
- What are we capable of achieving?

- What resources will we need?
- What resources can we afford?
- How productive will they be?

The answers to all these questions come from the linked processes of developing objectives and preparing budgets. They apply to organizations as a whole, separate functions (marketing, finance, personnel, production, administration), departments, sections and teams.

### What do we want to achieve?

There is no objective way of answering this question. The simplest approach would be to take last year's performance and add a percentage to it. A more rounded approach would be to consider what the organization's main stakeholders – shareholders and customers, but possibly also government and the general public – expect or require from it. Yet another approach would be to take the organization's long-term aims (perhaps for growth, expansion or an increase in market share, or for productivity improvement or cost reduction) and to work out next year's contribution to them. Regardless of how the answer is reached, it will ultimately result in performance objectives and financial targets.

### What are we capable of achieving?

There are both internal and external factors to consider here. The internal factors relate to capacity, resources and productivity. The external factors are to do with what the market wants from us and how much customers are willing to pay.

Organizations typically prepare three levels of budget:

- Cash budget
- Sales budget
- Production budget.

They may have different titles but the main purposes are the same:

- The *cash* budget sets out how much money will be available to pay for inputs or resources like staff, materials, equipment, training, transport, heat, light and so on.
- The *sales* budget appears to be the most commercial of the three. But think of it as setting out the anticipated demand for

the organization's products or services. Then you will see that it applies equally to the likely demand for consultancy services; the number of children likely to apply to a local school; or the number of VAT enquiries which are likely to be received by the local Customs and Excise office.

- The *production* budget sounds as if it relates mainly to manufacturing. However, it is equally relevant to a road haulage business (how many trucks? how many drivers?), to a training business (how many courses? how many participants?) or to an accounts department (how many invoices? how many queries?).

For any organization, one of these three budgets provides the limiting budget factor. This is the factor which determines the maximum size of the other budgets. That factor may be:

- The availability of skilled staff
- Machine time
- Market demand
- Cash flow.

Regardless of what it is, the limiting budget factor will be the starting point for the preparation of all other budgets.

**Case Study**

Last year, the new intake into Wallcorn School was 56 children. It has two reception class teachers, each of whom has a classroom with 30 desks. Neither has space for more. The education authority is prepared to fund a further teacher but all classrooms are being used. Sixty-eight children have applied to join the school next year.

**What is the limiting budget factor in this situation?**

The school has more demand than it can cope with, so its equivalent of a sales budget will not limit its activities. It has access to extra money to pay another teacher so the cash budget will be adequate. Its limiting factor is space – the two reception classrooms can accommodate more than 60 pupils together and nowhere else is available.

### What resources will we need?

We identified resources in an earlier chapter as consisting of:

- People
- Plant
- Equipment
- Materials.

Historical data will identify the quality and quantity of production these resources can achieve. A comparison with planned output will reveal whether they will be sufficient. This in turn will show whether:

- New people need to be recruited or existing staff trained to produce more
- Plant needs to be extended or reorganized
- Equipment needs to be upgraded or replaced
- More or better materials need to be sought.

If any of these are not possible, they will become the limiting budget factor and output plans will need to be revised. Alternatively, the comparison may show excess resources and a need to reduce the scale of the operation.

### What resources can we afford?

This is another potential limiting budget factor, related to the cash budget. Increasingly, public sector organizations are subject to tight cash limits and are being required to deliver more for less. Even in commercial organizations, the drive for increased competitiveness and cost reductions is making cash saving a priority. Which leads us to our final question.

### How productive will they be?

The era when productivity was not a key issue is over. If existing resources did not produce enough, you added more. The emphasis now is on gaining more output from the same, or fewer, resources. An increasing adoption of the internal customer–supplier relationship also means that help from other teams or departments such as training, machinery adjustment, or maintenance comes at a price.

Any action necessary to improve productivity will need to be included in your budgets, unless it is something you can do for yourself.

## Budgets and people

Like any other performance objectives, budgets need to be achievable. Otherwise they are seen as irrelevant and will be ignored. Equally, budgets that are too easy to achieve will also be ignored, because those responsible will soon recognize that they can exceed the budget without making a conscious effort.

The 'top-down, bottom-up' approach to planning means involving the people responsible for achieving budgets in the preparation of them. This has the following advantages:

- The budgets are realistic
- The people involved understand them
- They are motivated to achieve them
- And, surprisingly, the budgets are likely to be more demanding because people set higher standards for themselves than is generally recognized.

However, if budgets are to be realistic, motivating and achievable they must be kept up to date if circumstances change. There are countless examples of production budgets remaining the same while cash budgets are cut, making the output targets neither realistic nor achievable.

## The master budgets

Sales, production and cash budgets, together with subsidiary budgets like the labour budget, materials budget, administration budget, transport budget and capital budget will be brought together to produce a set of master budgets. These will consist of a budgeted profit and loss account, balance sheet and a cash flow forecast.

Consider the following situation.

# Case Study

Roland has just started in business as a sub-contract builder. He has taken on Alan as an assistant, he is paying himself £800 and Alan £600 per month. He has borrowed £10,000 from the bank and bought a van. His business bank manager has insisted that Roland prepares a cash flow statement shown in Figure 22.1. Roland has also secured a brick-laying contract with a larger builder, which he estimates will bring in £2,000 a month, this is paid one month in arrears. He has saved £3,000 which he will pay into the business in May, when he also expects to make the first payment on his van and start work on his new contract.

Unfortunately, the weather in August is terrible and the building site is shut down for a month.

| | May (£) | June (£) | July (£) | August (£) | September (£) | October (£) |
|---|---|---|---|---|---|---|
| Income | 3,000 | 2,000 | 2,000 | 2,000 | 2,000 | 2,000 |
| Expenditure | | | | | | |
| Bank loan | 500 | 500 | 500 | 500 | 500 | 500 |
| Wages | 1,400 | 1,400 | 1,400 | 1,400 | 1,400 | 1,400 |
| Van running costs | 50 | 50 | 50 | 50 | 50 | 50 |
| Total Expenditure | 1,950 | 1,950 | 1,950 | 1,950 | 1,950 | 1,950 |
| Balance | 1,050 | 50 | 50 | 50 | 50 | 50 |
| Balance Brought Forward | Nil | 1,050 | 1,100 | 1,150 | 1,200 | 1,250 |
| Balance Carried Forward | 1,050 | 1,100 | 1,150 | 1,200 | 1,250 | 1,300 |

*Figure 22.1*

### When will Roland run out of money?

According to Roland's forecast, the work he did in July will be paid for in August and he will carry forward £1,200 into September However he will not have worked in August. If he does not use the van, he can save £50 of expenditure. He may also be able to lay Alan off for the month saving another £600.

The bank loan interest is fixed however and will have to be paid. We must also assume that he needs his own £800 wages to meet household expenses. His expenditure for August will therefore be:

| | |
|---|---|
| Bank loan | £500 |
| Wages | £800 |
| Total | £1,300 |

This will allow him to carry forward £1,850 into September. However, assuming work on the site starts again, his expenditure in September will return to £1,950 and he will get no cash into the business. He will therefore run out of money in September.

## Monitoring and controlling budgets

Budgets are statements in financial terms of:

- The quality of outputs required to meet the organization's objectives.
- The inputs which the organization has decided it can afford to meet those objectives.

As we explained in an earlier chapter, different teams, sections and departments in an organization depend on each other and supply each other. Consequently, the plans and budgets of individual parts of an organization should reflect the needs of its internal customers and what they can afford or are prepared to pay. They should provide a way of co-ordinating diverse activities in an organization to ensure they contribute what is required to achieve its overall objectives.

That means budgets are not just the results of some tedious number-crunching, prepared and issued at the start of the plan period, which can then be filed and forgotten while you get on with managing the real work of your team. Instead, they make a valuable contribution to monitoring and controlling that work which, as we have seen, is a central part of management.

Budgets are normally prepared to last for a year then broken down into monthly targets. Properly prepared budgets take account of monthly variations in demand and the difference in level and type of activity during that month. So budgets are only estimates based on the best available information at the time.

# Analysing budget statements

At the end of each monthly budget period, you are likely to get a statement showing you and your team's performance against the budget. Any differences between planned and actual performance will be shown as a variance.

Variances can be favourable or adverse. Favourable variances indicate that more output has been achieved, or less money spent, than planned. Adverse variances result from producing less output or spending more money than planned. It is tempting to assume that adverse variances are negative and need action, but favourable variances are positive and can be ignored. But that is not always true, as the Case Study shows.

**Case Study**

> Performance against budget in June for the staff canteen of Healthwise Pharmaceuticals.

|  | June | | | Year-to-date (Jan–June) | | |
|---|---|---|---|---|---|---|
|  | Budget (£) | Actual (£) | Variance (£) | Budget (£) | Actual (£) | Variance (£) |
| **Income** |  |  |  |  |  |  |
| Meals sold | 1,500 | 1,000 | 500A | 9,000 | 7,000 | 2,000A |
| Snacks and drinks sold | 1,000 | 1,200 | 200F | 6,000 | 6,400 | 400F |
|  | 2,500 | 2,200 | 300A | 15,000 | 13,400 | 1,600A |
| **Expenditure** |  |  |  |  |  |  |
| Snacks and canned drinks | 800 | 960 | 160A | 4,800 | 5,120 | 320A |
| Ingredients | 750 | 500 | 250F | 4,500 | 3,500 | 1,000F |
| Wages | 800 | 800 | — | 4,800 | 4,800 | — |
| Staff training | 100 | — | 100F | 200 | — | 200F |
| Maintenance | 50 | 50 | — | 3,000 | 3,000 | — |
|  | 2,500 | 2,310 | 190F | 17,300 | 16,420 | 880F |

*Figure 22.2*

**Which of these variances concern you?**

**Do they show any pattern?**

The canteen output (measured by its income) is below budget both in June and in the year to date. However, the variance in June (expressed as a percentage of budget) is higher than in the year to date. In other words, the situation is worsening. There is another pattern here, too. Staff are buying fewer meals but more snacks. This trend is also more pronounced in June than in the year to date.

Looking at expenditure, the overall variance is favourable but this masks the presence of an adverse variance in the value of snacks and canned drinks bought. However, this is what you would expect as sales of these are above budget. You might have noticed though that the profit margin on snacks is lower than that on meals. So if present trends continue, the canteen will find it harder in future to break even, which is the apparent intention. It is also worth noting that the apparently favourable variance on staff training results from the fact that no training has been done this year at all.

The budget is just a set of figures. It does not include explanations so you cannot draw any definite conclusions without doing some investigation. The variances may result from a badly constructed budget. But the other possible explanation is that the meals are poor and staff are moving to more palatable snacks instead. And could the lack of training be contributing to poor quality meals?

## Investigating variances

If you were involved in preparing your budget, you should know the assumptions on which it was based. You should know the anticipated output demand and where it was expected to come from. You should also know the basis on which costs and expenditure were calculated.

So the first step in investigating variances is to compare reality with the assumption on which the budget was based. For example:

- Was output down because your team was less productive than expected, or because your customers required less? In either case, why?
- Were material costs higher because more were wasted, or because central purchasing changed supplier?
- Were wage costs up because of extra overtime, or because of a general wage increase that was higher than expected?

252

# Controllable and non-controllable variances

The next step in investigating variances is to decide whether the causes of them were inside or outside your control. Of the examples just given, team productivity, waste and overtime costs are usually within a manager's control. Customer demand, central purchasing and organization-wide wage increases are not. Unless, of course, customer demand has fallen because they are not satisfied with your output.

There is clearly nothing you can do directly about non-controllable variances. But if their causes are likely to continue, they will have an impact on your future performance against budget rendering your budgets both unreliable and irrelevant. This is a matter to refer to your line manager. Ask yourself in advance:

- Can my manager influence changes to my budget?
- Can my manager control causes which I cannot?
- If so, what do I want my manager to do?

Controllable variances are different and we have looked at problem-solving and change processes in earlier chapters. Use the following as prompts when investigating controllable variances:

- What is the real cause of the variance?
- Who else will be involved in putting it right?
- What will an ideal solution look like?
- What choices do I have?
- Which is the best?
- And how will I implement it?

Add to these the overriding questions:

- Is the variance important enough to deal with?
- Or is it a one-off and likely to disappear of its own accord?

# Flexible budgets

The standard way for organizations to prepare budgets is as we have described:

- Overall objectives are agreed and set
- The cost of achieving them is agreed and set
- Local budgets are determined in accordance with them.

253

This process assumes that the future can be predicted accurately. Of course, this is not the case:

- Demand will vary
- Efficiency and productivity will vary
- Costs will vary.

Changes in any of these factors will have a significant impact on budgets. Some are in the control of the organization and its managers. But others are not. This is the issue which flexible budgets are designed to address.

Typically they are based on a series of predictions. They assume a:

- Most likely case
- Best case
- Worst case

for each budget. Separate budgets are then worked out for each case.

This involves you as the manager constantly updating budgets, either in line with organizational guidelines or by individual analyses of the current situation. However, computer spreadsheets that allow extensive 'what if?' analysis, make flexible budgets possible to introduce, if not easy to monitor and control.

## Review your learning

Check your understanding of this chapter by completing the following:

1. What is the purpose of a budget?
2. Organizations typically prepare three budgets, what are they?
3. Give three advantages for involving people in the preparation of budgets.
4. In budget terms what is the difference between planned and actual performance?
5. How does a flexible budget operate?

## Theory to practice

Apply this chapter to your own experience by answering the following:

1. What is the limiting budget factor for your operation?
2. How much do you contribute to the preparation of your own budget? If your answer is 'not enough', how could you influence it more?

3 Which of the factors in your budget are under your control? And outside your control?

4 How much freedom do you have to change factors that should be under your control? What more would you like?

5 What, if anything, can you do to change non-controllable factors?

6 Does your organization operate fixed or flexible budgets? What are their positive and negative aspects for you?

# Resource bank

## References

Denzler, D. (2004) Shell One Operations Management circa 2003, www. clubpom.com

Mullins, L. (2002) *Management and Organizational Behaviour*, 6th edn, Prentice Hall

## Additional reading

Fleming, I. (2003) *The Time Management Pocketbook*, Management Pocketbooks

Hawkins, A. and Turner, C. (1995) *The Managing Budgets Pocketbook*, Management Pocketbooks

ILM Super Series (2003) *Information in Management*, Elsevier

ILM Super Series (2003) *Understanding Finance*, Elsevier

## Website addresses

www.clubpom.com
Operations management information

# Section 5  Focusing on Results

- *Who monitors results?*
- *Who controls results?*
- *Are customers important?*
- *How can I improve the layout of the workplace?*
- *What are my responsibilities in maintaining a healthy and safe environment?*
- *How can I contribute to continuous improvement?*

# 23 Planning, organizing and controlling work

| Chapter Objectives | • *Who monitors results?* |
| | • *Who controls results?* |

Managers achieve results – through people and other resources. That summarizes (though in a much over-simplified way) the message of the first chapter of this book. But it leaves several basic questions unanswered. It does not explain:

- What results managers should achieve
- How to make the best use of people
- How to use other resources
- What to do to ensure that work achieves the desired results.

This chapter provides answers to all of these questions.

## Setting management objectives

People at work must know what is expected of them; they otherwise have no way of telling whether they have succeeded or failed. Even more importantly, they cannot decide what to do, what their priorities are or where to focus their effort. Equally, without objectives as a manager you will have no means of measuring performance.

Most organizations tackle this issue by ensuring that managers have a set of objectives to achieve. Traditionally those objectives were set using a cascade system. In other words, the organization would decide its corporate objectives through the strategic planning process, then pass those down, translating them at each level into objectives that would contribute to the achievement of the organization's corporate goals, as shown in Figure 23.1.

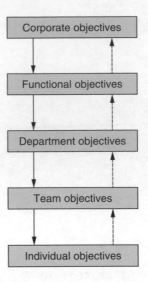

*Figure 23.1*

Many organizations still follow this traditional approach. Others, however, use what is known as a 'bottom-up, top-down' approach: this embraces the philosophy of greater staff consultation and involvement. This approach involves the organization setting broad corporate aims then asking managers and staff at lower levels to specify what they can do to achieve them. The 'bottom-up, top-down' approach can be messy and time-consuming because it involves several cycles of consultation and amendment before final objectives are agreed. Nevertheless, it is far more effective at ensuring that objectives are realistic, achievable and gain commitment from those responsible for delivering them and therefore is well worth the additional effort required.

You may have objectives imposed on you, you may set them for yourself, or you may sit somewhere between those two extremes. Regardless of your situation, you will need to ensure that your objectives and those you set for your team are sufficiently detailed and complete for you to know exactly what you and they are expected to achieve. To be truly useful objectives should be SMART:

Specific

Measurable

Agreed

Realistic

Time-based

In other words, the outputs should be clearly defined such that performance can be quantified, agreed between you and your manager, achievable within the constraints of time and resources and with a target date so that achievement can be measured.

There are obvious motivational and practical reasons why objectives should be agreed and realistic. But you may be wondering why the SMART definition places so much emphasis on quantified and measurable objectives. That is because objectives are of little value on their own. They only become valuable as a basis for measuring performance.

This brings us to the idea of the control loop: a mechanism developed originally for engineering applications but now extended for use in management. A central-heating thermostat is a good example of how a control loop works. Imagine a thermostat at work. It measures the temperature in a room, recognizes when it is not warm enough and then triggers the boiler to send hot water through the radiator. When the room is warm enough the thermostat switches off the boiler.

There are various elements operating in this process:

Input – heat from the boiler

Process – heating and circulating water

Output – a warm room

Standard – the desired room temperature

Comparator – a way of comparing actual with desired temperature

Actuator – a mechanism for turning on the boiler (see Figure 23.2).

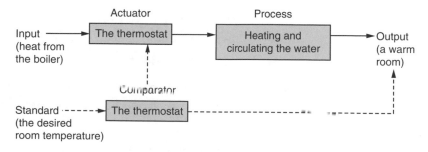

*Figure 23.2*

In more general terms, a control loop is a system that recognizes when output performance does not meet the required standard (quality, quantity, time, cost) and then triggers action to correct the process so that the standard is achieved. That is why it is so important for objectives to be specified, measurable and time-based.

Being in a position to set your own objectives may sound desirable but is actually both fraught and complex. Your objectives should take account of:

- Corporate direction
- Long-term survival
- Current financial position
- Available resources
- Customer requirements.

The order may well be different according to the organization's priorities! Long-term survival depends ultimately on customer satisfaction, so your objectives should come as close as possible to meeting customer requirements within the limits of available budget and resources. These considerations come next.

## Organizing your team

People are the only resource that does not wear out over time and can be developed to achieve more than when it started.

Unfortunately people are also the only resource that will disagree with you and cannot be relied on to perform properly when you press the button!

In order to achieve results through people you need to ensure that your team:

- Knows what to do
- Knows the standards to which it should be done, and
- Is motivated to do it.

Motivating people was the key theme of Chapter 10. This chapter focuses on the other two key themes of giving instruction and setting standards.

The basic principles of organizing staff are common sense and can be summarized in the following questions:

- What are the objectives – what do we need to achieve?
- What resources do we have?

- What are the requirements in terms of quality and quantity?
- What are the time-scales for achieving the objectives?
- How can I get the best out of the team to achieve these objectives?

You should not expect members of your team to help you achieve your objectives if they do not receive the necessary pay, praise, recognition and development to compensate for their efforts.

We often refer to shop-floor staff as operatives. The word somehow gives the impression that they are pieces of machinery – there to follow commands in the same way as an industrial lathe or a conveyor belt. This way of thinking can be traced back to the last century and the writing of F. W. Taylor. Taylor invented worthwhile modern techniques like time-and-motion study, functional specialization and technical training. Taylor intended all of these to improve productivity and efficiency by ensuring that each worker was doing the job best suited to them, had the necessary skills to do it and was doing it in the most efficient way. The drawback though is that 'in Taylor's system there was a strong element of dehumanising the workforce' (Clutterbuck and Crainer, 1990), this is because the emphasis on the 'one best way' of carrying out every task suggests robotic obedience to it.

We now recognize the importance of individual differences, acknowledge people's right and ability to influence the nature of their own work and therefore consult and involve staff.

**Insight**

All production line and administrative staff at Premier Plastics are selected on the basis of rigorous ability tests. They punch a time clock when they arrive. All production line jobs are given a daily output target and workers receive a bonus for exceeding it. In recent years, the company's profitability has declined. Senior management are seeking ways of improving efficiency and have set up small groups of staff to review and recommend changes to operating procedures.

**What examples of Taylorism can you see in this example?**

**What examples of a modern approach to management can you see?**

**What difficulties might the company encounter in moving from one to the other?**

Selection on the basis of ability-testing, time-clocks, output targets and production bonuses are all Taylorist techniques. Involving staff in changing procedures is a modern approach. The main difficulty in moving from one to the other is likely to be that staff who have previously had no chance to think for themselves will now find themselves expected to 'do management's thinking for them'. As Adam Smith pointed out in 1776:

*A man who spends his life carrying out a small number of very simple operations with perhaps the same effects has no room to develop his intelligence or to stretch his imagination so as to look for ways of overcoming difficulties which never occur. He therefore loses quite naturally the habit of using these facilities.*

Consequently, a culture of consultation needs to be supported by a programme of staff education, management encouragement and example.

## Organizing other resources

The physical resources available to a manager are:

- Stock or inventory (raw materials)
- Consumable items (which are used up in the production process)
- Tools and equipment.

In an ideal world, raw materials would always be available, customer demand would always be predictable, equipment would never break down or need maintenance, and staff would never go off sick, take holidays, resign or retire!

Under those circumstances, organizing resources would be a one-off event. It would be possible to calculate resource requirements once only, make those resources available and continue to meet customer needs completely without making any adjustments. However, we are concerned with reality, and know that managing the real world is very different:

1 *Raw materials* should be readily available, but at times demand for them may outstrip supply, or there could be a transport strike, or a price increase, or a fall in quality which may necessitate a search for an alternative supplier.

2 The *demand for an organization's products or services varies* according to:

- Customer confidence, disposable income and other external factors
- Seasonal demand (e.g. garden furniture in summer, Christmas trees in winter)
- Levels of local, national and international competition.

3 *Equipment needs maintenance*: all equipment requires 'down time' in order for staff to carry out checks and maintenance.

4 *Staff availability will vary*: of course those who resign or retire will normally be replaced but there will be a delay before new staff reach the performance standard of those they are replacing; gaps resulting from sickness or holiday can be filled by temporary staff, but these are unlikely to have the relevant experience or expertise to achieve the same level of productivity.

Of course you could just shrug your shoulders and say 'not my problem'. But this is not an acceptable response from a manager, for three reasons:

- Your team looks to you to provide the resources and support they need to do their jobs. Your credibility as a manager will suffer if you fail to do so
- Other customers in the supply chain depend on you
- Leaving others to make your decisions means you get no practice in a key management skill.

# Forecasting demand

The first stage in organizing resources to achieve results is to calculate demand for the outputs you produce.

### The organization's strategic plans and objectives

Part of strategic planning involves analysing customer expectations, competitive pressures and overall changes in the market. Some of this analysis will be based on informed guesswork, but it will result in a set of quantified objectives which will then become the organization's targets for the planning period.

### Historical demand

It would be a mistake to assume that future demand will be an exact repetition of past demand. Many organizations have gone out of business as the result of making that false assumption! Nevertheless, an intelligent examination of past demand patterns can give a good indication of likely future demand.

**Insight**

> Alice Hay is a dental surgeon. The average number of patients she treated daily is shown in Table 23.1, split between NHS (public) and private patients, for each of the months of last year and this year to date.

**Table 23.1**

| Last year | | | This year to date | | |
|---|---|---|---|---|---|
| January | Public | 14 | January | Public | 15 |
| | Private | 4 | | Private | 6 |
| February | Public | 15 | February | Public | 16 |
| | Private | 3 | | Private | 5 |
| March | Public | 16 | March | Public | 17 |
| | Private | 4 | | Private | 7 |
| April | Public | 17 | April | Public | 18 |
| | Private | 4 | | Private | 6 |
| May | Public | 17 | May | Public | 18 |
| | Private | 5 | | Private | 7 |
| June | Public | 16 | June | Public | 17 |
| | Private | 5 | | Private | 6 |
| July | Public | 13 | July | Public | 14 |
| | Private | 5 | | Private | 5 |
| August | Public | 11 | | | |
| | Private | 4 | | | |
| September | Public | 15 | | | |
| | Private | 6 | | | |
| October | Public | 14 | | | |
| | Private | 4 | | | |
| November | Public | 13 | | | |
| | Private | 7 | | | |
| December | Public | 10 | | | |
| | Private | 6 | | | |

What trends and patterns can you see in these figures?

How many public and private patients would you expect Alice Hay to treat in August of this year?

What are the resource implications of this analysis?

Last year and this year both show a seasonal pattern. The number of patients treated drops in the summer (perhaps as people go on holiday) and in December. A comparison between last year's and this year's figures shows a further trend – numbers are consistently higher this year, and the proportion of private patients rose steadily last year and continues to rise this year. Alice may have decided to accept no new NHS patients.

The seasonal pattern suggests that Alice's patient numbers will again drop in August but the steady increase in both overall numbers and private patients makes it likely that she will treat 12 public patients and 5 or 6 private patients daily in August of this year.

With this information, Alice can:

1 Insure she has enough raw materials to carry out the treatments which will require more detailed analysis of average usage.

2 Negotiate holiday arrangements for herself, her nurse and receptionist.

3 Work out likely revenue and profitability for the month. Make decisions about equipment maintenance.

4 Decide whether, in view of the rising trend in patient numbers, she should take on extra staff or find a partner to join her in the practice.

## Quantitative production

Historical demand data is an accurate reflection of what actually happened. However, as the last insight shows, it rarely repeats itself exactly. Quantitative production provides a fairly accurate picture of short-term demand and can be used either as an alternative to historical data, or as a complementary technique. It normally involves a basic form of market research, asking customers what their needs will be for the following week or month. Customer–supplier partnerships are a useful source of quantitative production. Regular internal production meetings attended by supplying and receiving departments are another good example.

### Qualitative prediction

Forecasting from historical data and quantitative production rely on the assumption that future demand will be fairly similar to past demand. But in the case of new products and services where there is no historical data, and in environments where external factors are going through major change, such assumptions are not safe. Qualitative prediction, otherwise known as the Delphi technique because it involves 'asking the oracle', is a matter of finding a team of experts and asking them to make a best guess about levels of future demand, based on their expert analysis of customer expectations and environmental change.

## Smoothing demand

Regardless of the sophistication of the techniques used, demand forecasting can only be an approximate science. New customers, changes in customer requirements or external influences and seasonal patterns will all make demand uneven: higher at some periods, lower at others. Organizations can take certain actions to smooth demand by:

- Offering price reductions and discounts at periods of low demand
- Producing 'summer goods' and 'winter goods' to reflect seasonal fluctuations
- Manufacturing products at a consistent level throughout the year but warehousing excess production when demand is low and supplying from stock when demand is high – although risky and costly
- Encouraging customer loyalty by providing, for example, loyalty discounts, season tickets on the railways, or offering retail incentives like vouchers or supermarket saver cards.

## Adjusting capacity

However, none of these techniques will totally remove the inconsistency and unpredictability of customer demand. It is therefore important for organizations to be able to adjust resource capacity in line with demand. They can do this by:

- Maintaining excess capacity: this involves forecasting peak demand and making resources available to meet it; for example, holiday resorts and airlines have more capacity than they need except at peak holiday times but offer discounts and other incentives to off-set this excess capacity out-of-season

- Automation: this involves the adoption of automated, computer-controlled methods to allow easier adjustments to the nature and volume of output

- Flexible staffing: as the name suggests, this involves techniques like overtime and part-time working, flexitime and the use of temporary and agency staff

- Multi-skilling: ensuring that staff have a range of skills which will enable them to move between tasks according to market demand

- Revising maintenance patterns: this involves bringing forward equipment maintenance and staff training when demand is low and deferring them when demand is high

- Subcontracting: this involves keeping operations in-house when demand is light but buying in from subcontractors when it is heavy.

**Insight**

Peter King owns and operates a motor business where he sells used cars and offers a repair and maintenance service. His peak periods for car sales are at the beginning of the summer and in March and August when people sell their old cars in order to buy new ones registered with the bi-annual number plate. Peak periods for service work are again at the start of the summer, preparing cars for holiday trips and at the start of the winter, so that they are reliable during the bad weather.

**In practical terms how could Peter smooth demand/adjust capacity?**

Peter could smooth demand by:

- Promoting discounts at quiet times of the year
- Offering special deals to existing customers.

In order to adjust capacity he might:

- Arrange for staff to work overtime
- Negotiate more flexible working patterns so that staff work long hours during busy periods but take time off at slack times
- Train workshop staff to sell cars or salespeople to carry out repairs (difficult but not impossible)

- Use quiet periods for maintenance, refurbishment and training
- Bring in temporary staff
- Use subcontractors and accept a lower profit margin (perhaps to prepare used cars or carry out specialist repair work like tyre or exhaust fitting).

## Managing stock

Stock or inventory provides a buffer between variations in demand and supply. But holding goods or stock is expensive. The physi-cal and administrative processes of monitoring stock levels, re-ordering and replenishing stock are expensive, as is the stock itself. Efficient inventory management involves a balancing act between ensuring availability and keeping costs to a minimum. The past few years have seen an increase in high street retailers, for example, using distribution and warehousing companies to manage their stock/goods. Instead of storing large quantities of goods in a stock room, the stores order and receive goods on a daily basis ensuring they have adequate supplies to meet production or customer demands.

This has proved a more cost-effective way to manage the stock and has reduced the need for large stock rooms, which in turn has increased the floor space available in which to promote and sell goods.

Organizations use a number of differing techniques and systems, many of which are now computer-based, to ensure they are managing the supply and demand of their goods or stock in the most cost-effective way. One such technique is called *ABC Analysis*.

ABC Analysis works on the recognition that consumable resources can be divided into three categories, based on the volume of items and the value compared with total stockholding:

*Category A* items represent a small proportion of total volume but a high proportion of total value (typically 10–15% of volume, but 70–80% of value). These items will be tightly controlled, frequently re-ordered in small quantities.

*Category B* items represent a higher volume (say 20% of the total) but a lower value (maybe 15% again). These items will require a less sophisticated stock control system and will be held in greater quantities.

*Category C* items represent high volume but low value. They do not justify the expense of tight control and are typically ordered by the box or container load and held in large quantities.

The following Case Study illustrates how a furniture manufacturer uses ABC analysis.

**Case Study**

> Riley and Sons is an old-established company which manufac-turer's high-quality furniture. The furniture is then sold through a limited number of shops on a 'made to order' basis. Customers can choose different finishes, including upholstery fabric for each style of furniture.
>
> As each item of furniture is made following the customers order, Riley's only carry a small quantity of, for example, upholstery fabric and solid brass handles (Category A). The solid wood which is used in all the furniture is imported from Scandinavia at a substantially discounted price to Riley's (Category B). Hidden castors are fitted to most of the furniture cabinets and tables, which are 'best sellers' for Riley's (Category C).

**Do you consider Riley's is managing its stock in the most cost-effective way?**

You have probably answered yes to that question. Riley's makes a good profit from the fabrics and such items as brass handles but despite this they are still costly for Riley's to buy. However, it is more cost-effective for Riley's to buy in the fabric for special orders rather than storing rolls of fabric just in case it is to be used. All of Riley's products are made from the imported wood so they pur-chase and use large quantities hence their good discount. The fac-tory is kept busy on a fairly constant basis throughout the year so it makes sense to buy-in large quantities of wood. The castors are one of the cheapest components, made and imported from abroad, and are supplied in boxes of 500.

Many organizations, not just manufacturing, have adopted the Just-in-Time (JIT) principle. Originally from the automotive indus-try, JIT is a simple concept that ensures that stock is delivered at precisely the time it is needed to be transferred into finished prod-ucts or services. Stock levels are kept to a minimum but are always available when required. As you can see the principle depends on working closely with suppliers to ensure that quality goods – there is no time to replace faulty items – arrive at precisely the right time.

*Materials Requirement Planning (MRP)* is the general name for computer software that is increasingly available for organizations, which enables them to more accurately calculate their purchasing needs based on their current stocks and expected future requirements.

Organizations may use one or a combination of these techniques to ensure that they achieve the balance of meeting customer demand whilst keeping the cost of stockholding to a minimum.

# Monitoring and controlling results

An effective control mechanism not only measures performance against standards, but also initiates corrective action when these standards are not being met. Typical standards are likely to include:

- Budget
- Quality
- Timeliness
- Use of renewable resources
- Use of consumable resources.

In order to monitor performance successfully you will need:

- Quantified standards
- Systems to compare performance with standards
- Regular and timely feedback to enable corrective action.

Case Study

> Kevin is a business link adviser. He compiles and receives weekly reports on the numbers of consultations he has performed which are compared with monthly targets. His performance is also assessed on the basis of how much trade is generated as a result of his work. His success rate is set by Business Link.

How effective are these monitoring systems?

Will they work as control mechanisms?

The feedback Kevin receives on the number of consultations is quantified regularly and quick enough for him to take corrective action in order to meet his monthly targets.

His assessment on the basis of the amount of trade generated is a different matter. Again, it is quantified and regular. But once he has put companies in contact with each other he can do nothing. The ball is in their court. A deal could be done, on the other hand the deal could fall through. There is little corrective action he can take after he has introduced the firms to each other. Each deal between firms will take time to come to fruition, so there are sometimes very long delays before he is able to clarify how much business he has created.

Monitoring results costs money. But failure to detect errors or variances also costs money. To be cost-effective the frequency of monitoring should balance the cost of the monitoring with the cost of failing to take necessary corrective action in time.

Assuming that monitoring takes place early enough and frequently enough for you to take corrective action, what form might that action take? Consider Adam's situation:

**Case Study**

A major high street bank is offering a particularly low interest rate mortgage which they have advertised on national television and newspapers. The offer is for a limited period only with all applications having to be processed by the end of May before the bank starts another promotional offer. Adam Parker supervises a team in the regional office of the bank. Their task is to process the applications. It is the end of April and Adam has received a flood of applications. Adam has four weeks, 1,000 applications to process and five staff. By the end of the first week his team has dealt with 200 applications.

**What corrective action could Adam take?**

Adam has several choices:

- He could bring in more staff, either temporary staff from an agency or by borrowing them from elsewhere in the regional office. That is provided his budget is sufficient and the new staff can be trained quickly enough.

273

- He could ask his staff to check the applications less carefully and spend less time on each one.

- However, this will lower quality and the bank risks losing money if they make wrong decisions.

- He might adjust work priorities. If his staff are also processing other applications which are less time-critical he could put these on hold and concentrate on the mortgage applications.

- He may be able to make the checking procedure more efficient, thus saving time and maintaining quality.

- It is too late to help with this promotion, but he could learn for the future by putting in a bid for more sophisticated equipment – a computer program, for example, to automate part of the process.

Failure to achieve results may be because:

- Output volume is too low
- Output quality is not good enough
- Output costs are too high
- Output is too slow.

Any of these may be subject to correction by:

- Increasing resource outputs
- Improving process efficiency
- Changing the input specification
- Changing the output specification.

All of these corrective actions are dependent on budget constraints and customer requirements.

# Controlling quality

There are three main approaches to controlling quality. They are very different in:

- Their objectives
- The operational stages to which they apply
- The systems necessary to support them
- The actions resulting from these.

Nevertheless, they all have one thing in common – they start by defining quality as 'conformance to customer requirements' or 'conformance to specification', that specification in turn being derived from what the customer requires.

Quality control is the traditional and most basic approach. It compares outputs with customer requirements, in order to identify which outputs meet, and do not meet, the quality standard. Typical quality control systems include:

- Quality inspection, where inspectors assess whether the outputs meet the desired standard
- Sampling the output, which reduces inspection costs by assessing only a proportion of outputs (e.g. testing every other one)
- Statistical process control, which identifies the causes of changing output quality.

Quality control is applied to outputs after they have been finished. In a manufacturing context, it is applied to finished components and completed products. Elsewhere it might involve:

- Trying on a coat to see if it fits after alteration
- Checking the $CO_2$ emission from a car after it has been serviced
- Proof-reading a letter after it has been typed.

As a result of quality control we either accept or reject the output.

Quality assurance differs from quality control in that it concentrates on processes rather than outputs. It is designed to ensure that the methods used to transform inputs into outputs achieve the required output quality.

Typical quality assurance systems include:

- ISO 9000, 9001/2/3
- Process reviews and flow-charting.

Since quality assurance places an emphasis on monitoring processes, it is likely to involve:

- Process redesign
- Clarification of procedures
- Implementation of new systems
- Improved control documentation.

Such a system is therefore likely to prevent quality problems rather than solve them after they have occurred.

We have already referred to total quality management (TQM). It is an all-embracing philosophy intended to put customer satisfaction at the heart of every organization. It makes every individual, team, activity and operation responsible for achieving quality and extends the idea of quality to include delivery, customer relations and added value, among other things.

Because TQM applies before, during and after the transformation process, the systems which support it cover such widely diverse activities as:

- Customer consultation and feedback
- Staff training
- Systems design
- Process improvement.

The outcomes of TQM are more diverse and have an effect not only on processes, procedures and controls but also on the overall culture and attitudes of the organization.

Therefore the success of TQM is dependent on the commitment and involvement of everyone throughout the whole organization.

| **Review your learning** | Check your understanding of this chapter by completing the following: |

1  What do you understand by a 'top-down, bottom up' approach to objective setting?

2  Objectives should be (fill in the missing letters):

S

M

A

R

T

3  A control loop is a system which compares o _ _ _ _ _ _ with s _ _ _ _ _ _ _ _ _ and initiates c _ _ _ _ _ _ _ _ _ _ a _ _ _ _ _ when these are not being met.

4 Why do organizations seek to smooth demand?

5 What is the difference between quality control and quality and assurance?

<table>
<tr><td>**Theory to practice**</td><td>Apply this chapter to your own experience by answering the following:</td></tr>
</table>

1 How SMART are your objectives? How could they be improved?

2 What systems do you use to compare outputs with standards? How effective are they and why?

3 What techniques does your organization use to smooth demand?

4 How much scope do you have to adjust capacity to demand? What more would you like?

5 How does your organization assess the quality of its outputs? What more could it do?

6 How could you improve the quality control of your team's outputs?

# 24 Meeting customer needs

| Chapter Objectives | • *Are customers important?* |
|---|---|

*Customers are our most important asset. They are the life-blood of our business and their satisfaction is the ultimate objective of all we do.*

*Without customers we could not exist.*

The majority of organizations these days recognize that without satisfied customers they would not exist. Many organizations, particularly those in the retail sector, are continually looking at different ways of both anticipating and satisfying the needs of their customers. As we have shown in other sections of this book this encompasses areas such as total quality, the supply chain, stock control.

However, as we all know customers can be extremely demanding, unreasonable and fickle!

Being able to meet those unreasonable demands, retaining customers and having customer satisfaction as a principal objective, differentiates those organizations that will survive and thrive from those that fail.

Many writers suggest that the key to achieving this is managing the business from the perspective of satisfying the customer rather than focusing on the product or service.

*Starting with customer wants and needs ... enables the organization to develop appropriate products and services for which there is a requirement.*
Proctor (1996)

*The purpose of a business is to create and keep a customer.*
Levitt (1983)

Attracting new customers costs an organization eight times as much as it does to keep an existing one so it makes business sense to develop a customer-oriented organization.

However, ensuring that customer focus is part of an organization's culture requires time and effort invested to change attitudes and may require:

- Introducing processes to assist the organization to identify customer wants, needs and expectations
- Review of current systems and procedures
- Training all levels of staff.

# Identifying customer needs

It is essential for an organization to understand their customers in terms of:

*who buys, how they buy, the choice criteria used, where and when they buy.*
Jobber (1995)

Finding out what the end customers want, need and expect, and how satisfied they are with what they get, involves using a range of marketing techniques and may involve:

*Telephone interviews*

These are quick, relatively cheap to conduct but not suitable for in-depth research.

*Postal questionnaires*

Take longer than telephone interviews before the results are received but can include more questions. The questions must be carefully designed to avoid misunderstanding. The major problem associated with researching via questionnaires is that only a small number are ever returned completed. An average of only 2–5% will be returned unless some form of incentive is given.

*Face-to-face interviews*

Are costly and time-consuming to conduct but do allow a more in-depth exploration of issues and give scope for the interviewer to use visual prompts and to show physical products.

*Focus groups*

These involve a small group of people meeting, often for a whole evening, to discuss complicated issues like buying motives and personal preferences, under the guidance of a skilled researcher. Expensive and time-consuming, they nevertheless provide complex research information which could not otherwise be gathered.

*Customer response cards*

Included with products or sent to selected customers, these provide a way of finding out why customers made their purchase and their level of satisfaction.

These are all valid market research methods and can be used in differing sectors. For example, if your organization sells cars you may send out customer response cards to find out if they are satisfied with their new purchase. Equally you could send out customer response cards to patients within a GP catchment area to find out if they are satisfied with the service they are receiving from the doctors and the surgery.

The techniques are used mainly for final customers. They all result in what is known as 'primary data' because they collect facts, figures and opinions for the first time and for a specific purpose.

'Secondary data' is the phrase used to describe information on statistics already collected for a different purpose. Sources of secondary data include:

- Internal records like past sales records, customer complaints or letters of praise
- Industry data available from trade magazines, trade association reports and academic journals
- Government statistics related to topics like car ownership, numbers of students attending school and university, how old people are and where they live.

Although these are generally used to find out more about external customers, it is worth pointing out that several of these methods are equally applicable to internal customers. For example, if you manage the accounts department you could use a questionnaire

280

to gain information about levels of satisfaction from the departments in the organization who use your service.

Another approach which is equally relevant to both external and internal customers is what is known as customer–supplier partnerships. The principles on which this approach is based are that:

- The closer customers are to suppliers, the more they can influence the products or services they receive.

- The greater their influence, the more likely it is that products and services will meet their needs.

- Customers and suppliers should work together in cooperation rather than opposing each other as enemies.

In practical terms, customer–supplier partnerships involve customers developing accurate and comprehensive specifications for what they want and communicating those specifications to the supplier. But the process goes further than that. Partnerships also involve customers and suppliers working together to design and develop the product or service and, where necessary, modifying the original specification, or production methods, or quality standards to the point where the final output is acceptable to both parties.

# Satisfying customer needs

The Chartered Institute of Marketing defines marketing as 'the management process for identifying, anticipating and satisfying customer requirements profitably'. That definition suggests that at our peril we ignore the needs of our customers. Satisfying customer needs is not simply about providing a product or service, it is also about doing it in the right way. Marketing involves providing:

> **The right *product*, in the right *place*, at the right *time*, at the right *price* and in the right *way*.**

What constitutes right in each case will of course depend on the individual customer's needs. And the extent to which customers can find an exact match with their needs will depend on how specific they are. In most cases, however, customers, whether they are internal or external, will have to make a compromise choice depending on which of the five rights are most important to them.

**Case Study**

Alan's daughter is getting married in three weeks' time. He has gone out to buy a new suit for the wedding. Ideally he wants a dark grey, three-piece suit, in a traditional style, costing no more than £250.

He does not usually wear a suit so he wants reliable advice from the salesperson. The suit may need some minor alterations so he wants to buy it this afternoon. He works long hours so can only get to the shops after work and has gone to his nearest large shopping mall where he knows there are several shops that sell suits.

He soon finds that most suits are only two-piece and their styles are far too modern. He finds one in a traditional style which fits perfectly but the waistcoat will have to be specially made. It may be ready in three weeks but could take a month. Another is exactly what he wants – but is only available in blue. Finally the local branch of a national high street chain appears to have the answer. The colour and style are right. The trousers can be shortened in a week. Unfortunately the nearest jacket in his size is located in a store in another city. The salesperson is helpful and can arrange for the jacket to be transferred. The transfer will take seven days and Alan can try it on when it arrives. The total price of the suit is £285.

**What are the five rights in Alan's case?**

**What compromises may he have to make?**

> Right product is a traditional dark grey, three-piece suit that fits him
>
> Right place is his nearest shopping mall
>
> Right time is ready for him in three weeks
>
> Right price is no more than £250
>
> Right way is with reliable advice from the salesperson.

None of the available alternatives is an exact match with his needs. He may choose to compromise on product (give up the waistcoat, accept a different colour, risk a jacket that does not fit) or on price. He cannot compromise on time – the wedding is not going to be delayed for the sake of his suit – nor on place – he has limited time to get to the shops. But if he could find the perfect suit which fitted him at the price he wanted to pay, he could probably do without reliable advice from the salesperson.

In Alan's situation, time is the prime driver in his buying decision. For other customers in other situations it may be product, price or location. It is rare for the way in which a sale is made to be the main consideration and then only in situations where competing alternatives are identical in all other ways.

# Improving customer satisfaction

We can group the five rights under just three headings:

- Product factors (the right product at the right price)
- Convenience factors (in the right place at the right time)
- Human factors (in the right way).

In most organizations the staff who have direct contact with final customers are in a minority. They are typically limited to:

- Sales staff
- Telephone/call centre staff and receptionists
- Accounts staff who prepare invoices
- Customer service staff.

Using our three headings, these are the people who constitute the human factor for final customers, whose attitude to the organization will depend on their:

- Promptness of response
- Friendliness and courtesy
- Knowledge and expertise.

However, sometimes these frontline staff have little or no control over product and convenience factors.

**Insight**

Sally is the receptionist working in the outpatients department of the local NHS Trust hospital. The clinic is particularly busy and the patients are having to wait at least an hour before seeing the doctor. Many of the patients are cross about having to wait so long and complain to Sally.

**What action can Sally take?**

**Which of our factors can she control?**

**What changes would be necessary to improve the situation and who would be responsible for them?**

Sally's scope for action is very limited. She can apologize, sympathize, direct patients to the magazine rack and the coffee machine. She can give them as accurate information as possible about how much longer they will have to wait.

These are all human factors – important to get right but not central to the problem.

There appears to be nothing wrong with the product factors – we assume that the doctors are prescribing suitable treatment and the issue of price is not relevant in this situation.

The problems stem from convenience factors – primarily availability and time. They could be solved by:

● Scheduling more doctors into the clinic rota

● Allowing more time for each appointment so that they do not over-run

● Booking fewer patients in at the same time.

However, none of these are Sally's responsibility. They are likely to be medical and administrative decisions which, once taken, will be set into formal procedures. Unfortunately they may not be aware of the impact they have on Sally.

This takes us back to the supply chain concept. To improve customer satisfaction it is important for everyone working in the organization to understand the needs of the final customer so that they are aware of how they contribute to satisfying them. Some organizations arrange for all staff, as part of their induction or other training, to experience frontline contact with final customers.

If that is difficult or impossible, the total quality principle of internal customers achieves a similar objective. But both approaches go no further than identifying needs.

Improving customer satisfaction requires the manager to take the lead in asking and answering some fundamental questions. Oakland (1989) listed these questions as:

- Who are my immediate customers?
- What are their time requirements?
- How do I, or can I, find out what the requirements are?
- Do I have the necessary capability to meet the requirements? (If not then what must change to improve the capability?)
- Do I continually meet the requirements? (If not then what prevents this from happening when the capability exists?)
- How do I monitor changes in the requirement?

To this list we would add five further questions:

- How much scope do I have to make changes?
- What organizational constraints may prevent me from making changes?
- How do I encourage my team to contribute to improving customer satisfaction?
- How effective am I in persuading others to be involved?
- How can I gain the agreement of my line manager?

These questions raise issues related to informing, persuading and influencing and managing change, which are covered in Chapters 7 and 15 of this book.

<table>
<tr><td>Review your learning</td><td>Check your understanding of this chapter by completing the following:<br><br>1 List three 'primary' techniques for identifying customer needs.<br><br>2 What is a customer–supplier partnership?<br><br>3 What are the five areas to focus on in satisfying customer need?</td></tr>
<tr><td>Theory to practice</td><td>Apply this chapter to your own experience by answering the following:<br><br>1 List your main internal and external customers.<br><br>2 How do you and your team identify their needs?<br><br>3 How could you use the techniques described in this chapter to find out more about their needs?<br><br>4 What can you do to involve your team in improving customer satisfaction?</td></tr>
</table>

## 25 Managing the work environment

| Chapter Objectives | • *How can I improve the layout of the workplace?* |
|---|---|
| | • *What are my responsibilities in maintaining a healthy and safe environment?* |

Most of us go to the same place of work every day. As a result, over time we stop seeing it – we simply take for granted that it is the way it is and come to accept its imperfections. The purpose of this chapter is to encourage you to take a fresh look at the workplace and to be critical about the way its design and layout affects the efficiency of production and the health and safety of your staff.

## Operational design and efficiency

Work flows. Depending upon your industry, raw materials may flow through a manufacturing process, information may flow through an administrative process being analysed, interpreted and applied as it goes or clients may flow through a health club using sports equipment and leisure services.

Work flow is subject to a host of potential inefficiencies. Consider the following Case Study:

**Case Study**

Wanda and her team produce monthly management accounts for a firm assembling computer hardware systems to individual customer orders. Sales information comes monthly from the sales team, normally collated during the first week of the following month. This enables the sales team to claim all commission due on sales made that month. Customer orders are identified by a unique job code, although members of the sales team are careless about getting the code right. As soon as a sale is made, individual salespeople also send details through to the production facility so that assembly can start. These details include a technical specification but not the value of the order. Production costs for each job come to the management accounts team as soon as the job is finished. The production facility uses a different system of job coding from that used by the sales force.

**What are the inefficiencies in this system?**

**How could they be removed?**

Here are some of the inefficiencies (you may have recognized others):

*Waiting time*

The management accounts department needs to monitor sales values and production costs, but these arrive at different times and at different frequencies.

*Inconsistent systems*

The sales team and production facility use different job coding systems. Wanda and her team, or someone else in the company, will need to make the two incompatible systems consistent with each other.

*Double-handling and repetition*

The sales team produces two incomplete sets of data but with common elements (customer details, for example). In other words, they are providing some data twice.

*Inaccuracy*

Not only are the job codes different for sales and production but the sales team sometimes get their codes wrong, which will make reconciliation even more time-consuming (or, at worst, impossible!).

Managers are responsible for ensuring, as far as they can, that the operations they control are efficient. Most of the inefficiencies we have identified are not directly under Wanda's control. However she and her team are still internal customers of the sales team and production staff. She needs to make them aware of her need for:

- Information inputs at the right time, to reduce or avoid waiting
- The right inputs (no inaccuracies, consistent information).

287

She could point out that such inefficiency could be reduced by simplifying and streamlining the system. The process of identifying and removing inefficiencies is part of operations scheduling. This involves analysing the flow and sequence of operations to ensure that they are logical and efficient. It needs to take account of:

*Activity duration*

How long the activity takes to complete, the resources currently used and its impact on the next activity in the sequence.

*Activity frequency*

The more frequent the activity, the more important it is to identify and remove inefficiencies because of their cumulative effect.

*Activity sequence*

The analysis of activity sequences involves a critical examination of the whole chain of activities which make up an operation, in order to identify inefficiencies like double-handling, repetition, waiting time and excess distance between activities.

The most helpful technique for analysing activities is the use of an activity flow-chart, otherwise known as a network diagram. Figure 25.1 shows an example, using for simplicity the preparation of a meal.

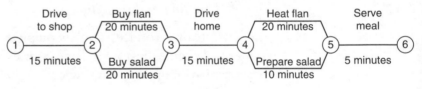

*Figure 25.1*

The conventions of a network diagram are as follows:

- All activities start and finish with a circle (called a 'node')
- Nodes are numbered for ease of reference
- Activities are described in action words above the line with the duration below
- Durations can be in anything from seconds to months, provided they are all consistent
- 'Burst' nodes are points where several activities can start when one is completed (the later activities are said to 'depend' on the completion of the preceding one).

Network diagrams contribute to operations scheduling by:

- Enabling you to identify the sequence of activities which determines the minimum duration of an operation (called the 'critical path') through the network
- Encouraging you to think critically about the duration of individual activities as a first step in improving efficiency
- Helping you to streamline an operation by finding activities which could be carried out simultaneously (like preparing the salad whilst the flan is being heated, in our example)
- Highlighting waiting time.

# Workplace layout

We referred earlier to inefficiencies caused by the need for work-in-progress to travel excessive distances. Picture an office worker who has to refer frequently to the contents of a manual filing system. If the filing cabinets are at the other end of a large open plan office, each reference will require several extra minutes that could be eliminated by repositioning them close to the desk. Similarly, if Just-in-Time deliveries are made to a manufacturing business where goods inwards are a long way from production, the frequency and cost of transporting the deliveries could be reduced by holding stocks on the production line.

If you have the authority to re-arrange your team's working area you will need to start by putting together information about:

- The location of fixed structures like walls, doors and windows
- The position of equipment which cannot be moved, including items like radiators and extractor fans
- Where services like water and electricity are located
- Typical flows of people and materials.

You will, of course, consult with your team sourcing the inefficiency they are experiencing and asking for their suggestions for improvement.

An efficient workplace layout should provide:

- Easy accessibility to all parts of the work area
- Maximum flexibility so that it can be changed easily to accommodate, for example, temporary staff, meetings or changes to the work flow

- Maximum productive use of space, including wall-height for storage and avoiding 'dead space'
- Minimum distances for people and materials to travel, to save on time and handling
- Maximum comfort and safety, ensuring adequate lighting, heating, ventilation, access to emergency exits and avoidance of hazards
- Efficient work flow avoiding cross-traffic by ensuring that people and materials move only in one direction as far as possible.

**Insight**

Trish Walker is supervisor in the accounts department of Taylor's a builders merchant. Figure 25.2 shows the office layout.

Trish receives and distributes work from her desk. The filing cabinets and photocopier are used by all the staff.

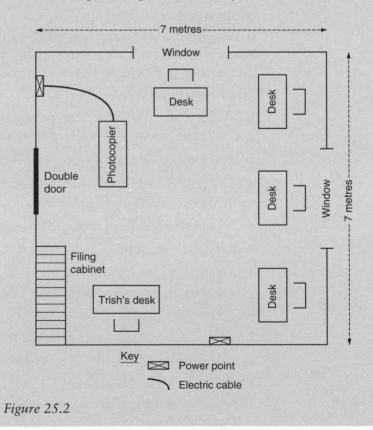

*Figure 25.2*

**What is wrong with this office layout?**

**How could it be improved?**

The obvious problems with the layout are:

- The photocopier blocks the door, obstructs access to three desks and the electric cable is a safety hazard
- Much of the centre of the office is unproductive space
- Access to the filing cabinets involves covering long distances and obstructs Trish's work area
- There is no natural light to Trish's desk
- Distributing work involves a considerable walk round the office.

Possible improvements, based on the limited information given might involve:

- Moving the photocopier to the top left corner of the office
- Re-organizing files and relocating cabinets closer to individual desks
- Moving Trish's desk to a more central position with better lighting.

Of course these are only proposals. A more detailed analysis of work flow and staff movements could result in more suitable changes.

# Health and Safety – everyone's responsibility

There are three reasons why a manager should treat health and safety issues as priorities:

- A manager's responsibility for staff is generally accepted to extend to caring for their welfare
- UK law makes health and safety a legal duty of managers, individual staff members and of organizations
- Sick and injured staff significantly reduce productivity.

# Health and Safety – part of a manager's job

Health and safety in the workplace is *everyone's* responsibility, not just that of the health and safety team.

Everyone in the organization needs to understand the standards of Health & Safety expected by the organization, and their role in achieving and maintaining those standards.

The workplace is a potentially dangerous environment – you may be working with machinery, heavy loads, hazardous material, you and your team may be under pressure and have to work at speed to complete tasks in the required time. An office may have trailing cables, drawers left open, boxes poorly stacked – any of which has the potential to cause serious injury. Organizations need to actively plan for safety to prevent accidents and injury from occurring.

As a manager you have a key responsibility to ensure that your team works in a healthy and safe environment. You need to walk around your workplace looking out for potential hazards and risks.

*A hazard is anything that could cause harm – for example, chemicals, electricity, movement of people and materials.*

*Risk is the chance – big or small – of harm being done.*

Fortunately the law is there to assist you in the process of maintaining a healthy and safe working environment.

# Health, safety and the law

Legislation reflects society. As social attitudes change, so new legislation is introduced to ensure that the law keeps up with society.

Health and safety legislation culture is an example of this trend. In the UK, the first tentative steps to protect workers were introduced in the latter part of the nineteenth century. The Factories Act was passed in 1937, followed by a series of further Acts in the 1960s and early 1970s.

It is important to recognize that health and safety are vital issues – and failure to take them seriously can have significant legal and financial implications.

The Health and Safety at Work Act (HASAWA) 1974 is an unusual piece of business legislation in that it places obligations on both employers and employees. The Act sets out the duty of every employer with five or more employees, as:

*... to ensure, as far as reasonably practicable, the health, safety and welfare at work of all his employees.*

The Act ensures that the following should be adhered to:

- The preparation of a written health and safety policy which must be communicated to all staff contractors who work regularly on the employer's premises
- Consultation with safety representatives or a safety committee appointed by a recognized trade union
- Informing employees about health and safety law and providing them with the local addresses of the authorities which enforce that law, by displaying approved posters or circulating leaflets
- Reporting all fatal accidents and cases of major injury
- Keeping records of reportable injuries for at least three years
- Providing adequate first-aid facilities.

In addition to the 1974 Act, the Workplace (Health, Safety and Welfare) Regulations 1992 set standards for temperature, ventilation, lighting, workspace, seating, windows, escalators, toilet and washing facilities. All this is on top of an employer's general duties to provide:

- Safe work systems
- Training and supervision
- Maintenance of sites and systems
- The provision of safe ways into and out of places of work
- The provision of a safe and healthy work environment.

Importantly, the HASAWA makes it the duty of employees to:

*take reasonable care for the health and safety of himself and of other person's who may be affected by his acts or omissions at work.*

This includes responsibilities to:

- Cooperate with their employers and others to enable them to comply with the law
- Avoid the intentional or reckless misuse of equipment or materials
- Follow health and safety instructions
- Report to the employer any dangerous situations in the workplace or any shortcomings in health and safety arrangements.

In addition to HASAWA there are a number of key Acts that control health and safety at work. Many of these have derived from Europe. These include:

- Management of Health and Safety at Work Regulations 1999
- Workplace (Health, Safety and Welfare) Regulations 1992
- Manual Handling Operations Regulations 1992
- Personal Protective Equipment at Work Regulations 1992
- Reporting of Injuries, Diseases and Dangerous Occurrences Regulations 1995
- The Working Time Regulations 1998.

So far, we have described an employer's responsibilities and those of an employee. But where do you as a manager fit in? As a manager you should make sure that you are familiar with your own company's Health, Safety and Environmental policies and procedures and ensure that these are adhered to effectively. Whilst you are not expected to know everything about the law you should, however, have sufficient knowledge to ensure that you and your team comply.

From the viewpoint of health and safety legislation, managers are in the uncomfortable position of needing to fulfil both employers' and employees' responsibilities. As representatives of their employer, managers have a duty to:

- Monitor the extent to which the work environment meets the requirements of health and safety legislation
- Identify and take remedial action
- Instruct and train their staff on the health and safety policy and procedures
- Encourage and provide opportunities for staff to identify shortfalls and recommend improvements.

As employees, managers have a duty to:

- Point out shortcomings in their employer's approach to health and safety
- Recommend improvements
- Highlight remedial action which is outside their own authority.

All of these duties and responsibilities result from health and safety legislation. But there are others which simply stem from good management practice. These include:

- Learning from the incident: by identifying the cause, taking action to ensure it is not repeated and recording it for future reference
- Planning processes with an eye to health and safety considerations
- Making regular health and safety checks of all operations and activities under their control.

Much of this is fairly obvious though not always straightforward to implement. But what about situations where the manager's responsibilities as employer and employee appear to conflict? In other words, when the organization's demands cannot be met without damaging the health, safety or welfare of the workforce?

This raises some important questions:

- How should you pass issues and concerns higher up the organization?
- Is senior management aware of the consequences of their demands?
- Do they recognize the financial and practical costs of ignoring health, safety and welfare issues?

# The costs of health and safety

In 2003/04 the number of workplace fatal injuries in the UK reported to both the Health and Safety Executive and Local Authorities was 235.

For the same year the number of reported major injuries was 30,666.

Over a third of all reported major injuries were caused by slipping and tripping.

This equates to an average annual loss of 170,000 working days per 100,000 workers.
(Source: Health & Safety Executive, Safety Statistics)

So, there is an *enormous* cost to the national economy.

For organizations health and safety costs money because it involves all managers and staff spending part of their time in maintaining a healthy and safe working environment. However, this cost becomes insignificant compared with the costs to an organization of ignoring the health, safety and welfare of its employees.

For simplicity we can consider these in terms of legal, recruitment and productivity costs.

*Legal costs* may arise from the financial penalties incurred when an organization breaks health and safety law. In the UK because the Health and Safety at Work Act 1974 is a piece of criminal legislation, employers who break it are liable to fines or even imprisonment.

In addition, managers who fail to implement policies and procedures set up by their employers are also liable under the Act, as are employees who ignore their own health and safety responsibilities.

Also, if the employer has already been convicted under criminal law, it is likely that an employee will seek damages if he or she brings an action in civil law because the criminal conviction will provide proof of negligence.

Legal costs though are only the beginning.

**Insight**

Two light engineering firms in the same town are wanting to recruit staff. One has a history of injuries to staff and has been prosecuted under the Health and Safety at Work Act. The other has a better reputation for health and safety. The first pays higher wages.

**Which in your opinion will find it easier to attract staff?**

The answer to that question will of course depend on more factors than just health and safety. Nevertheless, assuming other things are roughly equal, it is unlikely that potential recruits will accept a higher risk of personal injury, or even death, in exchange for a little more pay. And they may well assume that a firm which gives little or no attention to health and safety matters is unlikely to care for its staff in other ways either.

In consequence an organization with a poor health and safety record will find it difficult to recruit and keep the staff it needs to meet its output and revenue targets. There will also be an ongoing impact on existing staff. In organizations where ill-health, accidents and injuries are commonplace:

- The workforce loses confidence in both the organization and its management.

- Individual workers are more concerned about their own well-being than they are about that of the business.

- And, of course, accidents and injuries cause disruption and loss of output, not only from the victims but also from their colleagues, from managers and from others with a first-aid responsibility.

## Review your learning

**Check your understanding of this chapter by completing the following:**

1 What are the three factors related to an activity which operations scheduling should take into account?

*Activity d _ _ _ _ _ _ _*

*Activity f _ _ _ _ _ _ _ _*

*Activity s _ _ _ _ _ _ _*

2 A critical path is the s _ _ _ _ _ _ _ _ of activities which determines the m_ _ _ _ _ _ _ _ _ duration of an operation.

3 List four reasons for providing an efficient workplace layout.

4 HASAWA places legal duties on three groups of people. Who are they?

5 What are the potential costs to an organization if it ignores health and safety issues?

## Theory to practice

**Apply this chapter to your own experience by answering the following:**

1 How could the work flows for which you are responsible be improved?

2 How could your workplace layout be made more efficient?

3 Are the members of your team aware of their health and safety responsibilities? If not, how could you change this?

4 Who is your local safety representative?

5 Are you aware of your own health and safety responsibilities? How could you find out more?

6 Carry out a safety audit of your workplace. What hazards can you find and how can you remove them?

# 26  Continuous improvement

| Chapter Objectives | • *How can I contribute to continuous improvement?* |
|---|---|

The importance of organizations adapting successfully to change is a theme throughout this book. In this final chapter we examine the key role a manager has in continually looking for new ways of working. Management literature contains reference to a need for 'creative dissatisfaction' involving:

- A continual search for better ways of doing things
- Recognition by managers that effective responses to change are the key to survival.

## Improvement in context

However, making improvements is not necessarily a straightforward process. As we have shown earlier in this book:

- Ease of making improvements depends on the culture of your organization
- People who are not used to change find it difficult and threatening to cope with
- For change to succeed, managers – and particularly senior managers – need to give a positive lead
- Even if your organization is geared to adapt to change and improvement, it is often not easy to identify the form that change should take.

At this point, we need to distinguish between change and continuous improvement. Managing change is a radical process. It is likely to cause short-term disruption and upheaval and may require significant inputs of time, money and other resources. It will by definition have a major impact on those involved:

- Their jobs may change or even disappear
- They may need to learn new skills, systems and routines
- The work involved in implementing change will be significant.

Continuous improvement, on the other hand, is an incremental process of smaller changes. In other words, it involves a continuing series of minor adjustments which are easier to incorporate than radical change and reduce the need for it.

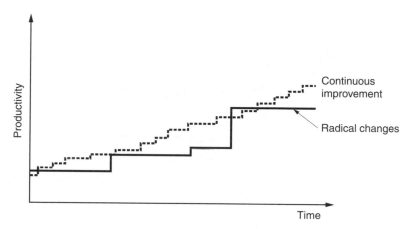

*Figure 26.1*

Continuous improvement is sometimes referred to as kaizen – a concept that was started in Japan. The word *kaizen* translates as 'good change'.

The principle of kaizen is to empower as many people to make relatively small, but good or positive changes, within their area of expertise.

# The need for improvement

Continuous improvement involves a large number of detailed improvements, over a long period of time, and on an ongoing basis. It works on the assumption that improvement is always possible, always necessary and always desirable. In many cases, all these are true.

Continuous improvement may be necessary to:

- Improve the contribution made to achieving the goals of the organization
- Improve customer satisfaction
- Reduce costs
- Increase efficiency
- Reduce or eliminate waste
- Increase job satisfaction.

However, making improvements can only be justified if they are relevant and cost-effective.

Alan Studley's team of five assembly workers make components used in the manufacture of double-glazed window units. His output targets reflect the demand from the final assembly team – internal customers in the supply chain.

Their targets are in turn based on the firm's sales forecasts. His team are currently meeting their targets comfortably. A process review has shown that replacing a current piece of equipment with a more sophisticated version costing £5,000 would increase output by 10%.

**What questions should Alan ask before taking this proposal further?**

We know from the Case Study that Alan's customers have no need at the moment for more outputs than his team are producing. But we do not know:

- What future demand there will be for them
- Whether they are satisfied with output quality and whether the new machine will improve it
- The company's long-term plans (expansion? new technology?) and how the new machine fits in with them
- The cost savings that might arise (for example, from maintaining current output levels but reducing staff).

Consequently, we cannot tell whether what is apparently a desirable improvement has any relevance either to current needs or future plans.

Equally we do not know whether it is likely to be cost-effective without more information about both overall costs and potential savings. We know how much the machine will cost, but:

- Will staff need re-training?
- Will other aspects of the assembly process need changing?
- If long-term cost savings can only come from making someone redundant, what will be the short-term cost and how will other staff react?

Whilst it therefore makes sense to be on the lookout for possible improvements, that does not always mean implementing them. The decision to take no action is a perfectly valid one, provided it has been made deliberately, following a careful comparison between the costs of the improvement and the benefits that will arise from it.

# Designing improvements

A formal approach to continuous improvement involves regular meetings of improvement teams. The team will be involved in:

- Assessing the need for improvement
- Designing the improvement
- Implementing the improvement.

Other types of improvement teams are:

- Project teams – brought together to deal with a specific issue, then disbanded when the issue has been resolved.
- Cross-functional teams, with representatives from, for example, customer services, marketing, support and the finance department.

As a manager you may find yourself as a member of the team or, in the case of a project, actually managing and leading the process.

# Managing a project

Whether you are introducing a new operating procedure or moving people from one building to another the same tools and techniques of project management apply.

301

Every project, large or small, has its own set of specific tasks and activities – this is often referred to as the project life cycle. These are:

- Defining/scoping the project
- Planning and project organization
- Implementing the plan
- Monitoring and review.

Defining the desired outcome is the starting point of the cycle. This may sound obvious but many projects fail because of lack of clarity of purpose, with people involved who do not fully understand what they are trying to achieve.

As the project manager you need to be clear about what it is you have been tasked to achieve, at what cost, to what standard and within what time-scales.

Use SWOT analysis and SMART principles to assist you in defining the objectives.

Involve the project team members as early as possible in order to gain maximum commitment and understanding. Which means that, even if the project objectives are set by senior managers or by you as project leader, the team must be at least consulted about and involved in the planning process.

To be effective a project team needs:

- A clear statement of the objectives it is there to achieve (which may be set by others or the team itself)
- To understand the budgeting and resource constraints within which it is working
- Knowledge of the organization's direction, its general aims and its values.

These are all necessary in order to ensure that the project team is aware of the limits to the types and scope of improvement they can reasonably expect to make. This is to avoid situations where the team is encouraged to make improvements, only to be told that their recommendations are too expensive, require resources which are not available or are not in line with wider organizational thinking, or have simply missed the point of the exercise.

In addition, teams should have:

### Meeting guidelines

Giving a general idea of how often they will meet, at what time of day and for how long. Meetings will also need a chair, a note-taker, an agenda and some general principles concerning the degree of formality, the team's authority and how it will tackle problem-solving and decision-making.

### Rules for allocating action

These will include: setting deadlines, a fair sharing of workload and the recognition that delegated tasks are compulsory, not optional.

### Team-working principles

These will deal with issues like: reliable attendance; time-keeping; listening to and involving others; conflict resolution.

### Process and progress reviews

It is tempting for project teams to become so wrapped up in the problems they are addressing that they fail to keep track of their effectiveness. Regular process reviews should consider: individual commitment and contributions; interpersonal relationships; team cooperation. Progress reviews should assess achievement against deadlines, success to date and progress towards the overall project.

**Case Study**

> The Foodstore is a cash and carry warehouse on the outskirts of a market town in the South of England. The warehouse is a freestanding building surrounded by its own car park. After several years' success, the volume of traffic through the car park is becoming an issue. Customers park so that delivery vehicles cannot get to the warehouse and the car park entrance is so narrow that customers' cars and delivery vehicles often block each other. Tom the warehouse manager has

now started to receive complaints from both customers and the delivery drivers.

Tom has a plan to widen the entrance and clearly mark out entrance and exit routes, customer parking bays and delivery vehicle access in the car park. However, he has been told by the contractor that these changes will require three days of disruption and two days when the car park cannot be used.

**What action should Tom take to implement his plan?**

We assume that Tom has senior management approval for his plan and that a budget has been allocated. These are certainly the first action steps he should take if he has not already done so.

Following those, he would be well-advised to check records of turnover and deliveries to identify the time of year and the five days in a week when traffic is lightest. It would then be a good idea to write to customers and suppliers explaining the benefits of the plan, his proposed timing for implementation and asking for comments. Of course, there is no point in doing that unless he is prepared to change his plan if there is a strong resistance, either to the plan or to the proposed timing.

When details have been finalized he will need to bring people up-to-date, asking them to keep visits and deliveries to a minimum while the work is going on. And if the plan changes he must communicate those changes urgently.

So now the contractor is at work but, as often happens, he finds he will need an extra day. It will now be important for Tom to:

- Negotiate with the contractor ways of finishing the job while keeping most of the car park free from obstruction
- Display notices so that customers and delivery drivers know what is going on
- Brief staff to answer questions and queries and deal with any complaints
- And, finally, would it be good marketing for the Foodstore to invite new and existing customers and suppliers to a celebration marking the successful completion of the project?

# Monitoring improvements

Earlier, the concept of the control loop was introduced. It referred to a process of:

- Setting performance standards
- Initiating action to achieve those standards
- Monitoring resulting performance or outputs
- Taking further action as necessary.

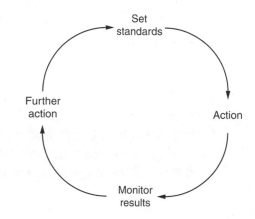

*Figure 26.2*

That process is central to just about every kind of management action. It applies to:

- Managing quality
- Managing outputs
- Problem-solving
- Decision-making
- Staff performance review
- Training evaluation
- Budget management.

So, to suggest that it is equally applicable to making and managing improvements should come as no surprise to you!

Monitoring the results of the improvement process is apparently the final stage in the improvement cycle. But, in fact, it would be a mistake to view it as coming at the end of the process. Instead, monitoring the results should be a consideration at the very beginning of the process and should continue to be a key issue as it unfolds.

At the start, any improvement initiative needs objectives and they should be set in quantified terms. This is easier in some cases than in others. It is relatively easy to say that an improvement initiative should:

- Increase output by 10%
- Improve energy efficiency by 3%
- Reduce waste by 5%
- Cut overtime costs by £3,000 per month.

But it is less easy to quantify factors like:

- Customer satisfaction
- Staff motivation
- Team cooperation.

Difficult it may be, but it is nevertheless not impossible. It is usually possible either to find quantitative measures of less obvious factors, or else to translate qualitative factors into numbers even if this is done in a somewhat arbitrary way.

For example:

- Customer satisfaction can be assessed on the numbers of customer complaints or the quality of rejected inputs.
- Staff motivation can be interpreted from levels of absenteeism.
- Team cooperation might be measured from a questionnaire.

Although factors like these take more thought and creativity to turn into numbers, the process nevertheless remains essential. This is because improvement monitoring is a comparative process. It involves comparing actual results with:

- The original objectives
- Historical performance
- And, sometimes, external or internal benchmarks to identify whether there is need or scope for further improvement.

Such comparisons are only meaningful if they are based on numbers.

Earlier we linked monitoring with control. That is we suggested that monitoring performance against standards was of little use unless it was followed by corrective action if performance did not meet the standards. That principle applies equally to monitoring improvements.

## Case Study

Elaine Wilson has been brought in to Premier Plastics as the new Human Resources Manager. The company's staff turnover is at an all time high of 27% – three times the average for the industry. Elaine has been told she has a free rein to improve the situation.

She investigates the situation and finds that:

- Wages and salaries are lower than in other companies
- Managers have had no management training
- The company offers shorter holidays and longer working weeks than others in the area
- Most local companies offer flexi-time but Premier Plastics does not.

Armed with this information Elaine receives approval to increase wages by 5%, introduce intensive training for managers, make holidays and working hours more competitive and introduce flexi-time.

After six months, staff turnover has dropped to 7%.

**How successful have Elaine's improvements been?**

There are two answers to this question. At one level, they have been extremely successful. Staff turnover is now below the industry average, with the consequent reductions in recruitment and induction costs, and lost output. But, at a different level, it is not possible to identify how successful individual initiatives have been. Something has worked – but was it: the combination of all four initiatives? Only one, two or three? If so, which?

That in turn raises the very practical question: Could Premier Plastics have achieved the same result by spending less?

That Case Study contains elements of: performance monitoring; performance comparison (against both historical performance and external benchmarks); and corrective action. But it also throws up another consideration. If you work in an organization with a philosophy of continuous improvement, you are bound to find it difficult to know which improvements have led to which results. In order to be able to quantify the results of improvement initiatives, it is advisable to let the dust settle after each one, so that you

307

can measure what happens without confusing the results through another initiative.

Interestingly, continuous improvement also prepares the way for radical change by encouraging people to accept and contribute to change. Nolan (1987) explains:

*The great paradox of innovation is that the biggest risk of all is not to innovate, never to do anything new, even at the experimental level. Yet it feels safe and comfortable to stick to the tried and tested.*

*Experiments are vital for several reasons:*

- *They identify new possibilities, some of which will probably be an improvement on what we are currently doing. Even if they are not, we have ensured that we are not missing anything – a valuable insurance in a changing world.*

- *A multiplicity of small risks is actuarially safer than one or two big ones – the risks are spread.*

- *The experiments are steps on a learning curve; the new knowledge obtained from each one can be used to minimize the risks of the next one.*

- *They keep the innovative muscles in trim; they provide practice in creating newness, taking new initiatives and handling the consequences. People who are used to doing new things are able to respond positively to unexpected new developments.*

## Review your learning

Check your understanding of this chapter by completing the following:

1 What does continuous improvement mean and what does it involve?

2 What are the stages of a project life cycle?

3 Why do improvement teams need objectives?

4 How might an improvement initiative affect others outside the team?

## Theory to practice

Apply this chapter to your own experience by answering the following:

1 How innovative is your organization in identifying problems and implementing solutions?

2   How could these processes be improved?

3   Think of an improvement initiative in your organization which has gone well. Why was that?

4   Think of an improvement initiative that did not go well. Why was that?

5   How do you involve your team in contributing to continuous improvement? Could you involve them more?

# Resource bank

## References

Clutterbuck, D. and Crainer, S. (1990) *Makers of Management: Men and Women who Changed the Business World*, Macmillan

Jobber, D. (1995) *Principles and Practice of Marketing*, McGraw-Hill

Levitt, T. (1983) *The Marketing Imagination*, Free Press

Nolan, V. (1987) *The Innovators Handbook*, Sphere

Oakland, J. (1989) *Total Quality Management*, Butterworth-Heinemann

Proctor, T. (1996) *Marketing Management: Integrating Theory and Practice*, McGraw-Hill

Smith, A. (1776) *The Wealth of Nations*, Penguin Classics

Taylor, F. W. (1911) *Principles of Scientific Management*, Harper & Row

## Additional reading

Hughes, P. and Ferret, E. (2003) *Introduction to Health and Safety at Work*

## Website addresses

**www.cim.co.uk**
Chartered Institute of Marketing

**www.hse.gov.uk**
Information, publications and downloadable resources from the Health and Safety Executive

**www.quality-foundation.co.uk**
British Quality Foundation provides help for organizations to improve their performance including best practice benchmarking

# Answers to 'review your learning' questions

## Section 1    Managing in Context

### Chapter 1    Achieving results

1   (a) Plan; (b) Organize; (c) Command; (d) Control;
    (e) Co-ordinate.

2   Information; People; Activities; Resources.

3   The individual involved, their levels and scope of authority and
    the nature of the decision.

### Chapter 2    Using resources

1   Adding value.

2   Inputs.

3   Consumable; Renewable.

4   Customer choice; Political decisions; Weather; Social change;
    Competition; Technology.

5   Managers do not work in isolation; Management is an ever-
    changing dynamic process.

### Chapter 3    Customer focus

1   Knowing and understanding customer needs enables us to
    satisfy them.

2   Internal and external.

3 Fitness for purpose or use.

4 Political; Economics; Social; Technological; Legal; Environmental.

### Chapter 4  Understanding the culture

1 The way we do things round here.

2 History; Size; Ownership; Purpose.

3 Power culture – spider's web. Depends on a strong leader; the culture is responsive and opportunistic.

Role culture – Greek temple. Work is controlled by formal rules and procedures, typical of large organizations e.g., banks, public sector.

Task culture – a net. Organizations that value innovation and creative thinking; hierarchy and status are not important; people are respected for their knowledge and expertise.

Person culture – a cluster. It is the individual rather than the organization that matters. Typically found in professional groups e.g. doctors, lawyers.

### Chapter 5  Understanding the environment

1 Political; Economics; Social; Technological; Legal; Environmental.

2 Economies of other countries; Levels of demand from other countries; Levels of competition; Social change; Overall rate of technological development; Customer preferences; Customer confidence.

3 Production and distribution methods; Customer demand and expectations; Product desirability and price; Administrative efficiency.

## Section 2  Providing Direction

### Chapter 6  Developing professionally

1 Emotional awareness; Accurate self-assessment; Self-confidence.

2 The adverse reaction people have to excessive pressure or other types of demand placed on them.

3 Demands; Control; Support; Relationships; Role; Change.

4 Higher productivity and competitiveness; Increased flexibility and customer service; Increased morale and motivation; Reduction in absenteeism; Meeting legal requirements.

## Chapter 7    *Principles of effective communication*

1 Accurate; Brief; Clear.

2 Formal feedback is a conscious response from the receiver; Informal feedback is a subconscious response from the receiver.

3 What is the purpose of the communication? Does it require immediate feedback? How long is the message? How urgent is the message? Who is going to receive the message? Where are the receivers based?

4 Clear; Concise; Complete; Correct; Courteous.

5 Managers are increasingly working in global markets with customers, suppliers and colleagues possibly working in other countries. It is important to understand the differences and local customs.

6 Cannot ensure confidentiality, email facility may be accessed by other users.

## Chapter 8    *Communicating at work*

1 Decide what you want from the interview; Allocate sufficient time; Gather relevant paperwork; Plan the structure; Book and arrange the room.

2 What do I want from this briefing? What does my manager want from this briefing? What information does my manager need? How should I present the information?

3 Decide the purpose; Decide on content; Plan the structure; Make notes; Prepare support material; Practice.

## Chapter 9    *Leading and delegating*

1 Your own views are valid, you may have answered that they are not necessarily synonymous.

2 Good.

3 Action-centred leadership.

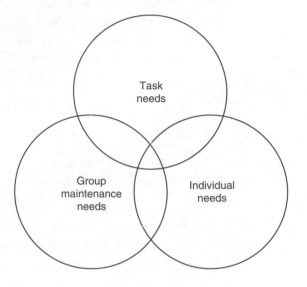

4 Makes productive use of time; Avoids managerial overload; Improves the job satisfaction of the team; Develops their skills; Improves their promotion prospects.

5 Joins or consults.

### Chapter 10 Motivating

1 The art of helping people to focus their minds and energies on doing their work as effectively as possible.

2 Physiological; Safety; Love; Esteem; Self-actualization.

3 Salary = hygiene; Opportunity for promotion = motivator; Responsibility = motivator; Status = hygiene; Working conditions = hygiene; Supervision = hygiene; Sense of achievement = motivator.

4 Expectancy theory:

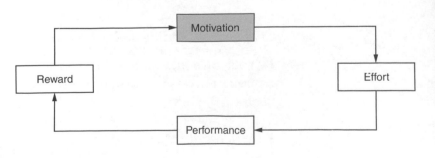

5 Expectancy theory suggests that if you do not honour your promises, your staff will come to expect you NOT to honour your promises in the future. Therefore, this is likely to have a negative effect on staff motivation.

### Chapter 11    Developing productive work relationships

1 Lack of information or understanding; Impossible/incompatible objectives; Failing to follow team norms, principles or procedures; Latent hostility.

2 Productive conflict centres on the task and ways of tackling it. It results in debate leading to agreement on the best way forward.

3 Destructive conflict focuses on the individual. It results in bad working relationships and poor performance.

4 Communicate; Encourage discussion; Focus on the task; Show respect and fairness; Contribute.

# Section 3   People and Performance

### Chapter 12    Managing teams

1 Common purpose; Interdependency; Respect; Selection; Commitment.

2 Forming; Storming; Norming; Performing; Adjourning.

3 Co-ordinator – mature, confident, trusting, chairman, clarifies.

Innovator – creative, unorthodox, solves difficult problems.

Monitor–evaluator – sober, strategic, discerning, makes judgements, lacks ability to inspire.

4 Because the group's objectives may supersede those of the organization.

### Chapter 13    Improving performance

1 Managing by walking about means spending more time with team members informally, to get to know them and their problems.

2 Distrust; managers or reviewers don't understand the system; lack of preparation; complicated paperwork; process is rushed; different managers apply different standards; managers are biased.

3 Immediate; limited; shows respect; puts the improvement into context; is two way.

4 Training is for short term – now and near future; Development is longer term – satisfies career ambitions and future promotions.

5 The difference between where we are now – current skills, knowledge, attitudes and behaviours – where we need to be to move the business forward.

## Chapter 14   Discipline and grievance

1 Advisory, Conciliation and Arbitration Service.

2 Be in writing; state who they apply to; non-discriminatory; confidential; allow employees to appeal; require management to investigate fully before any disciplinary action is taken.

3 Not seeking help; not checking rules and procedures; not keeping records; acting hastily; acting inconsistently; being prejudiced; avoiding issues.

4 Talk to your team, encourage informal discussion on a day-to-day basis.

## Chapter 15   Managing change

1 If they are informed about the reasons for the change. If they understand the benefits and are involved in the planning and design and afterwards encouraged to recognize what they have gained from the change.

2 A *Push* strategy involves making the driving forces stronger; a *Pull* strategy involves reducing the pressure of the restraining forces.

3 Fear of the unknown; fear of loss; ambiguity; insecurity; loss of control.

4 Review the outcome; confirm ownership; evaluate.

### Chapter 16 Solving problems and making decisions

1 What is the current situation? Why is it unacceptable? What has caused it? What are the likely consequences? To whom is it important? What objectives should a decision achieve? What are the constraints? What are the alternatives? Which is the best fit? How do we implement it? What have we learnt?

2 To keep asking 'why'. Establish the circumstances under which the problem does or does not occur.

3 Fishbone.

4 To ensure clarity, prevent ambiguity and that everyone involved understands.

5 To generate ideas; benefit from their experience; increase ownership and commitment.

### Chapter 17 Recruiting to the team

1 Job title; main purpose of the job; responsibilities and accountability; conditions of employment and performance measures.

2 The skills, knowledge, experience and qualifications and personal qualities required to do the job.

3 One-to-one interviews; panel interviews; assessment centres; numeracy and literacy tests; personality questionnaires; psychometric tests; online tests.

4 Enables the new employee to: Get to know the organization; Learn about their own work/team environment; Adjust to their new workplace.

# Section 4 Effective Resource Management

### Chapter 18 Managing and controlling costs and resources

1 Machine hours; Raw material volumes; Output targets; Labour hours.

2 Output quantities expected from a member of staff under normal circumstances.

3 *Variable costs* vary in line with output; *Fixed costs* remain fixed regardless of the levels of output.

4 Failing to define priorities; Inefficient delegation; Procrastination; Holding unnecessary meetings.

### Chapter 19    Changing inputs into outputs

1 Activities carried out that provide a source to customers which is its basic reason for existing.

2 Economy – how cheaply resources can be bought; Efficiency – achieving greater outputs with fewer resources; Effectiveness – the extent to which outputs meet desired standards.

3 Transforming raw materials and human inputs into goods and services of higher value.

### Chapter 20    Information management

1 *Data* are raw facts, figures – on their own – they mean nothing. *Information* is data which have been processed and analysed and therefore can be used to justify decisions.

2 Timely; Relevant; Accurate; Concise; Complete.

3 The number and location of people using the system; The required ease and speed of access; Complexity and volume of information; Processing power; Cost of equipment and inputs and outputs.

4 To protect individuals who have data or information about them stored on computer.

### Chapter 21    Financial information and management control

1 What markets we should attack; What products we should make; What services we should provide; Measure customer loyalty; Measure staff morale; Calculate break-even point; Make investment decisions.

2 Because there will be qualitative arguments to take account of.

3 *Fixed costs* remain relatively unchanged. Examples: rents, rates, heating, lighting. *Variable costs* vary directly according to the level of output. Examples: materials used in processes, products, bonuses.

4 Revenue which exceeds costs and contributes to the payment of fixed costs.

318

5 The costs of additional salary, equipment, training. The availability in the budget, what the contribution would be, projected profit; return on investment. The cost to the organization of not having the additional resources.

### Chapter 22    Preparing and using budgets

1 To monitor and control revenue and expenditure in order to achieve corporate objectives.

2 Cash; Sales; Production.

3 The budgets are realistic; the people involved understand and are motivated to achieve them.

4 Variance.

5 Flexible budgets are renegotiated upon; External changes that might affect revenues or expenditures.

# Section 5    Focusing on Results

### Chapter 23    Planning, organizing and controlling work

1 Where senior management set broad organizational aims, lower levels then say how they can contribute towards attaining these aims.

2 Specific; Measurable; Achievable; Realistic; Time-based.

3 Outputs; Standards; Corrective; Action.

4 A company which has demand that varies greatly works inefficiently because when it is busy, it is too busy and therefore unable to keep up with demand for its products. It may then have to contract out work which is expensive or turn work down. Conversely when it is not working to capacity it will have staff and equipment being under-utilized. Smoothing demand allows a company to constantly work at manageable levels whilst maximizing the efficiency of its resources.

5 *Quality control:* quality inspection and control. *Quality assurance:* focuses on the process rather than the output.

### Chapter 24  Meeting customer needs

1 Telephone interviews; Postal questionnaires; Face-to-face interviews; Focus groups; Customer response cards.

2 It involves customers developing accurate and comprehensive specifications for what they want and communicating those specifications to the supplier.

3 The right product, in the right place, at the right time, at the right price and in the right way.

### Chapter 25  Managing the work environment

1 Duration; Frequency; Sequence.

2 Sequence; Minimum.

3 Easy access; Flexibility; Productive use of space; Comfort/safety; Efficient work flow; Reduced travel distance for people/resources/products.

4 Employers; Employees; Managers.

5 Legal costs from civil actions from injured parties; Cost of lost working days – replacement staff costs; Recruitment costs; Production costs to cover down time due to stoppages for injuries or incidents; Management time.

### Chapter 26  Continuous improvement

1 Continuously improving productive efficiency in small incremental steps through empowered employees, i.e. continuous improvement.

2 Defining/scoping the project; Planning and project organization; Implementing the plan; Monitoring and review.

3 Gives the team focus; Ensures a common direction; Defines spheres of responsibility and the extent to which they are expected to improve processes/outputs.

4 Changes processes/information flows/documentation systems. May cause disruption.

# Index

**INDEX**